Measuring Customer Satisfaction and Loyalty

Survey Design, Use, and Statistical Analysis Methods

Also available from ASQ Quality Press:

Managing the Customer Experience: A Measurement-Based Approach
Morris Wilburn

Customer Satisfaction Research Management
Derek Allen

Competing for Customers and Winning with Value: Breakthrough Strategies for Market Dominance
R. Eric Reidenbach and Reginald W. Goeke

Analysis of Customer Satisfaction Data
Derek Allen and Tanniru R. Rao

Measuring Customer Satisfaction: Survey Design, Use, and Statistical Analysis Methods, Second Edition
Bob E. Hayes

Measuring and Managing Customer Satisfaction: Going for the Gold
Sheila Kessler

Customer Satisfaction Measurement Simplified: A Step-by-Step Guide for ISO 9001:2000 Certification
Terry G. Vavra

ANSI/ISO/ASQ Q10002-2004: Quality management — Customer satisfaction — Guidelines for complaints handling in organizations
ANSI/ISO/ASQ

The Certified Manager of Quality/Organizational Excellence Handbook, Third Edition
Russell T. Westcott, editor

The Quality Toolbox, Second Edition
Nancy R. Tague

Making Change Work: Practical Tools for Overcoming Human Resistance to Change
Brien Palmer

Innovation Generation: Creating an Innovation Process and an Innovative Culture
Peter Merrill

To request a complimentary catalog of ASQ Quality Press publications, call 800-248-1946, or visit our Web site at http://qualitypress.asq.org.

Measuring Customer Satisfaction and Loyalty

Survey Design, Use, and
Statistical Analysis Methods

Third Edition

Bob E. Hayes

ASQ Quality Press
Milwaukee, Wisconsin

American Society for Quality, Quality Press, Milwaukee, WI 53203
© 2008 by ASQ
All rights reserved. Published 2008.
Printed in the United States of America.

14   13   12   11   10   09   08   5   4   3   2   1

Library of Congress Cataloging-in-Publication Data

Hayes, Bob E., 1963-
Measuring customer satisfaction and loyalty : survey design, use, and statistical
analysis methods / Bob E. Hayes.—3rd ed.
    p. cm.
Includes bibliographical references and index.
ISBN 978-0-87389-743-3
1. Consumer satisfaction—Statistical methods. 2. Questionnaires. I. Title.

HF5415.335.H39 2008
658.8'12—dc22

                                2008020729

Publisher: William A. Tony
Acquisitions Editor: Matt T. Meinholz
Project Editor: Paul O'Mara
Production Administrator: Randall Benson

ASQ Mission: The American Society for Quality advances individual,
organizational, and community excellence worldwide through learning, quality
improvement, and knowledge exchange.

Attention Bookstores, Wholesalers, Schools, and Corporations: ASQ Quality
Press books, videotapes, audiotapes, and software are available at quantity
discounts with bulk purchases for business, educational, or instructional use.
For information, please contact ASQ Quality Press at 800-248-1946, or write
to ASQ Quality Press, P.O. Box 3005, Milwaukee, WI 53201-3005.

To place orders or to request a free copy of the ASQ Quality Press Publications
Catalog, including ASQ membership information, call 800-248-1946. Visit our
Web site at www.asq.org or http://www.asq.org/quality-press.

♾ Printed on acid-free paper

Quality Press
600 N. Plankinton Avenue
Milwaukee, Wisconsin 53203
Call toll free 800-248-1946
Fax 414-272-1734
www.asq.org
http://www.asq.org/quality-press
http://standardsgroup.asq.org
E-mail: authors@asq.org

For Marissa

*This book is dedicated to you. You have grown into a beautiful
person. You are a kind, loving, and forgiving person, qualities
I admire. You make the world more joyful, and remind me that there
is nothing more important than family and friends. Thank you for
being there for me in my greatest time of need. Your support, love
and acceptance have helped me immeasurably. I love you.*

Contents

List of Figures and Tables

Preface

The first edition of this book was published in 1992. At that time, there were no books that covered the topic of customer satisfaction questionnaire development and use. Since then, the field of customer satisfaction measurement has flourished. In 1997, the second edition was published with more information about real-life examples of customer satisfaction questionnaires. It is hard to believe that 11 years has elapsed since the second edition. The growth of the field of customer satisfaction measurement has proliferated greatly, with articles and books being written by both researchers and practitioners. I have learned much about the field of customer satisfaction measurement through my professional experience. I have been fortunate enough to have conducted survey research for top-level enterprise companies including Siebel Systems, Agilent Technologies, Oracle, and Cisco Systems, and have managed customer satisfaction research as an employee to Fortune 500 firms and as an independent consultant. Much of the new content in this edition is based on that experience.

This edition, like the first two editions, includes topics such as customer requirement determination, uses of customer satisfaction questionnaires, reliability and validity of questionnaires, sampling techniques, item generation, and real-life examples of customer satisfaction questionnaires. The third edition contains information about customer loyalty measurement. There is no shortage of articles and books on the concept of customer loyalty, but some of the books, I feel, have given a simplistic look at the measurement of customer loyalty that detracts from the scientific underpinnings of psychological measurement. I have dedicated a chapter to the measurement of customer loyalty that examines both the meaning and measurement of customer loyalty. Specifically, this chapter includes a critique of the research behind the Net Promoter Score (NPS) and presents research that extends the field of customer loyalty measurement.

I have included discussions on Web-based surveys and have included information on customer loyalty management.

I had a desire to write this third edition for some time now. I put off writing the book for too long. Due to certain life-changing events, I now have the time and, more importantly, the motivation to complete this edition. Although writing is sometimes difficult for me, I do enjoy the process of trying to convey important scientific principles in simple, understandable terms. All too often, important scientific principles in textbooks are not presented in a way that allows for easy comprehension. I hope I have accomplished my goal of sharing what I know in a meaningful way.

I present these scientific principles in relation to the development of customer satisfaction questionnaires, but these issues are equally applicable in an attempt to develop any attitude measure (for example, employee attitude surveys). Although I do discuss several topics in scale development, my intent is not to cover the entire content of this area, but to present information directly related to the development of customer satisfaction questionnaires.

The book contains eight chapters. One chapter discusses the importance of customer satisfaction in the American economy, and the other chapters cover specific aspects of customer satisfaction questionnaire development and use. The chapters are designed to be complementary and to develop a coherent picture of customer satisfaction questionnaire development and use. The book contains several appendices that present important statistical concepts to aid readers who lack a statistical background. An understanding of the information in the appendices is helpful but not essential to developing customer satisfaction questionnaires.

Chapter 1 introduces the concept of quality and emphasizes the importance of assessing customer satisfaction and customer loyalty. Awareness of the importance of customer satisfaction/loyalty stems from two sources: (1) a national quality award given to outstanding American companies that demonstrate outstanding product and service quality, and (2) the desire to achieve financial security of companies that are able to satisfy their customers and subsequently able to increase customer loyalty. In addition, this chapter presents a model of customer satisfaction questionnaire development and use designed as an overview for the remaining chapters. This model will help readers see the big picture of customer satisfaction questionnaire development and use before reading about the specific steps in subsequent chapters.

Chapter 2 covers two methods of determining important service or product characteristics as perceived by customers. Identification of these characteristics is necessary in generating questions for the customer survey. These methods are called the *quality dimension development process* and the *critical incident technique.* The quality dimensions include those general aspects of the service or product that customers say define the quality of the service or product. The two methods also identify specific examples of these important characteristics that will help determine the types of questions that can be included in a customer satisfaction questionnaire.

Chapter 3 covers measurement issues related to customer satisfaction questionnaires, discusses reliability and validity, and contains formulae to estimate reliability. It is important to evaluate the quality of any measurement system. When we measure parts that come from an assembly line, we want to be sure that the measurement process accurately reflects the true size of the parts we are measuring. Similarly, we want to ensure that the measurement of our customers' attitudes accurately reflects their attitudes. Imprecise measurement can lead to poor business decisions. This chapter shows you how to evaluate the measurement properties of your questionnaires.

Chapter 4 presents guidelines for developing questionnaires, including the types of questions to be included, characteristics of good questions, response formats, and information to be included in the introduction. Additionally, this chapter discusses the benefits of conducting Web-based customer surveys over more traditional survey approaches. This chapter closes with some information about standard questions that are commonly used to measure customer loyalty.

Chapter 5 covers different sampling methods. As is often the case, due to financial constraints, it is not possible to administer a survey to all customers. When this occurs, we administer a survey to a small subset of customers and analyze those data to determine the satisfaction level of all of our customers. The process of sampling ensures that the results based on the sample of customers are generalizable to all customers. Additionally, this chapter covers topics to show you how confident you can be in customer satisfaction results and how to determine an appropriate sample size for your customer satisfaction survey. This chapter also covers research that shows how to increase response rates to surveys.

Chapter 6 covers the measurement and meaning of customer loyalty. It critiques the Net Promoter Score and presents research that dives into the measurement and meaning of customer loyalty. Real examples are presented that use the new customer loyalty measures and highlights how companies can use these new measures to grow their business through both new and existing customers.

Chapter 7 includes five examples of customer satisfaction question-naires. The first three involve the manufacturing industry, the service industry, and the software industry. The latter two cover support functions within an organization (an internal statistical support group and a facilities group). This chapter discusses methods of presenting the data and suggests specific uses, including identifying which aspects of the service or product are especially important in customer satisfaction. In addition, this chapter applies customer satisfaction questionnaires to the traditional quality improvement techniques of control charting and describes their use in conducting organizational research. Finally, this chapter includes a discussion on customer loyalty management that outlines both a micro and macro approach to improving customer loyalty.

Chapter 8 includes various real-life examples of customer satisfaction questionnaires. Readers are shown how three companies actually used them. These examples are helpful because they show how the approaches in this book are applied to real-life situations. This chapter shows how the various companies developed both long and short customer satisfaction questionnaires, the application of sampling error, confidence intervals, and control charts. Readers will see that the development and use of questionnaires is one of compromise; it may not always be possible to follow all of the guidelines stated in this book. Nonetheless, the companies represented in the examples employed many of the guidelines from this book and were, at least, aware of the guidelines; they could make informed decisions regarding what they wanted to do for their particular survey process. Not all customer satisfaction survey processes will be identical, not even within the same organization. It is ultimately up to each reader to decide how he or she will use the information contained in this text and apply it to his or her specific customer survey process. It is hoped that the examples in this chapter will help readers better understand the survey process as it is applied in the real world.

Several appendices are included as well. Each appendix covers a specific topic related to statistical analysis. These appendices aim to help readers understand key statistical concepts that complement the material presented in the main body of the book. These appendices present a very general overview of statistics. Topics include measurement scales, frequencies, descriptive statistics, sampling error, the concept of hypothesis testing, and formal hypothesis testing procedures (t-tests, analysis of variance, and regression analysis).

I would now like to take this opportunity to thank my friends and colleagues who have influenced my thinking on customer satisfaction and loyalty measurement. Not in any particular order of importance, these people include Jeremy Whyte, Mike Moore, Margot Topp, David Zierman, Wade Gibson, Tom Hayes, and Lamona Foster. With their feedback and insight, they have helped me better understand and more clearly communicate what I know about this field.

I am blessed to have the love and support of beautiful friends and family. Like true friends, they have cheered me during my finest hours and held me during my lowest points. They make my life more interesting and fun. They are: Brandie Smith, Craig Silva, Wade Gibson, Stephen King, Stephanie Kincaide, Renah Seay, Audineh Asaf, Optimus Rhyme, Tiffany Tannahill, Jenn Meyers, Stephen Foster, Jonathan Foster, and Lauren Foster. I am honored to be called their friend. Mom, watakushi wa anata o ai shimasu. You are beautiful.

After working as an employee in major technology companies, I have since ventured out into the consulting world where I am able to have a more flexible lifestyle and am now free to publish what I want on this topic without the constraint of management's review of my work. In short, I get to research and write about topics that, I feel, should be addressed in this field. For those of you who are interested in reading more of what I have to say about the field of customer satisfaction and loyalty, you can find my blog and research at my consulting business, Business Over Broadway (www.businessoverbroadway.com).

I like to think that I am more than customer satisfaction and loyalty. After all, all work and no play makes Bob a dull boy. I have several interests related to science, and social causes. To understand the other side of me, you can check out what I do in my spare time: www.loyaltywidget.com (loyalty management for small and medium-sized businesses), www.withouttheplanet.com (raising money and awareness to help fight global warming), www.worldvotesforthepresident.com (a social experiment to see who the world would elect for our president).

Bob
Seattle, WA
April 2008

1
Introduction

There is a continual emphasis on a company's ability to produce high-quality products and/or provide high-quality services. In fact, many companies, in their attempt to compete in the marketplace, form either an organization to address various quality-related issues for the entire company or quality improvement teams to address specific quality-related problems. Not only do companies rely on their own employees for quality improvement, they also rely on consultants who specialize in quality improvement techniques and methodologies. The primary goal of these specialists is to increase the quality of the products and services of the companies they serve.

To increase the quality of products and services, we first need to define quality. I will use the definition presented by Montgomery (1996): Quality is the extent to which products meet the requirements of people who use them. He further distinguishes between two types of quality: quality of design and quality of conformance.

Quality of design reflects the extent to which a product or service possesses an intended feature. For example, an automobile with power steering, a sun roof, and many other luxury options would be considered to have better quality of design than a car without these options. Quality of conformance, however, reflects the extent to which the product or service conforms to the intent of the design.

Both of these aspects of quality can be measured. The measures give businesses an accurate indication of the "well-being" of their business processes and determine the quality of products and services resulting from these processes. Measures allow a business to: (1) know how well the business process is working, (2) know where to make changes to create improvements, if changes are needed, and (3) determine whether the changes led to improvements. Various measurement techniques can index the quality of business processes, products, and services. Measures of quality often focus on objective or *hard* indices. For example, in manufacturing industries, the process of producing parts is conducive to measurements of size (such as parts) and amount (for example, scrap or rework). In non-manufacturing industries, measurements could include the time to complete a service or the number of written errors on a particular form.

With the advent of Customer Relationship Management and Customer Experience Management in the past decade, however, there has been a focus on using more subjective or *soft* measures as indicators of quality. These measures are soft because they focus on perceptions and attitudes rather than on more concrete, objective criteria. It is often necessary to use these measures because objective indices are not applicable in assessing the quality of services. Also, companies are simply interested in gaining a more comprehensive understanding of their customers' perceptions. These soft measures include customer satisfaction questionnaires to determine customers' perceptions and attitudes concerning the quality of the service or product they received, as well as employee attitude questionnaires that assess employees' perceptions about the quality of their work life.

Knowledge of customers' perceptions and attitudes about an organization's business will greatly enhance its opportunity to make better business decisions. These organizations will know their customers' requirements or expectations and will be able to determine whether they are meeting those requirements.

To use customers' perceptions and attitudes to assess the quality of products and services, customer satisfaction instruments must accurately measure these perceptions and attitudes. If the instruments are poorly developed and inaccurately represent customers' opinions, decisions based on this information can be detrimental to the success of the organization. On the other hand, organizations with accurate information about customers' perceptions about the quality of the services and products can make better decisions to better serve their customers.

The combination of a competitive marketplace and the Baldrige National Quality Award (BNQA) has heightened the awareness of American companies of the need to focus their quality improvement efforts on customer-related issues. To incorporate customers' perceptions and attitudes into their quality improvement efforts, companies must be able to gauge customers' attitudes accurately. One way to measure customers' attitudes is through questionnaires. These companies should design customer satisfaction questionnaires that accurately assess customers' perceptions about the quality of services or products.

Measuring customers' attitudes continues to be an important element in the quality effort of American organizations. For instance, the Baldrige Award, given annually to American companies that demonstrate high standards of business practice, includes seven criteria or categories on which companies are judged. From its inception, the Baldrige Award has included customer satisfaction measurement issues as part of its award criteria. The BNQA point allocation in the recent iteration appears in Figure 1.1.

As can be seen by the point allocation for each criterion, customer satisfaction issues remain an important criterion in the BNQA. Of the 1000 points in the award, customer satisfaction issues account for 16 percent (Customer and Market Knowledge, 40 percent; Customer Satisfaction and Relationship Enhancement, 45 percent; Customer Focused Outcomes, 70 percent).

	Point values
1. Leadership	**120**
1.1 Senior Leadership 70	
1.2 Governance and Social Responsibility 50	
2. Strategic Planning	**85**
2.1 Strategy Development 40	
2.2 Strategy Deployment. 45	
3. Customer and Market Focus	**85**
3.1 Customer and Market Knowledge. 40	
3.2 Customer Satisfaction and Relationship Enhancement. 45	
4. Measurement, Analysis, and Knowledge Management	**90**
4.1 Measurement, Analysis, and Improvement of Organizational Performance 45	
4.2 Management of Information, Information Technology, and Knowledge. 45	
5. Workforce Focus	**85**
5.1 Workforce Engagement 45	
5.2 Workforce Environment 40	
6. Process Management	**85**
6.1 Work System Design. 35	
6.2 Work Process Management and Improvement. 50	
7. Results	**450**
7.1 Product and Service Outcomes. 100	
7.2 Customer-Focused Outcomes 70	
7.3 Financial and Market Outcomes. 70	
7.4 Workforce-Focused Outcomes 70	
7.5 Process Effectiveness Outcomes 70	
7.6 Leadership Outcomes 70	
Total Points	**1000**

Figure 1.1 2008 Baldrige National Quality Award Criteria.

Each of the following four customer satisfaction categories emphasizes the importance of understanding your customers. The Criteria for the 2008 award appear below. In Category 3.1, companies are judged, in part, on their method of determining customer requirements, expectations, and preferences:

1. How do you identify customers, customer groups, and market segments? How do you determine which customers, customer groups, and market segments to pursue for current and future products and services? How do you include customers of competitors and other potential customers and markets in this determination?

2. How do you use the voice of the customer to determine key customer requirements, needs, and changing expectations (including product and service features) and their relative importance to customers' purchasing or relationship decisions? How do your listening methods vary for different customers, customer groups, or market segments? How do you use relevant information and feedback from current and former customers, including marketing and sales information, customer loyalty and retention data, customer referrals, win/loss analysis, and complaint data for purposes of planning products and services, marketing, making work system and work process improvements, and developing new business opportunities?

3. How do you use voice-of-the-customer information and feedback to become more customer focused, to better satisfy customer needs and desires, and to identify opportunities for innovation?

4. How do you keep your customer and market listening and learning methods current with business needs and directions, including changes in your marketplace?

In Category 3.2, companies are judged on their method building relationships with their customers and how they determine and enhance the satisfaction level and loyalty of their customers.

A. Customer Relationship Building

1. How do you build relationships to acquire customers, to meet and exceed their expectations, to increase loyalty and repeat business, and to gain positive referrals?

2. How do your key access mechanisms enable customers to seek information, conduct business, and make complaints? What are your key access mechanisms? How do you determine key customer contact requirements for each mode of customer access? How do you ensure that these contact requirements are deployed to all people and processes involved in the customer response chain?

3. How do you manage customer complaints? How do you ensure that complaints are resolved effectively and promptly? How do you minimize customer dissatisfaction and, as appropriate, loss of repeat business and referrals? How are complaints aggregated and analyzed for use in improvement throughout your organization and by your partners?

4. How do you keep your approaches to building relationships and providing customer access current with business needs and directions?

B. Customer Satisfaction Determination

1. How do you determine customer satisfaction, dissatisfaction, and loyalty? How do these determination methods differ among customer groups? How do you ensure that your measurements capture actionable information for use in exceeding your customers' expectations? How do you ensure that your measurements capture actionable information for use in securing your customers' future business and gaining positive referrals, as appropriate? How do you use customer satisfaction and dissatisfaction information for improvement?

2. How do you follow up with customers on the quality of products, services, and transactions to receive prompt and actionable feedback?

3. How do you obtain and use information on your customers' satisfaction relative to their satisfaction with your competitors? How do you obtain and use information on your customers' satisfaction relative to the customer satisfaction levels of other organizations providing similar products or services, and/or industry benchmarks?

4. How do you keep your approaches to determining satisfaction current with business needs and directions?

In Category 7.2, companies are judged on their customer-focused performance results:

1. What are your current levels and trends in key measures or indicators of customer satisfaction and dissatisfaction? How do these results compare with the customer satisfaction levels of your competitors and other organizations providing similar products and services?

2. What are your current levels and trends in key measures or indicators of customer-perceived value, including customer loyalty and retention, positive referral, and other aspects of building relationships with customers, as appropriate?

The purpose of this book is to outline some guidelines that will aid in the development of customer satisfaction questionnaires. In addition, this book contains specific examples applying these guidelines. These guidelines are based on information combining both practical standards and scientific standards (AERA, APA, and NCME 1985). This book is written for professional practitioners in quality-related or marketing fields, which can use customer attitude measurements. In addition, companies with quality improvement programs will find this book useful in developing measures to assess their clientele's level of satisfaction.

It should be mentioned that the use of customer satisfaction questionnaires seems most appropriate for organizations in the service sector and other non-manufacturing fields. Unlike the manufacturing industry, in which quality can be assessed by an objective index such as the size of produced parts, the service sector offers little in the way of objective quality measures. Even hard measures (for example, time) used in the non-manufacturing environment might not reflect the true quality of the service. For example, if the transaction completion time for a service is measured by a stopwatch and indicates a fast completion time, this does not ensure that customers perceive the completion time as fast. The customer may have expected an even faster time. Because quality is determined, in part, by the extent to which goods meet the customers' requirements, the measurement of quality in non-manufacturing settings is probably best indexed by customers' perceptions of the service they received.

Due to the differences in the output between manufacturing and non-manufacturing companies, customer satisfaction questionnaires will more likely find greatest use in non-manufacturing settings. However, questionnaires can still be applied in manufacturing environments. For example, although the quality of manufactured products is assessed by objective indices (in fact, automobiles are rated in *Consumer Reports* by objective indices such as number of repairs), automobile manufacturers are using the term *customer satisfaction* to advertise and market their automobiles. Some automobile manufacturers claim they are designing their cars to make the driver feel better. Although customers' perception of quality is probably correlated with objective indices of quality, automobile companies that make statements concerning customers' perceptions about their cars can and should use customer satisfaction measures to assess the customers' perception about the quality of their cars.

Therefore, customer satisfaction questionnaires can be used in both non-manufacturing and manufacturing fields. The use of customer satisfaction questionnaires offers companies another approach in the assessment of the quality of their goods. It focuses an organization's attention on the customers and on how they perceive the organization's products and services.

The entire American economy revolves around customers. Improving the customer relationship is seen as the key to improving business performance (Ang & Buttle, 2006; Reinartz, Krafft & Hoyer, 2004). In the course of this endeavor, popular business strategies emerged that have shined a spotlight on the importance of understanding customers' attitudes, expectations, and preferences. Customer-centric business strategies, such as CRM (customer relationship management) and CEM (customer experience management), focus on managing customers' attitudes about their experience and fueling the proliferation of customer feedback programs (CFPs). There is a strong desire to establish and use measures of customers' attitudes as indices of the company's quality. Often, this desire stems from the lack of quality measures available to some companies (especially service companies) or results from an interest in satisfying customers. This desire to measure customers' attitudes should be paralleled by the knowledge of customer satisfaction questionnaire development. To enable companies to assess their customers' attitudes, technical guidelines on the development of customer satisfaction questionnaires must keep pace with this ever increasing emphasis on customer satisfaction issues. The following chapters contain guidance on an appropriate method for developing and using questionnaires.

MODEL OF CUSTOMER SATISFACTION QUESTIONNAIRE DEVELOPMENT AND USE

As an introduction to the remainder of the book, I would like to present a basic model describing the development and use of customer satisfaction questionnaires. This model appears in Figure 1.2 and illustrates the process in general. Each phase of the process contains specific steps, each focusing on an important element in the understanding of customers' opinions. As you read the book, it might be beneficial to keep this model in mind. It will help you incorporate the details of each chapter into a "big picture." This model also allows you to see how different parts of each chapter are interrelated.

Figure 1.2   A general model for the development and use of customer satisfaction questionnaires.

Step 1 in the process is to identify customer requirements or quality dimensions, the important characteristics of a product or service. Customer requirements define the quality of your products or services. In this step, not only do you identify the quality dimensions, you also identify specific examples of these dimensions.

Knowledge of customer requirements is essential for two reasons. First, it provides a better understanding of the way your customers define the quality of your services and products. If you understand customer requirements, you are in a better position to know how to satisfy your customers. Second, knowledge of customer requirements will facilitate the development of the customer satisfaction questionnaire. Its questions should assess the extent to which customers are satisfied on each of the quality dimensions. Chapter 2 includes information on identifying customers' requirements.

Step 2 in the process is to develop the questionnaire. This step includes many specific components. The ultimate goal of this step is to develop a questionnaire that allows the assessment of specific information about your customers' perceptions. The specific information should correspond to the underlying customer requirements you identified in Step 1. Chapter 3 includes information concerning the evaluation of questionnaires. Chapter 4 covers the development of the questionnaire, including the selection of questions (characteristics of good items), the choice of response formats, and the method of selecting the best items to be included in the questionnaire. Additionally, this chapter lists the benefits of Web-based surveys and presents standard questions used to measure customer loyalty. Chapter 5 covers various sampling methods and shows you how to determine an appropriate sample size in order to obtain reliable results.

Once the questionnaire has been developed, the next step is to use it. Step 3 represents the many specific uses of customer satisfaction questionnaires. Each use allows you to obtain specific information about your customers' perceptions. The uses vary from identifying the current status of customer satisfaction and loyalty to assessing customer satisfaction over time. Chapter 6 covers the measurement and meaning of customer loyalty and presents in-depth research that questions the effectiveness of the Net Promoter Score. Chapter 7 includes some specific uses of customer satisfaction questionnaires and a discussion on customer loyalty management. Chapter 8 includes examples of customer satisfaction questionnaires.

Tables at the end of Chapters 2, 4, and 7 summarize the text of each chapter. These tables provide practical guides and a general outline for the development and use of customer satisfaction questionnaires; consult the text to obtain the exact procedures involved at each general step.

All survey processes within an organization (for example, employee, customer) should be documented in a written format. This written document is designed to help the organization understand how and why the survey process was developed and to help you present your survey process to interested parties. For example, the Baldrige Award could use this written documentation to help decide the extent to which you truly understand your customers' perceptions and satisfaction levels. This book not only offers guidelines regarding the customer survey process; it can also help you organize and present your survey process in a documented format. Following the guidelines in the book will help you create a written document that outlines the customer survey program in clear and precise terms, from the determination of customer requirements, the development of the sampling plan, and creation of the survey, to the use of the information gained from the survey. This type of information will show readers the exact process and methodology that were used to develop the survey. Only through clearly written documentation can you support the quality of the entire survey process and lend credibility to the people who developed the survey.

2

Determining Customer Requirements

We usually describe a product or service in terms of several dimensions or characteristics. For example, after receiving a service, we might describe the service provider as fast, always available when needed, and unpleasant. These descriptions represent three different aspects of the service: *responsiveness, availability,* and *professionalism,* respectively. These are a subset of all possible dimensions by which the service can be described. The composite of all possible dimensions describes the entire product or service.

We can regard customer requirements as those characteristics of the product or service that represent important dimensions. They are the dimensions on which customers base their opinions about the product or service. I will use the term *quality dimensions* to describe these important dimensions. Also, I will interchange the terms *customer requirements* and *quality dimensions* throughout the book.

The purpose of determining customer requirements is to establish a comprehensive list of all the important quality dimensions that describe the service or product. It is important to understand the quality dimensions in order to know how customers define the quality of your service or product. Only by understanding the quality dimensions will you be able to develop measures to assess them.

Although there may be some standard quality dimensions that generalize across many products or services, some dimensions will apply only to specific types of products or services. Quality dimensions applicable to many service organizations include availability, responsiveness, convenience, and timeliness (Kennedy and Young 1989). These quality dimensions seem applicable to many service industries such as banking, hotels, and hospitals. This list of quality dimensions, however, is not comprehensive for each of these industries. The hospital industry might include additional quality dimensions such as quality of food and quality of care. Similarly, other industries may possess quality dimensions that uniquely define their services and products.

It is important that each company identify all relevant quality dimensions in order to ensure understanding of the definition of quality for its products or services. Analyzing the services or products will provide a comprehensive picture of these dimensions.

This chapter will present two methods designed to identify important quality dimensions of products or services. The first method is the *quality dimension development approach*. This approach calls for the provider to establish the quality dimensions of its service or product. The second method is the *critical incident approach* (Flanagan 1954); it involves customers in determining the quality dimensions.

QUALITY DIMENSION DEVELOPMENT

This method involves the people who provide the service or product. This might be individuals within a quality circle addressing a particular problem or individuals working independently to better understand their customers' requirements. In either case, these people are closely involved with the business process and should be in a good position to understand the purpose and function of the services or products they provide. Essentially, this process involves two steps: first identifying the dimensions and then defining these dimensions with specific examples.

Identification of Quality Dimensions

The first step involves identifying the dimensions that define the quality of the service or product. This list of dimensions can be generated in various ways, using different sources of information. One way is to investigate literature (such as scientific, professional, and trade journals) that discusses specific industries. These publications might provide dimensions of the service or product.

As an example of information found in scientific journals, researchers (Parasuraman, Zeithaml, and Berry 1985) have concluded that service quality can be described on the basis of 10 dimensions. Attempts to measure these 10 dimensions, however, reveal that customers can only distinguish between five dimensions (Parasuraman, Zeithaml, and Berry 1988). This suggests that the original 10 dimensions overlap each other considerably. The five dimensions of service quality are *tangibles, reliability, responsiveness, assurance,* and *empathy.* Definitions of these dimensions are available in a publication on service quality by Zeithaml, Parasuraman, and Berry (1990).

Some trade journals include articles that pertain to a particular industry. For example, various quality dimensions of staff support areas were presented by Kennedy and Young (1989). Five dimensions of staff support and their definitions appear in Figure 2.1. These quality dimensions were identified as important characteristics of staff support areas.

These examples demonstrate the value of journals, either scientific or trade, as resources for establishing lists of quality dimensions. By reading journals, you can gain insight from knowledgeable people who have extensive experience in a particular field.

Another way to establish a list of quality dimensions is to study the service or product. This study should include people involved in the business process, people who are in a good position to understand the purpose or function of their jobs in relation to meeting customer expectations. This examination of the service or product should lead to identification of numerous quality dimensions.

Some dimensions might include those found in Figure 2.1, or the dimensions might be specific to a particular industry or organization. An initial list of quality dimensions will be identified by general terms such as *timely* or *professional,* each term representing a particular customer requirement. These terms are to be used as guides toward understanding the dimensions of the service or product.

It is important to define these terms so that someone reading the definition will understand precisely what is meant. To clarify the definitions of the quality dimensions further, write specific examples for each definition. This process follows.

Establishing Specific Examples of Quality Dimensions

The process of clarifying quality dimensions is one of generating specific examples. Each example defines a particular dimension, and each dimension may include multiple examples. These examples take the form of

---

1. *Availability of support:* the degree to which the customer can contact the provider

2. *Responsiveness of support:* the degree to which the provider reacts promptly to the customer

3. *Timeliness of support:* the degree to which the job is accomplished within the customer's stated time frame and/or within the negotiated time frame

4. *Completeness of support:* the degree to which the total job is finished

5. *Pleasantness of support:* the degree to which the provider uses suitable professional behavior and manners while working with the customer

---

Figure 2.1   Some quality dimensions for staff support areas and their definitions.

specific declarative statements, each describing a specific instance of the quality dimension it represents. Each statement could be a specific task or behavior performed by a person within the process or it could describe a specific example illustrating the dimension. The former statement type should include an action verb describing a specific behavior of the service provider or product. The latter statement should include a specific adjective reflecting the content of the dimensions. Example statements that contain both specific behavior and specific adjectives are included in Figure 2.2. These statements were generated by the author using definitions presented by Kennedy and Young (1989).

These statements should reflect instances of performance by the staff or of product that customers can assess. It is important that your list include all possible examples for a particular dimension. This list of examples reflects the content of the dimensions; if the list is deficient, a complete understanding of each dimension will also be deficient. You should try to include at least four or five statements for each dimension. After generating the list of statements, you may take the additional step of combining any that seem redundant or repetitive. Some of the statements may overlap considerably and may not warrant separate dimensions.

The two steps in this process (generating dimensions and developing specific examples), although presented as independent of each other, are sometimes performed simultaneously. In some situations you may first generate specific examples that, in turn, lead to the generation of customer requirements. In either case, it is important that quality dimensions be defined by specific examples. Ultimately, the quality dimension development process will result in a list of customer requirements or quality dimensions, each defined by specific statements. The following software industry example illustrates the process and outcome of the quality dimension development process.

Software Industry

Murine (1988) discusses the measurement of software quality and lists 13 software quality factors. These factors are user oriented and can be evaluated by the customer. I have extracted the dimensions and their definitions directly from the article and have written statements to provide specific examples of each. The dimension, a brief definition, and the specific statements are presented in Figure 2.3. These specific statements are only a small portion of the possible statements that could have been generated. Other questionnaire developers, examining the same quality dimensions, could generate additional statements similar in content to the ones presented here.

Availability of support
1. I could get help from the staff when I needed.
2. The staff was always available to help.
3. I could contact the staff at any time I needed.
4. The staff was there when needed.
5. I could arrange convenient meeting times with the staff.

Responsiveness of support
1. They were quick to respond when I asked for help.
2. They immediately helped me when I needed help.
3. I waited a short period of time to get help after I asked for it.

Timeliness of support
1. They completed the job when expected.
2. They met my deadline(s).
3. They finished their responsibilities within the stated time frame.
4. The project was completed on time.

Completeness of support
1. They ensured that every aspect of the job was completed.
2. They completed everything they said they would do.
3. They were there to provide help from the beginning to the end of the project.

Professionalism of support
1. The staff members conducted themselves in a professional manner.
2. The staff listened to me.
3. The staff was courteous.
4. The staff cared about what I had to say.

Overall satisfaction with support
1. The quality of the way the staff treated me was high.
2. The way the staff treated me met my needs.
3. The way the staff treated me met my expectations.
4. I am happy with the way the staff treated me.
5. I am satisfied with the way the staff treated me.

Overall satisfaction with product
1. The quality of the final job they provided was high.
2. The job met my expectations.
3. I am satisfied with the job the staff provided.

Figure 2.2 Declarative statements describing the quality dimensions of staff support areas.

I.   Correctness: the degree to which the software meets customers' specifications
1. I am able to complete my job with this software.
2. The software meets my specifications in getting my job done.

II.   Reliability: the extent to which programs perform intended functions with precision
3. I am able to perform functions with precision.
4. The software allows me to perform functions accurately.

III.   Usability: effort required to understand output from programs
5. I was able to learn about the output from programs in a short amount of time.
6. The output of the programs is easy to understand.

IV.   Maintainability: effort required to find and correct an error in operational programs
7. Locating an error in the operational program is easy.
8. Fixing an error in the operational program is easy.

V.   Testability: effort required to test programs to ensure they perform intended function
9. The testing of the program required a short amount of time.
10. Testing the program to ensure it performed functions was easy.

VI.   Portability: effort required to transfer programs between hardware configurations and/or software environments
11. Transferring the program between different hardware configurations is easy.
12. I am able to transfer programs between different software environments with little problem.

VII.   Interoperability: effort required to couple one system to another
13. Coupling one system to another is easy.
14. The software allows for simple coupling between systems.

VIII.   Intra-operability: effort required to communicate between software components
15. Communicating between software components is simple.
16. I am able to communicate between software components easily.

IX.   Flexibility: effort required to modify operational programs
17. I am able to modify the operational program with little effort.
18. Changing the operational program is easy.

Overall satisfaction:
19. I am very happy with the software.
20. The software meets my expectations.

Figure 2.3   Quality dimensions, their definitions, and statements for the software industry.

Summary

Quality dimension development is a process of identifying customer requirements through various sources. One source is industry-specific literature. People within the company are another potential source. You might ask them to examine the business process and determine the key quality dimensions of the service or product they provide. In addition to determining these dimensions, you should generate specific examples illustrating exactly what is meant by each dimension. This process will lead to the development of a list of customer requirements, each defined by several specific statements.

CRITICAL INCIDENT APPROACH

The critical incident technique (Flanagan 1954) is another approach to determining customer requirements. It has been used in establishing performance dimensions for performance appraisal systems (Latham, Fay, and Saari 1979; Latham and Wexley 1977). This method is applicable in developing customer satisfaction questionnaires and equally valuable in business process analysis in which companies attempt to define and understand customer requirements. The present method can greatly facilitate this process of definition and understanding.

The critical incident approach focuses on obtaining information from customers about the services and products they receive. *Customers* is a generic term referring to anybody who receives a service or product from some other person or group of people. It is clear that various customer satisfaction questionnaires can be developed for different types of customers and that customers can be people who are external to an organization or people from a different department within the same organization. In either case, the critical incident approach can identify customer requirements.

The strength of the critical incident approach lies in its utilization of customers in defining customer requirements. Customers are in a good position to help you understand these requirements because they are the recipients of your services or products. Relying solely on organization or department standards in determining customer requirements might lead to a poor list that does not include factors important to customers. Also, such a list may reflect imagined customer requirements that should not be included. The critical incident approach identifies specific performance examples that illustrate organizational performance related to the services or products they provide.

Critical Incidents

A critical incident is an example of organizational performance from the customers' perspective. That is, critical incidents are those aspects of organizational performance in which customers come in direct contact with your product or service. These incidents usually define staff performance (in service organizations) and product quality (in manufacturing organizations).

A critical incident is a specific example of the service or product that describes either positive or negative performance. A positive example describes a characteristic of the service or product that the customer would like to see every time he or she receives that service or product. A negative example describes a characteristic of the service or product that would make the customer question the quality of the company.

A well-written critical incident example defining customer requirements has two characteristics: (1) it is specific and (2) it describes the service provider in *behavioral terms* or describes the service or product with *specific adjectives*. The incident description should be written so that it is unambiguous, able to be interpreted the same way by different readers. These characteristics should be explained to those responsible for describing the critical incidents.

A critical incident is *specific* if it highlights a single behavior or characteristic of the service or a single characteristic of the product. The critical incident is not specific if it describes several aspects of performance. For example, a nonspecific critical incident description might say:

> *I went to the bank to cash a check and waited in line for a long time. While I was waiting, I noticed that the teller was quickly servicing her customers.*

This critical incident is not specific because it describes more than a single behavior or characteristic of service. The reader would not know whether to focus on the fact that the customer waited a long time or that the teller was quick in the service she provided. Improve this example by rewriting it to describe two separate characteristics:

1. I waited in line for a long time.

2. The teller was quickly servicing her customers.

A well-written description of a critical incident should focus on *behaviors* of the service provider and should use specific *adjectives* that describe the service or product. Saying "the teller was not able to help me" does not specify what the teller did and why the teller was unable to help. Improve this example by focusing on specific behaviors and including specific adjectives:

1. The teller carefully listened to my request.
2. I received immediate service for my transaction.

The first description focuses on the behavior of the teller while the second uses a specific adjective to describe the service.

GENERATING CRITICAL INCIDENTS

This procedure involves two steps. In the first, customers are interviewed to obtain specific information about the service or product. In the second, this information is categorized into groups, each group reflecting a quality dimension. A detailed discussion of both steps follows.

Interview

There are two approaches for identifying critical incidents: group interviewing and individual interviewing. The major difference is that either groups or individuals are the focus of the identification process. A minor difference is that individual interviews can be conducted either in person or over the telephone. In either group or individual interviewing, the method of identifying critical incidents is the same, and the following procedure is equally applicable.

For the first step, it is essential that you obtain input from people who have received the service or product. These people must be actual customers who have had several interactions with the service provider or the product, since they will be providing specific examples of service or product quality.

The recommended number of interviews ranges from 10 to 20. This high number of interviewees is recommended so that deficient information from one will be offset by sufficient information from another. Thus, information obtained from the interviews will more likely completely cover the spectrum of customer requirements. In group interviews, critical incidents described by one person may stimulate mention of incidents by other group members.

The interviewer should ask each participant to describe five to 10 positive instances and five to 10 negative instances of that service or product. These positive and negative instances constitute the critical incidents that define good and poor service or product quality.

Recall that the interviewee should avoid using general terms to describe critical incidents. If the interviewee uses general phrases such as "the service was nice" or "the product was good," the interviewer should determine what the merchant actually did, in behavioral terms, that made him or her "nice" or which aspects of the product made it "good."

For example, a customer may describe a critical incident in more than one way: "The merchant was quick to respond when I arrived" and "The merchant was good." The latter description does not specify why the merchant was good. The former provides specific information: the merchant was quick in responding to the customer. By pressing the interviewees to supply specific examples of performance or specific adjectives describing the service or product, the interviewer obtains critical information that more efficiently defines customer requirements. Such specific descriptions of critical incidents will facilitate the development of the customer satisfaction questionnaire.

Categorization of Critical Incidents

After interviewing 10 people, you may have a list of 200 critical incidents. This list is likely to include some incidents that are similar to others and these should be grouped together. The key to categorizing similar critical incidents is to focus on a specific adjective or verb they share. After forming the clusters, write a phrase for each cluster that reflects the content of its incidents. This phrase is called a *satisfaction item*. One guideline for writing satisfaction items is that they should contain a specific descriptive term of the service or product or a verb that describes an actual event involving the service or product. For example, the following critical incidents, experienced by three different people, would fall under one satisfaction item:

1. I waited too long before I was helped.

2. I was in a big hurry but had to wait in line for a very long time.

3. I waited in line for a very short time.

A satisfaction item that would encompass these three similar incidents could be

I waited a short period of time before I was helped.

As indicated by this example, both positive and negative critical incidents can be included under one satisfaction item. The three critical incidents just listed, even though they reflect positive and negative aspects of service, are all reflected by the verb *wait*. Therefore, the satisfaction item was written to include the word *wait*.

Writing satisfaction items may take some practice. The most important thing to remember is that satisfaction items, like critical incidents, should be specific in describing the service or product. Quite often, the satisfaction item might even be one of the critical incidents.

Once all of the critical incidents are categorized into their respective satisfaction items, repeat the categorization process using the satisfaction items. That is, group similar satisfaction items in order to identify a specific customer requirement or quality dimension. Label these customer requirements with phrases or a single word describing the content of the satisfaction items. These summary labels reflect specific quality dimensions. Unlike satisfaction items, these labels need not be specific. The only requirement is that the label should reflect the content of the satisfaction items. Using the previous example, we may generate a second satisfaction item that results in these two satisfaction items.

1. I waited a short period of time before I was helped.

2. Service started promptly when I arrived.

Both of these satisfaction items would be included under one customer requirement category labeled *Responsiveness of service.*

Having finished all the groupings, you will see a hierarchical relationship representing three levels of specificity falling on a specific-general continuum. The critical incidents fall on the specific end of the continuum, the customer requirements fall on the general end of the continuum, and the satisfaction items fall somewhere in between.

Although the outlined process leads from critical incidents to satisfaction items that lead, in turn, to customer requirements, this is not the only order in which the critical incidents approach can flow. It may be easier to first categorize the critical incidents directly into the customer requirement categories. Next, within each customer requirement category, categorize critical incidents into various satisfaction items. Thus, both methods result in a hierarchical relationship between critical incidents, satisfaction items, and customer requirements. This hierarchical relationship is illustrated in Figure 2.4. Customer requirements are defined by satisfaction items that are, in turn, defined by critical incidents.

Three forms are presented in Appendices A and B that will help you conduct interviews to determine the critical incidents. These forms are designed to facilitate each step in the critical incidents approach. The first form (Appendix A) will help you divide positive and negative aspects of the service and will make it easier to list all the critical incidents in a simple format. After conducting the interviews and recording the information, you can cut apart the form and allocate the critical incidents into separate satisfaction items. The second form (Appendix B) will allow you to place critical incidents into clusters and write satisfaction items as headings for each cluster. After writing all the satisfaction items, you can place similar satisfaction items in one customer requirement category. The third form (also Appendix B) allows you to list satisfaction items that fall under a particular customer requirement.

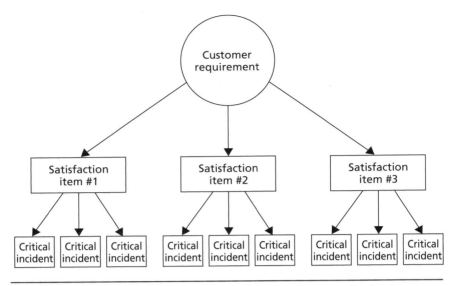

Figure 2.4   Hierarchical relationship among critical incidents, satisfaction items, and customer requirements.

QUALITY OF THE CATEGORIZATION PROCESS

The allocation process (from incident to satisfaction item and from satisfaction item to customer requirement category) is critical to understanding quality dimensions. Since the resulting customer requirements are derived from the initial solicitation and description of critical incidents, it is important to guarantee the quality of this allocation process.

Quality can be assured by having two people involved in the allocation process. These people are referred to as *judges* since their role involves judging the similarity of critical incidents and satisfaction items. The first judge will follow the previously described process, grouping incidents into satisfaction items and then grouping satisfaction items into customer requirement categories. The second judge looks at the customer requirement categories established by the first judge and allocates the critical incidents directly into them, bypassing the satisfaction items.

Inter-judge Agreement

The quality of the allocation process is indicated by the extent of agreement between the two judges. This "inter-judge agreement" is the percentage of incidents both judges place in the same customer requirement category. Inter-judge agreement is calculated by dividing the number of incidents both judges place in a customer requirement category by the total number of redundant and distinct incidents the judges place in the category. The index can range from 0 to 1.0. As this index approaches 1.0, it indicates that the judges are in high agreement. When the index approaches 0, it indicates that the judges are in low agreement. An index of approximately .8 should be used as a cutoff to determine whether the customer requirement was acceptable. This criterion has been suggested elsewhere (Latham, et al. 1979).

Let's look at an example to illustrate this index. Suppose the first judge grouped 100 critical incidents into 20 satisfaction items. Next, assume that this judge allocated two satisfaction items (a total of seven incidents) into one particular customer requirement category. Specifically, the first judge included incidents 1, 4, 6, 7, 9, 13, and 40 in the customer requirement category *availability*. Next, the second judge allocated all 100 critical incidents directly into the customer requirement categories that were established by the first judge, skipping the allocation of incidents into satisfaction items. Suppose the second judge included incidents 1, 2, 4, 6, 7, 9, 13, and 40 in the *availability* customer requirement category. The inter-judge agreement for this particular category would be .88 (7/8). The inter-judge agreement index would also be calculated for the remaining customer requirement categories.

If the criterion of .8 is not obtained, one or both judges may have made an error in the categorization process. A judge may have accidentally included or omitted a critical incident because he or she did not read the incident or category correctly. Thus, a brief check of the critical incidents could correct this problem. Also, a low inter-judge index could occur when a small number of incidents make up one customer requirement. If one judge omitted a single incident from a total possible set of four incidents, the resulting inter-judge agreement would be .75 (3/4). Although this value is below the recommended cutoff of .8, it seems to be an acceptable value given the small number of incidents that comprise the customer requirement category.

If a low inter-judge agreement index is apparent, the judges should discuss their disagreement and come to a consensus as to the appropriate incidents that comprise a particular customer requirement category. If they cannot agree, a third judge could be included to categorize the incidents. This third judge could highlight the differences between the first two judges, which may lead to consensus.

COMPREHENSIVENESS OF THE CUSTOMER REQUIREMENTS

Customer requirements obtained from the interviews should define comprehensively the quality of the service or product. If one important customer requirement category is overlooked during the initial interviewing process, the resulting customer satisfaction questionnaire would be deficient in measuring all customer requirements. In other words, you would be unable to assess your customers' perception of an important element of your service or product. Subsequently, you might not be able to improve overall customer satisfaction because you do not know why your customers are satisfied or dissatisfied.

You may also establish the quality of the content of critical incidents (Latham, et al. 1979). Do this by removing a random group of approximately 10 percent of the critical incidents from the initial list *before* they are categorized into satisfaction items and customer requirement categories. After the entire allocation process is completed with 90 percent of the critical incidents (determining customer requirements category), examine the remaining 10 percent to see whether they can be placed in the customer requirements categories.

If the 10 percent clearly can be placed into the customer requirement categories, then the categories are probably a comprehensive list of all possible customer requirement categories for that organization or group. If one or more of the 10 percent cannot be placed into any customer requirement category, then the list is probably deficient in defining all possible customer requirement categories. This problem can be handled by interviewing more customers to obtain more critical incidents. The recommended number of additional interviews, however, will depend on the extent of the deficiency; the more deficient, the more interviews are needed. As a general rule, you should conduct five additional interviews for every critical incident that could not be allocated in the initial list of customer requirements. Once you have conducted these additional interviews, reallocate all critical incidents into satisfaction items, then into customer requirement categories.

The next part of this chapter illustrates the use of the critical incidents technique to determine customer requirements in the service and manufacturing sectors. The service sector is represented by the banking industry, and the manufacturing sector is represented by the automobile industry. In addition, because customers can be internal to an organization, there is an illustration of the critical incidents approach as applied to a department that provides statistical support to other departments in the organization.

BANKING INDUSTRY

The first step in this process included interviews with 10 people who have had interactions with the bank's service. Critical incidents are confined to those related to customer interactions with personnel in the banking facility.

Responses from the 10 interviewees resulted in a total of 146 critical incidents. Some of these incidents appear in Figure 2.5. In addition, the figure includes the 10 satisfaction items (preceded by Roman numerals) that

Responsiveness of Service
I.   I waited a short period of time before I was helped.
    1. I waited too long before I was helped.
    2. Lines were too long.
    3. I waited in line for a very long time.
II. The service started immediately when I arrived.
    4. I went into the bank and the teller responded immediately to me.
    5. I received immediate service for my transaction.
    6. I could not get the teller's attention even though I was the only one in line.

Speed of Transaction
III. The teller handled transactions in a short period of time.
    7. The teller handled transactions fast.
    8. The handling of the transaction was quick after I told him or her what I wanted.
IV. The teller took a long time to complete my transaction.
    9. The entire transaction took too long.
    10. I waited a long time once I got to the window.

Availability of Service
V.   The financial consultant was available to schedule me for an appointment at a good time.
    11. I was able to set up an appointment with a financial consultant at a good time.
    12. The appointment time with the financial planner was when I wanted it.
VI. My appointment with the financial consultant was at a convenient time.
    13. The financial planner was available at a convenient time.
    14. My appointment was at an inconvenient time.

Professionalism
VII. The teller talked to me in a pleasant way.
    15. The teller took the time to talk to me to get all my requests completed.
    16. The teller was rude to me (specifically, he or she was short with me).
    17. The teller yelled at me when I could not open the depository canister.
VIII. The teller was very personable.
    18. The teller gave a personal compliment on my appearance.
    19. The teller had a friendly smile.
    20. The teller was not personal (did not say hello or goodbye).
IX. The teller carefully listened to me when I was requesting a transaction.
    21. The teller carefully listened to my request.
    22. The teller took the time to listen to me when I requested a lot of things.

Figure 2.5 Critical incidents, satisfaction items, and customer requirements related to the banking industry.   *(Continued)*

(Continued)

X.   The teller knew how to handle the transactions. 23. The teller knew how to handle a special transaction I requested. 24. The teller had to ask for help from another teller for a special transaction I asked for. 25. The teller looked confused when I asked for a special transaction. **Overall Satisfaction with Service** XI.   The quality of the way the teller treated me was high. XII. The way the teller treated me met my expectations. XIII. I am satisfied with the way the teller treated me.

Figure 2.5   Critical incidents, satisfaction items, and customer requirements related to the banking industry.

represent their respective critical incidents. Furthermore, satisfaction items are grouped into four customer requirement categories.

There is also a category labeled *Overall Satisfaction with Service.* The satisfaction items for this category are less specific than the items in different customer requirement categories and are not based on any critical incidents. This category represents overall service quality; it is not focused on any particular quality dimension. The value of these items will become clear in Chapters 3 and 6.

It is important to note that customer requirements reflect only aspects of the banking industry that are related to personal interaction. Not included are incidents related to other aspects of the banking industry, such as phone transaction banking, automatic teller machines, and account statements.

AUTOMOBILE INDUSTRY

The next illustration of the critical incidents technique applies to the automobile industry. Critical incidents were confined to aspects of the automobile's interior and its "drivability." Aspects of car driving quality were gathered in customer interviews. The categorization process resulted in three customer requirements. The critical incidents, satisfaction items, and customer requirements appear in Figure 2.6.

Another way to conceptualize the groupings of these satisfaction items is to place them all into one customer requirement category called *perception of driving quality.* This customer requirement could be paralleled by another aspect of car quality such as *reliability of car.* This customer requirement might be measured by more objective indices such as the number of repairs, amount of money spent on repairs, or number of breakdowns. Using this conceptualization could result in two customer requirements: (1) the customers' perception of driving quality and (2) the car's reliability.

Interior Quality
I.   The seating position was very comfortable.
    1. The seats are comfortable.
    2. The seats were very uncomfortable.
    3. There is ample leg room.
II. The visibility through the window was good.
    4. There were many blind spots from the driver's seat.
III. The inside of the car was noisy.
    5. There is loud interior noise.
    6. The interior noise interfered with the sound of the stereo.
    7. Air whistles through the window.
    8. There was little noise while I was driving.

Instrumentation
IV. The instrumentation panel was simple to understand.
    9. The instrumentation panel is difficult to read.
    10. The dials for the accessories were too complex to understand.
    11. The dials for the controls were easy to understand.
V.   The instrumentation panel was clearly visible from the driving seat.
    12. I could clearly see all the instruments and gauges.
    13. I had a clear view of the instrumentation.
    14. Instruments are within good reaching distance.

"Drivability"
VI. The car stopped smoothly when I applied the brakes.
    15. The car did not brake well. (It would vibrate when I was braking.)
    16. The car vibrated when I applied the brakes.
    17. The car stopped smoothly when I applied the brakes.
VII. The car vibrated at high speeds.
    18. The car vibrated at high speeds.
    19. The car rides smoothly, even at high speeds.
VIII. The car handled corners well.
    20. The car handles corners well.
    21. I could negotiate corners very well.
    22. The car would consistently skid around tight corners.

Overall Satisfaction with Automobile
IX. I enjoyed driving the car.
X.   I liked the overall driving experience of the car.
XI. The drive was excellent.

Figure 2.6 Critical incidents, satisfaction items, and customer requirements related to the driving quality of automobiles.

STATISTICAL SUPPORT

The next illustration of the critical incidents technique applies to a statistical department that provides support to other departments within the organization. A total of nine customers who have had previous contact with the staff in this department were interviewed. The categorization process resulted in five customer requirements. A partial list of the critical incidents, satisfaction items, and customer requirements is included in Figure 2.7.

Statistical Support

I. The staff person explained the statistical tests in understandable words.
   1. There was good explanation of the statistical tests.
   2. I received good explanation of the statistical analyses.

II. The statistical analyses were thorough.
   3. There was good analysis of data.
   4. Statistical help was minimal.
   5. The data analysis was incomplete.

III. The staff understood my software requirements.
   6. The software problem was never resolved.
   7. The staff understood the kinds of software I needed.

Enthusiasm

IV. The staff person was always willing to help.
   8. The person was always willing to help.
   9. The person would always help when I asked.

V. The staff person went out of his or her way to help.
   10. The person did not do the tasks.
   11. The person refused to do the project.
   12. The person did not do the project I asked him or her to do.

Final Written Report

VI. The written report was sufficiently detailed.
   13. The writeup of the project was not detailed.
   14. The written report was not complete.
   15. The document needed to be more comprehensive.

VII. The written report contained what I needed.
   16. Everything I asked for was in the final report.
   17. The report contained everything I asked for.

Responsiveness

VIII. The staff person completed the job quickly.
   18. Projects are completed quickly.
   19. The project started very late.
   20. I received fast turnaround time on my project.

Figure 2.7   Critical incidents, satisfaction items, and customer requirements related to the quality of a statistical support department. (Continued)

(Continued)

Project Management

IX. The staff person finished the project in the stated time frame.

    21. The staff person did not meet the specified deadlines.

    22. The staff person did not have the job completed for a meeting.

    23. The project was turned in late.

X. The staff person planned the entire project through its completion.

    24. The planning of the project was complete.

    25. The project was well organized.

XI. The staff person understood how much time the project required.

    26. The person did not understand my requirements.

    27. The person understood the magnitude of the project.

Overall Satisfaction with Support

XII. I am satisfied with the service I received.

XIII. The quality of the service met my expectations.

Figure 2.7 Critical incidents, satisfaction items, and customer requirements related to the quality of a statistical support department.

CHAPTER SUMMARY

This chapter demonstrated two techniques for determining customer requirements, those aspects of your service or product that define its quality. The first technique, the quality dimension development process, involves people closely linked to the service or product, those people who best understand the needs of the customer and the function and purpose of the service or product. They are responsible for determining and defining quality dimensions and citing specific examples of each dimension.

The second technique, the critical incident technique, involves obtaining information from customers about actual incidents they consider to define good and bad aspects of the product or service. These incidents define the satisfaction items, and the satisfaction items, in turn, define the customer requirements. Some examples demonstrated the effectiveness of the critical incidents approach in establishing customer requirements for both non-manufacturing and manufacturing organizations and internal customer support groups.

Figure 2.8 presents the basic steps to follow for each method when establishing your customer requirements. This figure includes some important points at each step to facilitate the process.

Quality Dimension Development

Steps	Important Points
1. Create list of quality dimensions.	• Read professional and trade journals to obtain list of quality dimensions. • Generate list from personal experience.
2. Write definition of each dimension.	• Definition can be in general terms.
3. Develop specific examples for each quality dimension.	• Examples should use specific adjectives reflecting the service or product. • Examples should include specific behaviors of the provider. • Examples should use declarative statements.

Critical Incidents Approach

Steps	Important Points
1. Generate critical incidents.	• Interview customers. • Critical incidents should be specific examples of good or poor service or product quality. • Each critical incident reflects only one example.
2. Categorize critical incidents into clusters.	• Categorization is based on similarity in content of the incidents.
3. Write satisfaction items for each critical incident cluster.	• Each satisfaction item should be a declarative statement. • Satisfaction items should be specific.
4. Categorize satisfaction items into clusters, each cluster representing a customer requirement.	• Categorization should be based on similarity of satisfaction items. • Customer requirement must reflect the content of satisfaction items.

Figure 2.8 Procedures for establishing customer requirements. (Continued)

(Continued)

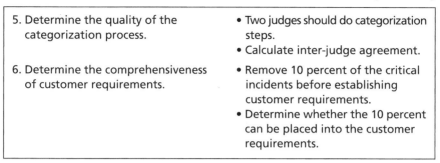

5. Determine the quality of the categorization process.	• Two judges should do categorization steps. • Calculate inter-judge agreement.
6. Determine the comprehensiveness of customer requirements.	• Remove 10 percent of the critical incidents before establishing customer requirements. • Determine whether the 10 percent can be placed into the customer requirements.

Figure 2.8   Procedures for establishing customer requirements.

The next chapter will discuss measurement issues related to question-naire development and use. These measurement principles should be considered when evaluating any type of questionnaire designed to measure people's opinions, perceptions, and attitudes.

3

Reliability and Validity

Measurement instruments can help us better understand and make predictions about our world. For example, we may be interested in measuring our customers' level of satisfaction in order to uncover any perceived problems with our services or products. In addition, we might want to change customer opinions about our services or products. In order to know our customers' current level of satisfaction and to recognize when changes in their opinion do occur, we need a measure that accurately assesses customer attitudes. When we develop questionnaires, it is important to ensure that the data obtained from them reflect reliable and valid information. This chapter discusses issues that demonstrate the importance of careful thought in the design of questionnaires that measure perceptions and attitudes.

THE MEANING OF CUSTOMER PERCEPTION AND ATTITUDE

Customers' perceptions of the quality of a service and their overall satisfaction have some observable indicators. Customers may smile when they talk about the product or service. They may say good things about the product or service. Both actions are manifestations or indicators of an underlying construct we might call *customer satisfaction*. The terms *customer satisfaction* and *perception of quality* are labels we use to summarize a set of observable actions related to the product or service. This idea of constructs and their relationship to observable variables is depicted in Figure 3.1.

As indicated by Figure 3.1, various observable criteria (such as items) might be manifestations of an underlying dimension (such as customer requirements). For example, we could make inferences about people's happiness by obtaining several types of observable indicators of the underlying *happiness* construct. Observable indicators could include smiling, laughing, and saying positive things. If a person is laughing, smiling, and

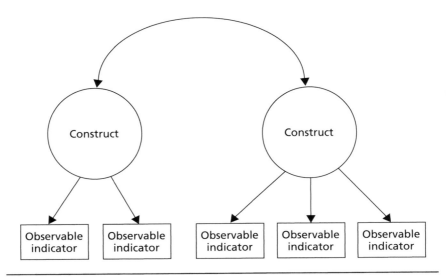

Figure 3.1   The relationship between observable indicators and the underlying constructs, and the relationship between the constructs.

saying positive things, we conclude that this person is happy by examining the observable criteria.

Similarly, we draw conclusions about customers' perceptions and attitudes about products or services by examining observable manifestations related to the product or service. These observable manifestations are the responses the customers give on a customer satisfaction questionnaire. If people indicate good things about the product on the customer satisfaction questionnaire and demonstrate other indications of positive behavior, we can conclude that they are satisfied with the product.

From Figure 3.1, we can draw conclusions about the concept of customer perception and attitude. First, we can never really know the true underlying satisfaction level of our customers. We develop measures to make inferences about the underlying construct, satisfaction. Second, we are interested in the relationship between underlying dimensions or constructs (such as customer satisfaction or perceived responsiveness). We want to understand how these underlying constructs, or customer requirements, are related to each other.

When constructing a questionnaire or scale that assesses customer attitudes and perceptions toward customer requirements, it is necessary to consider measurement issues to ensure that scores derived from such instruments reflect accurate information about these underlying constructs. Measurement issues in customer satisfaction are as important as issues related to the measurement of tangible objects such as machine parts. Gauge repeatability and reliability indices (gauge R&R), for example, are designed to reflect the quality of the measurement process in industrial settings. Similarly, statistical indices can reflect the quality of measurement of satisfaction questionnaires. Reliability and validity are two important measurement issues to consider when developing questionnaires.

RELIABILITY

I will introduce the concept of reliability with a simple measurement example. We could use a ruler to measure the length of one particular part. We could measure the part five times, obtaining five scores. Even though the part can be characterized by one true length, we would expect the five scores to be slightly different from each other. The deviation could be due to various random factors in the measurement process, such as variations in the ruler with each measurement or change in ruler length with each measurement. To the extent that random factors are introduced into the measurement process, any one score we obtain may not reliably reflect the true score.

When we develop a questionnaire that assesses customer perception of the quality of the service or product, we want to be sure that measurements are free from random error. That is, we want to be sure the true underlying level of perception of quality or satisfaction is accurately reflected in the questionnaire score. When random error is introduced into measurement, the observed score is less reliable in estimating the true underlying score. Errors of measurement are examined under the context of reliability.

Reliability is defined as the extent to which measurements are free from random-error variance. Random error decreases the reliability of the measurement. If we want to feel confident that scores on our questionnaire reliably reflect the underlying dimension, we want the questionnaire to demonstrate high reliability. There are three general forms of reliability: test-retest reliability, equivalent form reliability, and internal consistency. Discussions of reliability appear in various textbooks (Anastasi 1988; Brown 1983; Guion 1965; and Gulliksen 1987). I will first review information concerning classical measurement theory and then discuss indices used to estimate the reliability of questionnaires. A more detailed discussion of classical measurement theory, including underlying statistical assumptions, appears in various books (such as Gulliksen 1987).

Classical Measurement Theory

When assessing a customer's level of satisfaction, the best we can do is to ask the person to respond to questions. From the answers, we obtain a score that indicates that person's level of satisfaction with the product or service.

However, this only gives us an observed score. According to classical measurement theory, this observed score comprises a true score (the actual level of satisfaction) and a component of measurement error. Error is assumed to be random and is unrelated to the true score. The basic equation of classical measurement theory, known as the classical measurement model, describes the relationship between observed scores, true scores, and error. The model is

$$X = T + E$$

where X is the observed score, T is the true score, and E is error of measurement. To the extent that we have small error of measurement, this observable measure (X) is highly representative of the underlying true score, T.

An illustration concerning the relationship between these three components might make things clear. In Table 3.1, we have a hypothetical example of data collected from 10 customers. The first column (X) represents the score these people received on the questionnaire (their observed score) and indicates their level of satisfaction: the higher the number, the higher their satisfaction. Now, let's assume that we were somehow able to obtain the

Table 3.1   Hypothetical example illustrating observed scores, true scores, and error.

Customers	X	T	E
1.	5	5	0
2.	3	4	−1
3.	4	3	1
4.	3	2	1
5.	1	1	0
6.	5	5	0
7.	5	4	1
8.	2	3	−1
9.	1	2	−1
10.	1	1	0

$$M_X = 3.0 \qquad M_T = 3.0 \qquad M_E = 0.0$$
$$\text{Var}(X) = 2.88 \qquad \text{Var}(T) = 2.22 \qquad \text{Var}(E) = 0.66$$

Average for	Variance for
$X = M_X = \Sigma X_i / n$	$X = \text{Var}(X) = \Sigma(X_i - M_X)^2 / n$
$T = M_T = \Sigma T_i / n$	$T = \text{Var}(T) = \Sigma(T_i - M_T)^2 / n$
$E = M_E = \Sigma E_i / n$	$E = \text{Var}(E) = \Sigma(E_i - M_E)^2 / n$

customers' true level of satisfaction (the customers' true score)—perhaps we know God, and He informed us of the true level of satisfaction for each customer. The second column *(T)* represents the customers' true level of satisfaction. Finally, the last column *(E)* represents the random error and is calculated by subtracting the values in column *T* from the values in column *X*.

There are two approaches we can take in explaining reliability. One approach focuses on correlational analysis (see Appendix J), and the other focuses on variance for each of the components in the classical theory equation *(X, T,* and *E).* I will present the correlational approach first.

Using correlational analysis, we can determine the degree of agreement between the observed scores *(X)* and the true scores *(T).* We can calculate the correlation coefficient between *X* and *T* scores. A correlation coefficient can range from –1 to 1. A negative correlation indicates that as one variable increases, the other variable decreases. A positive correlation indicates that as one variable increases, the other variable also increases. A correlation of zero indicates there is no linear relationship between the two variables. A perfect negative or positive correlation indicates a perfect negative or positive relationship, respectively.

Using the data in Table 3.1, we can calculate the correlation coefficient between the *X* and *T* scores to be .88. This suggests that the differences in true scores are closely matched by differences in observed scores. That is, people who have truly high scores (true scores) also obtain relatively high scores on the questionnaire (observed score). Also, people who have relatively low true scores also obtain relatively low observed scores on the questionnaire.

Therefore, a form of reliability would be the correlation between observed and true scores. As the correlation between *X* and *T* increases, the differences in people's *X* scores more closely approximates the differences in people's *T* scores. When the correlation between *X* and *T* is 1.00, there is perfect linear agreement between *X* and *T.* That is, differences in *X* scores exactly match the differences in *T* scores. When the correlation between *X* and *T* is 0, there is no linear relationship between *X* and *T.* That is, there is no agreement between *X* and *T* scores.

We could also examine reliability of the measurement instrument by focusing on variance of the specific components (that is, observed, true, and error components). Variance is an index that reflects the spread of the data around the arithmetic average of the data. (See Appendix E for a discussion of average and variance.) The larger the variance, the larger will be the spread of the data around the average. The formula for variance is presented in Table 3.1, and the variance for each component has been calculated. The variances for each of the sets of variables are related in a similar fashion, as are the variables themselves.

$$Var(X) = Var(T) + Var(E)$$

where $Var(X)$ is the variance associated with the set of observed scores, $Var(T)$ is the variance associated with the set of true scores, and $Var(E)$ is the variance associated with the set of errors.

As error variance decreases, as indicated by the equation, the variance of the observed score approaches the variance of the true score; that is, as error decreases, the differences in observed scores between people become a *reliable* reflection of differences in their true scores. If the error variance is large, however, the observed score is not reliably related to the true score.

Reliability estimates can be indexed by a number that represents the percentage of variance of observed scores that is accounted for by the variance in true scores. In mathematical terms, this corresponds to the following equation.

$$\text{Reliability } (r_{xx'}) = Var(T) / [Var(T) + Var(E)]$$

where $Var(T) + Var(E) = Var(X)$.

This reliability index can range from 0 to 1.0. A reliability index of 1.0 indicates there is no measurement error; observed scores can be perfectly predicted by true scores. This is a highly desirable situation. A reliability index of 0 indicates there is no true score variation or that the variation in the observed scores can be completely explained by random error. This is a highly undesirable situation. For the data in Table 3.1, we can calculate the reliability of the observed score (X), which is $r_{xx'} = 2.22/2.88 = .77$. This indicates that our observed scores are somewhat related to the underlying true scores for the customers. In fact, the correlation between the X and T scores can be calculated by taking the square root of the reliability $(r_{XT} = \sqrt{.77} = .88)$. Conversely, reliability is the squared correlation between the observed scores and true scores.

Reliability, then, can be discussed in terms of both the relationship between observed and true scores and the variance of components of the classical measurement model. The two approaches should not be interpreted as representing two different types of reliability. They are merely two different ways of conceptualizing the degree to which observed scores are related to true scores (or the degree to which observed scores are free from random error). Readers are offered both approaches to help facilitate understanding of this important concept.

Standard Error of Measurement

Measurement error is often discussed in terms of the standard error of measurement (SEM). The SEM could be calculated for a given individual by administering the questionnaire or test to that individual many times (say, 100 times). Due to measurement error, the person might not get the same score on each administration of the test. Thus, these observed scores would form a distribution that would approximate a normal distribution described by a mean and a standard deviation (see Appendix F). The mean of this distribution would be our best estimate of the person's true score. The standard deviation of this distribution is technically called the *standard error of measurement*; it describes the amount of measurement error we have. Theoretically, we could calculate the SEM for each individual, but this would be tedious, if not impossible. We can more easily calculate SEM from the reliability of the questionnaire. The equation for the SEM is

$$\text{SEM} = s_x \times \sqrt{(1 - r_{xx'})}$$

where s_x is the standard deviation of observed scores for the sample of people to which the questionnaire was administered, and $r_{xx'}$ is the reliability of the questionnaire.

As this formula illustrates, SEM is inversely and monotonically related to reliability. That is, for a given s_x, an increase in reliability always leads to a decrease in SEM. As reliability approaches 1.0 (observed scores, X, are perfectly correlated with true scores, T), SEM goes to zero. Conversely, as reliability approaches zero (X scores are not related to T scores), SEM will equal the s_x.

The meaning of SEM and the relationship between reliability and SEM is illustrated in Figure 3.2. The top portion of the figure presents the expected distribution of random errors for a given individual using a particular questionnaire. The SEM describes the degree of error for observed scores we would expect for a given true score. As the SEM decreases, we are more confident that the observed scores are a good reflection of the true scores. For example, if the SEM for a given questionnaire was .50, then we could say with a 95 percent degree of confidence that for a person with a true score of 4, his or her observed score would fall between $3.0 = (4 - (2 \times .5))$ and $5.0 = (4 + (2 \times .5))$. If the SEM was .25, we could say with the same degree of confidence that the person's observed score falls between 3.5 and 4.5.

The bottom portion of Figure 3.2 demonstrates the relationship between X and T scores and shows how SEM is incorporated into this relationship. As this illustration indicates, if we have a high degree of measurement error, we are less confident that a particular observed score is associated with any one true score. For example, if SEM is high, which would be reflected in the widening of the distributions, then an observed score of 4 might represent a true score of 4 or it might also represent a number of other true scores. If SEM is low, which would be reflected in the narrowing of the distributions, then an observed score of 3 would most likely represent a true score of 3, and the possibility of the observed score representing other true scores is greatly decreased.

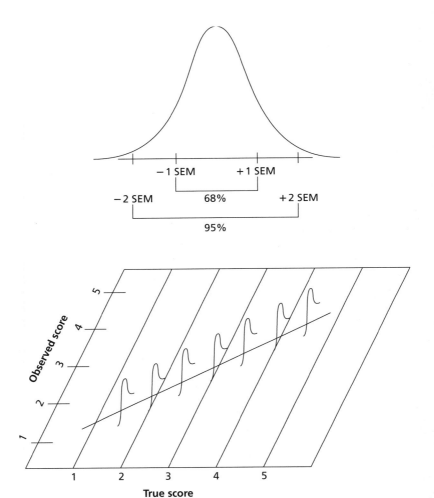

Figure 3.2 The top portion illustrates an expected distribution of observed scores for a given person. The bottom portion illustrates the relationship between observed scores and true scores and incorporates the standard error of measurement.

Some simple scatter plots of the relationship between the X and T scores are presented in Figure 3.3. Although T scores can never be assessed, a hypothetical scatter plot of the T scores with the X scores can be presented given a certain value of the reliability. In general, as reliability increases, the precision in predicting X scores from the T scores increases. In other words,

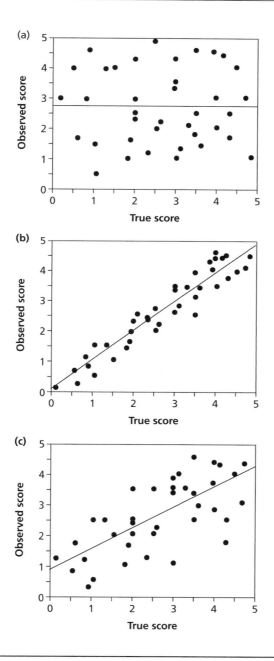

Figure 3.3 The hypothetical relationship between true scores and observed scores with varying degrees of reliability (a: $r_{xx'} = 0$; b: $r_{xx'} = .81$; c: $r_{xx'} = .25$).

as reliability increases, the variability in X for any given T score (represented as SEM) decreases. As seen in Figure 3.3(a), a reliability of 0 indicates that changes in X scores are unrelated to changes in T scores. In other words, a given observed score, X, could reflect many possible true scores, T. As seen in Figure 3.3(b), a reliability of .81 indicates that an observed score (X) is highly related to the underlying true score (T). Consequently, a given observed score is likely to reflect a limited number of true scores. Figure 3.3(c) illustrates a measure with a low degree of reliability.

SOURCES OF ERROR AND RELIABILITY ESTIMATES

The term *reliability* is a generic term used to describe the degree of error associated with a measure. Because we can never know the exact degree of true variance and error variance, we can never directly calculate the level of reliability for a set of scores. We can, however, estimate reliability. We will see that there are different methods of estimating reliability. These differ depending on what type of measurement error you want to examine. Next, I will cover the different types of estimates of reliability and the errors associated with them. There are three general classes of reliability: stability, equivalence, and internal consistency.

Measures of Stability and Test-Retest Reliability

It is possible to administer the same survey at two different times (time 1 and time 2) to the same set of people and get different results. The difference between their scores at time 1 and time 2 reflects error associated with a change in the characteristic that is being measured by the survey. Change from time 1 to time 2 indicates one of three things: (1) there may have been a change in the true score being measured, (2) there may have been measurement error, or (3) both.

An index of reliability to assess stability over time is referred to as *test-retest reliability*. This index of reliability is essentially the correlation between the survey scores for time 1 and time 2. As is seen in Table 3.2, we have a set of 10 people, each receiving a survey at two separate times. Their respective scores for each time period are listed. Using the formula in Appendix J to calculate the correlation, we see that the test-retest reliability is .66. This reliability estimate indicates that scores are relatively stable across the two time periods. People who have low scores at time 1 also tend to have low scores at time 2. People who have high scores at time 1 also tend to have high scores at time 2.

The stability of customer satisfaction over time might depend on the time interval between the administration of the two surveys. Given a short interval between time 1 and time 2, there may be carry-over effects to the second survey session. That is, customers may remember their scores from

Table 3.2   Test-retest reliability for survey X.

Person	Time 1 (X)	Time 2 (X')
A. Neumeister	4.5	5.0
A. Asaf	4.0	3.4
T. Hayes	2.0	3.0
B. Smith	5.0	5.0
C. Silva	1.5	3.0
S. Kincaide	5.0	3.0
S. King	4.0	4.0
R. Seay	2.6	3.5
L. Foster	2.0	1.0
O. Rhyme	4.5	4.0
Mean of X and X'	3.51	3.49
SD	1.35	1.16
ΣX and $\Sigma X'$	35.10	34.90
ΣX^2 and $\Sigma (X')^2$	139.51	133.81
$\Sigma (X\,X')$	131.70	

$$r = \frac{10(131.7) - (35.10 \times 34.90)}{\sqrt{([(10 \times 139.51) - 35.10^2][(10 \times 133.81) - 34.90^2])}}$$

$$r = .657$$

the first session and simply duplicate their answers in the second adminis-tration of the survey. Thus, a high test-retest correlation (say, .90) between the two sets of scores might not be due to the stability of the customer satisfaction being measured; rather, it might reflect carry-over effects. On the other hand, when there is a long interval between two administrations of the survey, many variables can intervene and influence customer satisfaction scores. For example, customers could be given a survey one month after they purchase a product and then again one year later. If we see a low correlation (say, .40) between these two scores, there are competing explanations for this result: (1) there is a change in the customer satisfaction level over this time period, (2) the customer survey is not highly reliable, or (3) both.

Even though interpretations of the test-retest correlation can be problematic for either short or long time intervals between administrations, there is still no standard rule for an appropriate length of time between survey administrations. A general rule would be that, when determining an appropriate time period between survey administrations, one must be cognizant of the types of factors that can influence survey scores and adjust the time interval accordingly.

Test-retest reliability is not commonly calculated with customer satisfaction surveys; it's difficult to design a survey process that allows for the administration of the survey to the same set of individuals across two time periods. Each customer must be identified so that his or her scores for time 1 and time 2 can be linked in order to calculate the correlation between the two sets of scores. For research purposes, this type of reliability estimation might be useful to see whether customer satisfaction does not, in fact, change over time. For practical purposes, however, this method of estimating reliability may not be worthwhile. However, test-retest reliability could be analyzed at group level to determine the stability of customer satisfaction across different office locations. For example, if a bank has hundreds of locations, it would be possible to calculate the average satisfaction scores for each bank branch across two different times. The correlation between the two sets of bank branch scores would indicate the degree of stability we see across time. A high correlation would indicate that customer satisfaction levels for branches are the same over time. A low correlation would indicate that customer satisfaction levels for branches change over time.

Measures of Equivalence and Parallel Forms Reliability

A survey contains a specific set of questions that are designed to assess a particular construct (such as service quality). When developing this survey of service quality, you include various specific questions. Our goal in developing the survey is to be able to generalize from the specific items in our measure to the content domain from which the items were drawn. The set of items used in the survey is just a small sample of possible items we could have used. To the extent that scores derived from this survey are unique to the items within the survey, we have error associated with the selection of those particular items.

An index of reliability to assess the extent to which scores are free from error associated with a particular set of items is referred to as *parallel forms reliability*. Essentially, this form of reliability indicates whether the scores of the survey can generalize beyond the specific items that are in the survey to the domain of all possible items. For this form of reliability, we compare two equivalent forms of a survey designed to measure the same construct. For example, it is possible to develop two different surveys of service quality, each survey containing slightly different questions to measure the same underlying construct of interest. To calculate parallel forms reliability, two surveys measuring the same construct are administered to the same set of people. The correlation between the two sets of scores is used as the estimate of reliability. If there is not much error associated with the item selection process, the two different surveys should be highly correlated with each other. Table 3.3 contains the scores of two different surveys that measure service quality for 10 people. The correlation between the two surveys is .93, suggesting that there is little error associated with the selection of the specific items within each survey. A low correlation between the two measures could suggest that it's not possible to generalize scores from one or both of the measures beyond the items in the scale.

Internal Consistency

Internal consistency concerns the degree to which the items in the survey are measuring the same thing. For example, in a customer survey, we could combine some items to get a single score of some quality dimension. The items that are combined should be assessing the same thing. If the items are not measuring the same thing, then the overall score would be meaningless. To the degree that the items in the survey are measuring the same thing, we have little measurement error. Two estimates of internal consistency will be presented next.

Table 3.3 Parallel forms reliability for survey X.

Person	Survey 1	Survey 2
A. Neumeister	4.5	5.0
A. Asaf	4.4	4.0
T. Hayes	2.0	1.5
B. Smith	5.0	5.0
C. Silva	1.5	2.0
S. Kincaide	5.0	4.0
S. King	3.8	4.0
R. Seay	2.4	3.0
L. Foster	2.0	1.5
O. Rhyme	4.5	4.0
Mean of X_1 and X_2	3.51	3.35
SD	1.38	1.27
ΣX_1 and ΣX_2	35.10	33.50
ΣX_2^2 and ΣX_2^2	140.31	126.75
$\Sigma(X_1 X_2)$	132.25	

$$r = \frac{10(132.25) - (35.10 \times 33.50)}{\sqrt{([(10 \times 140.31) - 35.10^2][(10 \times 126.75) - 33.50^2])}}$$

$$r = .93$$

Split-Half Reliability Estimate

This method estimates internal consistency by dividing the scale into halves (for example, odd versus even items, or first half of scale versus last half of scale), then correlating the scores on these halves. A high correlation indicates that the two sets yield consistent information; that is, if a person scores high on one set of items, then that person also scores high on the other set. Thus, the items are likely measuring the same thing.

When using the split-half method to estimate reliability, it is necessary to include a correction factor. Reliability estimates are affected by the length of the scale: the more items on the scale, the higher the reliability. Using the split-half method, we actually estimate the reliability for a scale that was half the original length (because the scale was divided in half). To control for test length, we use a correction formula, the Spearman-Brown formula, which results in a corrected reliability estimate. The general formula is

$$r_{cc'} = (nr_{12}) / (1 + (n - 1)r_{12})$$

where $r_{cc'}$ is the corrected reliability estimate of the questionnaire, r_{12} is the correlation between the two halves of the same questionnaire, and n is the number of items in the overall scale divided by the number of items in each of the halves.

For example, we may want to calculate the reliability of a questionnaire that has 10 items. Using the split-half method, we divide the questionnaire into halves containing five items each and calculate the correlation between the halves. Suppose we found that the correlation was $r_{12} = .7$. Next, because reliability estimates are affected by the length of the scale, we would correct this value to obtain a better estimate of reliability. The final reliability estimate, corrected for length, would be $r_{cc'} = .82$ ($r_{cc'} = (2 \times .7) / (1 + .7)$).

Cronbach's Alpha Estimate

The Cronbach's alpha estimate also tells us how highly the items in our questionnaire are interrelated. Unlike the split-half reliability method, however, this estimate need not be corrected for length. Calculation of Cronbach's estimate is usually done with the help of a statistical package designed to calculate this reliability estimate. Statistical packages are usually used when questionnaires have many items. Cronbach's (1951) estimate of reliability is calculated using the variance of individual items and covariances between the items. This estimate, however, also can be calculated using the correlations between the items. Given that items within a questionnaire use the same scale, both approaches give similar estimates. The latter approach is easier to understand and is presented here.

Generally, the formula for Cronbach's reliability estimate is

$$r_{xx'} = (K / (K - 1)) \times (1 - [(\Sigma X_{ii}) / (\Sigma X_{ii} + \Sigma X_{ij} \text{ where } i \neq j)])$$

where X_{iis} and X_{ijs} are the elements in the covariance matrix or correlation matrix, and K is the number of items within a given dimension. The numerator, (ΣX_{ii}), indicates that the elements in the diagonal of the covariance (correlation) matrix are to be added together. The denominator, $(\Sigma X_{ii} + \Sigma X_{ij})$, indicates that all the elements in the covariance (correlation) matrix are to be added together.

Table 3.4 represents a correlation matrix using actual data for the items from Figure 4.5 in Chapter 4. Customers responded to each item using a five-point scale ("1" represented strong disagreement, and "5" represented strong agreement). With this questionnaire, we think we are measuring two customer requirements, perception of availability (items 1 through 3) and perception of responsiveness (items 4 through 6). Therefore, we can combine the items in their respective scales (average of the items within each scale) to obtain two observed scores, each representing a customer requirement. We now want to see whether these observed scores are reliable indicators of an underlying dimension. The reliability estimate is .897 = $[1.5 \times (1 - 3/7.468)]$ for perception of availability and .904 = $[1.5 \times (1 - 3 / 7.556)]$ for perception of responsiveness. As indicated by these reliability estimates, the composite of the three items for each dimension gives us an overall observed score that is a reliable measure of the underlying dimension.

TYPES OF ERROR AND RELIABILITY ESTIMATES

Reliability indicates the degree to which measures are free from random error. As we have seen, however, there are different sources of error and corresponding estimates of reliability. Table 3.5 summarizes these different sources of error and the methods of estimating reliability. One type of measurement error is associated with time sampling. A survey given on two

Table 3.4   The correlation matrix of the items from Figure 4.5.

	Avail I	Avail 2	Avail 3	Resp I	Resp 2	Resp 3
Avail 1	1.00	.92	.80	.23	.00	.34
Avail 2	.92	1.00	.51	.49	.16	.49
Avail 3	.80	.51	1.00	−.25	−.25	.00
Resp 1	.23	.49	−.25	1.00	.78	.83
Resp 2	.00	.16	−.25	.78	1.00	.67
Resp 3	.34	.49	.00	.83	.67	1.00

Table 3.5   Sources of error and methods of estimating reliability.

Source of error	What are we asking?	Estimate of reliability	How to calculate reliability estimate
Time-specific	Is there stability in customer satisfaction over time?	Test-retest	Correlation between same survey given on two occasions
Item-specific	Can the items in the survey generalize to all possible items?	Parallel forms	Correlation between two different surveys designed to measure the same thing
Internal consistency	Do the items in the survey measure the same thing?	Split-half	1. Corrected correlation between two halves of the same survey
		Cronbach's alpha	2. See text

separate occasions might result in different scores. The method used to determine the degree of this error is the test-retest method of estimating reliability. Another form of measurement error is associated with the specific items used in a given measure. Different items are used in two different surveys to measure the same thing. If both surveys are measuring the same thing, the sample of items from both surveys should be representative of the same larger population of items. To the extent to which results from the survey are item specific, we have error associated with item sampling. Parallel forms reliability is the method used to determine the degree of this type of error. Finally, if we develop a survey to measure a single thing, then each item in that measure should be highly correlated with all others. Internal consistency estimates indicate the degree to which the items in the survey measure the same thing.

It is clear that the term *reliability* means different things depending on what source of error you are estimating. It is important to be aware of the distinction among the sources of error and methods used to estimate reliability. It is possible that each source of error would occur in a single instance in the use of a survey. For a given situation, a survey could be assessed on the error associated with time-specific factors as well as item-specific factors. Corresponding reliability estimates could be calculated for these respective sources of error. Be aware of the sources of error associated with these reliability estimates and what they mean.

BENEFITS OF SCALES WITH HIGH RELIABILITY

There are two benefits of having a scale with high reliability: (1) it distinguishes between varying levels of satisfaction better than a scale with low reliability, and (2) it makes it more likely that we will find significant relationships between variables that are truly related to each other.

Detection of Differences in Satisfaction Levels

Reliability indicates the degree to which observed scores are related to true scores. Therefore, if we use a scale with a high level of reliability, we can better distinguish between people on the continuum of customer satisfaction. As illustrated in the scatter plot in Figure 3.3(c) representing a scale of low reliability ($r_{xx'} = .25$), we would have considerable error of measurement. Consequently, we could find that customer 1, who has a true score of 3, could have an observed score between 1.0 and 4.5. Customer 2, who has a true score of 5.0, could have an observed score as low as 3.0. Although these two customers actually differ with respect to customer satisfaction (T scores), we might not be able to distinguish between them because our scale is unreliable. It is possible that customer 2 with a higher true score of customer satisfaction might get an observed score that is lower than the observed score of customer 1. With low reliability, there is a great deal of uncertainty as to what the observed score indicates for any person. This would limit the strength of the conclusions we can make about people's scores.

If we use a scale with high reliability such as $r_{xx'} = .81$ [see Figure 3.3(b)], we would have little error in measurement. Therefore, we would be able to distinguish between people whose satisfaction levels are close. Now, customer 1, who is truly less satisfied than customer 2, will more likely get an observed score that is lower than the score of customer 2. In the situation where reliability equals 1.0, customers who have a true score of 3 will get an observed score of 3, and customers who have a true score of 5 will get an observed score of 5.

In summary, when using scales with low reliability, only true differences that are very large are likely to be detected. A scale with high reliability will likely detect true differences that are either very large or very small. The strength of this detection is directly related to the reliability of the scale. Therefore, to increase the ability to make distinctions between customers, we need to increase the reliability of the scale.

Detection of Significant Relationships Between Variables

We might want to determine whether perceptions of availability are linked to overall customer satisfaction. This might be important to know if we wanted to determine where to allocate some resources in order to increase overall customer satisfaction. We would allocate resources to increase availability of the service if, in fact, it did significantly predict overall customer satisfaction. We could determine how strongly these two variables are related to each other by calculating the correlation coefficient between them (see Appendix J).

Even though we have an observed correlation between these two variables, we are really interested in the true correlation between them. Our observed scores possess some amount of measurement error that will decrease the correlation between these two variables. Due to error in measurement of the variables, observed correlations between variables are always smaller than the true correlations. The relationship between the true correlation and the observed correlation is

$$r_{X_oY_o} = r_{X_tY_t} \sqrt{r_{XX'}} \sqrt{r_{YY'}}$$

where $r_{X_oY_o}$ is the observed correlation between variables X and Y, $r_{X_tY_t}$ is the true correlation between variables X and Y, and $\sqrt{r_{XX'}}$ and $\sqrt{r_{YY'}}$ are the reliabilities for variables X and Y, respectively.

From this equation, we see that the observed correlation decreases as the reliability of either scale decreases. Also, as the reliability of both scales approaches unity, the observed correlation approaches the true correlation. Using the previous example, even though there might be a true relationship between availability and overall customer satisfaction, poor measures (low reliability) of either variable would attenuate the correlation and lead us to the wrong conclusion about the relationship between these two variables.

For example, let's suppose that we assessed the satisfaction level of 50 of our customers using a measure that included scales assessing perception of availability and overall customer satisfaction. The reliability of each of these scales is .50. Suppose that the true correlation between these two variables is $r = .40$. With our sample of 50 customers, however, we might find an observed correlation of $r = .20 = (.40 \times .71 \times .71)$. Calculating the significance of this observed correlation coefficient, we find that it is not statistically significant from zero, $t(48) = 1.41, p > .05$ (see Appendix J for an explanation of t-tests for correlation coefficients). Thus, we incorrectly conclude that there is no relationship between these two variables even though a true relationship exists. With this misleading information, we may not allocate the necessary resources to availability and would miss an excellent opportunity to increase the satisfaction level of the customers.

An acceptable level of reliability will depend on how the questionnaire is used (see Nunnally 1978). For basic research, as illustrated in the preceding paragraph, reliabilities should be .80 or higher. It has been stated, however, that increasing reliabilities above .80 will not dramatically affect the correlation between scales (Nunnally 1978).

In summary, reliability of the scales will necessarily influence the magnitude of the correlation found between any two scales. The correlation is attenuated as the reliability of the scales decreases. Incorrect conclusions about the relationship between two variables are likely when the reliability of either scale is low.

FACTORS AFFECTING RELIABILITY

Various factors affect the reliability of scales. Two factors are the number of items in the scale and the sample of people on which the reliability estimate is calculated.

Number of Items in the Scale

We can increase reliability by increasing the number of items in the scale. This is similar to the concept of decreasing sampling error by increasing sample size (see Appendix F). The more observations we have in our sample, the more confident we are that the sample mean is an accurate reflection of the population mean. Similarly, the more items we have in our questionnaire, the more confident we are that observed scores are accurate reflections of true scores.

If increased reliability is to be realized by adding more items to the scale, the additional items must be representative of the same concept that is being measured. For example, if we have two dimensions in our questionnaire, professionalism and responsiveness, we could increase the reliability of the responsiveness scale by adding more items related to the responsiveness concept. These items, however, would not necessarily increase the reliability of the professionalism scale because they do not reflect that concept.

Sample of People

A sample of people who are similar with respect to their levels of satisfaction might yield low reliability estimates of the scales. If a scale has potential scores ranging from 1 to 5, and if everybody in the sample has a true score of 5, then, theoretically, there is no true score variance in this sample. Recall that reliability is the true score variance divided by the observed score variance. Therefore, in our example, if the true score variance is 0, then reliability would be 0.

If we are to obtain high reliability estimates, we must base reliability estimates on a sample of people who are heterogeneous (they differ amongst themselves) with respect to the concept being measured. If people truly differ with respect to the concept being measured (true scores varying from 1 to 5), there would be true score variance in the sample. Consequently, because there will be considerable true score variance, we would more likely find a high reliability estimate.

THE NEED FOR MULTIPLE ITEMS IN MEASUREMENT

It must be noted that internal consistency indices can only be estimated with measures that have more than one item. In Appendix K, Figure K.1, the first three statements pertain to the dimension of availability. The next three statements pertain to responsiveness. A reader may ask: "Why use all these statements in the same customer satisfaction questionnaire? They seem to be redundant." The point of using multiple items to measure a given dimension is to ensure that our overall score, which is a composite of several observed scores, is a reliable reflection of the underlying true score. Measures that use only one item to assess a person's perception of quality of customer requirement categories or of overall customer satisfaction may be unreliable (not measuring the underlying true score). In fact, the reliability estimates presented previously cannot be calculated for a one-item scale. Therefore, people who use one-item scales to assess the level of satisfaction of various customer requirements run the risk of obtaining information that is not highly reliable; that is, the observed score on their one-item measure is not highly related to the actual levels of satisfaction of their customers.

I think an illustration of the importance of multiple-item scales is warranted. Suppose that you wanted to develop one test to assess both simple arithmetic ability and reading comprehension. One way to assess arithmetic ability is to ask people to solve a mathematical problem, and one way to assess reading comprehension is to have people first read a passage and then answer a question related to it. Does it seem reasonable to assess the level of mathematical ability by using a test that contains only one arithmetic question and to assess reading comprehension by using a test that contains only one problem? People who believe that one item reliably assesses the perception of customer requirements may also believe that one question is sufficient in measuring both the level of mathematical ability and the level of reading comprehension.

Mathematical ability and reading comprehension, like customer perceptions, are unobservable constructs measured by instruments (tests) that result in scores of some kind. According to classical measurement theory, these scores are only observable indications of the underlying level of satisfaction or level of mathematical or reading comprehension.

Intuitively we understand that, in order to get a better indication of arithmetic ability and reading comprehension, we should use more than one question (item) to assess each ability. The more items related to a particular ability, the more confident we feel that the overall scores on that test will be consistently related to people's arithmetic ability and reading comprehension. In other words, we should use a test that has multiple items for each category we are measuring. In fact, with a test that contains multiple items for both arithmetic ability and reading comprehension, the reliability of each subscale can be calculated using the split-half method of estimating reliability. With this test, we would obtain two reliability estimates, one for the arithmetic scale and one for the reading comprehension scale.

The same argument for the importance of multiple items applies to measurement of customer perceptions and attitudes. We should not feel comfortable with people who design customer satisfaction questionnaires to assess five quality dimensions using one item for each dimension. More than one item should be used when assessing customer attitudes if we want to determine how reliably each dimension is measured.

Summary

So far, I have discussed issues of reliability of measures. When we are measuring customer perceptions or attitudes, we want scores for that particular scale to be highly reliable. This will give us some confidence that observed scores derived from that measure reflect true levels of customer attitudes. Furthermore, we will be confident that the highly reliable measure will be able to distinguish between people who have a positive attitude and those who have a negative attitude.

Although reliability of a scale is crucial, it is not sufficient in determining the quality of a measure. We should also concern ourselves with the issue of validity.

VALIDITY

Validity refers to the degree to which evidence supports the inferences made from scores derived from measures, or the degree to which the scale measures what it is designed to measure. For example, if we make the inference that scores on a measure reflect levels of customer satisfaction, we need information to assess how well that inference is supported. Although we may have a highly reliable questionnaire, we still may want to question what the observed score actually indicates. Although the scale may reliably distinguish people on some underlying continuum, we still must ensure that the continuum is the correct continuum (for example, customer satisfaction). Unlike mathematical indices of reliability, there is no one statistic that provides an overall index of the validity of inferences about scores. There are several ways to obtain evidence to support the inferences made from test scores. These methods, referred to as *validity-related strategies* (AERA, APA, and NCME 1985), are content-related strategy, criterion-related strategy, and construct-related strategy.

Content-Related Strategy

Content-related strategy concerns the examination of the content of the items of the scale. Content-related evidence concerns the degree to which items on the scale are representative of some "defined universe" or "domain of content."

Let's look at the assessment of customer satisfaction to demonstrate what kind of evidence should be examined. The domain or universe of content refers to all possible items that could be included in the customer satisfaction questionnaire. If we define our universe of content as those items that reflect satisfaction with the service provided, the questionnaire developed should have items representative of this defined universe. The goal of content validity is to have a set of items that best represents the universe; these items will make up our final questionnaire.

Examples of items appropriate for assessing customer satisfaction with service include "I am not happy with the way I was treated" or "The service was pleasant." These items are representative of what people would say if they were either dissatisfied or satisfied with the service they received. On the other hand, items that seem inappropriate for assessing customer satisfaction with service include "I am happy with the product" or "I am happy with the price I paid." These seem to be related to customers' attitudes toward the product received and the price of the service or product, rather than customer satisfaction with the service.

Content-related evidence involves the judgment of people familiar with the purpose of the questionnaire. These people determine the correspondence between the content domain and the items of the measure. The critical incidents approach outlined in Chapter 2 is designed to ensure that the defined universe of important customer requirements is represented by the items in the customer satisfaction questionnaire.

Criterion-Related Strategy

Criterion-related strategy is concerned with examining the systematic relationship (usually in the form of a correlation coefficient) between scores on a given scale and other scores it should predict.

Again, I will use the customer satisfaction example to help illustrate a criterion-related strategy. You might be interested in how well the perception of various dimensions of quality predicts the extent to which people endorse the particular service (for example, telling friends about it). These two constructs are conceptually different. The former focuses on customers' perceptions of the product's quality characteristics. The latter focuses on a particular behavior that may be predicted by people's level of satisfaction. The correlation between the measures of perceptions of quality and endorsement behavior represents a systematic relationship between these two variables. We would expect to find some dimensions of quality (as perceived by the customer) to be related to endorsement behavior with that product. The higher the quality, the more frequent the endorsements.

Construct-Related Strategy

In the field of psychology, a construct can be defined as an attribute or characteristic inferred from research (Guion 1965). Construct-related evidence is derived from both previous validity strategies (content and criterion); it focuses on examining relationships between many variables. It is desirable to demonstrate two things when examining the correlations between measures. The first is that the scale correlates with variables with which it should correlate. This is termed *convergent validity*. The second is that the scale does not correlate with things with which it should not correlate. This is termed *discriminant validity* (Campbell and Fiske 1959). We can establish evidence of convergent and discriminant validity by correlating test scores designed to measure the same thing and correlating test scores designed to measure different things, respectively.

Another approach in obtaining construct-related evidence is through the use of a multitrait-multimethod (MTMM) matrix (Campbell and Fiske 1959). The MTMM approach requires the measurement of multiple constructs (or traits) through multiple measurement devices (or methods). The MTMM matrix is the correlation matrix of these constructs measured by different methods. The MTMM approach helps us determine the extent to which the correlations between constructs are due to the constructs (traits) being measured versus the methods being used to measure them. Various patterns of correlations in the MTMM matrix indicate the extent to which the underlying constructs are being measured. We want to see high correlations between the measures of the same construct using different measurement instruments (evidence of convergent validity). We also want to see relatively low correlations—lower than the convergent validities—between the measures of different constructs using the same measurement instrument (evidence of discriminant validity).

Construct-related evidence also can be provided by examining the correlation between a given variable and other variables. The variable of interest is embedded in a theoretical framework that can be theoretically derived; it helps to define the meaning of the constructs being measured. This framework can tell us that this variable should correlate with certain variables and not with others. Using our previous example in discussing criterion-related strategies, the constructs *perception of quality* and *customer satisfaction* should be embedded into the theoretical framework of customer satisfaction. We would expect a measure of perceived quality to be related to a measure of customer satisfaction if we believe that the perceived quality of a product leads to customer satisfaction. However, we would not expect a relationship between customer satisfaction and, say, shoe size, since there is no theoretical reason why these two should be related. If we did find a relationship between these two variables, it could suggest that our measure of customer satisfaction is actually a poor measure. (It is possible, however, that the theoretical framework of customer satisfaction should be changed to include shoe size.)

Summary

Validity refers to the extent to which inferences from scores are meaningful. There are three methods of providing evidence for validity of scores on a customer satisfaction questionnaire. A content-related strategy focuses on the sample of items in the questionnaire and how well they represent the entire domain of customer satisfaction items. A criterion-related strategy focuses on statistical relationships between measures and whether scores predict what they should predict. A construct-related strategy is composed of the two former strategies and is more of a theory-driven method. It specifies to what the measure should and should not relate.

CHAPTER SUMMARY

This chapter discussed measurement issues of reliability and validity. Reliability refers to the degree to which observed scores obtained from a questionnaire are systematically related to some underlying true scores (the degree to which observed scores are free from random error). Reliability of scales is especially important when studying the relationship between variables. Low reliability decreases the observed correlation between two variables. Thus, if reliability of either or both measures is low, incorrect conclusions about the relationship between the variables are likely. Although reliability is an important characteristic of a questionnaire, we must also concern ourselves with the meaning of the scores. We must ensure that the observed score represents the dimension we intend to measure. Validity refers to the degree to which we can make these types of inferences.

4

Customer Satisfaction Questionnaire Construction

Item Generation, Response Format, and Item Selection

This chapter will give you some practical guidelines to follow when developing customer satisfaction questionnaires. In addition to reiterating the significance of customer requirements and satisfaction items, I will include new information on the characteristics of good items, scaling procedures, and item selection. Finally, I will present a process for questionnaire construction integrating this information.

Customer satisfaction questionnaires are constructed in four phases: (1) determining questions (items) to be used in the questionnaire, (2) selecting the response format, (3) writing the introduction to the questionnaire, and (4) determining the content of the final questionnaire (selecting items from the initial set of satisfaction items that will compose your measure).

DETERMINING QUESTIONS OR ITEMS

Let's start with an example of an organization that would like to develop a customer satisfaction questionnaire. Suppose that the organization, in an attempt to gauge how well it services its customers, includes these requests in its questionnaire:

1. Please rate the availability of the service.

2. Please rate the responsiveness of the staff.

3. Please rate the professionalism of the staff.

These three requests were obviously designed to measure three customer requirements: availability of service, responsiveness of service, and professionalism of service.

Although these customer requirements may be meaningful and valid service characteristics, there are problems with the requests. There is ambiguity in the vocabulary; *availability* and *responsiveness* might be interpreted differently by different people. Responses to these questions will reflect this ambiguity. To illustrate how different people may have differing definitions for the same word, I asked 10 people to tell me the meaning of *some* using a number. Their answers ranged from *three* to *seven*.

Similarly, if you ask your customers to indicate how satisfied they are with the availability of service they received, they may have different definitions of the word *availability* and thus be thinking of different things when they respond. Subsequently, it would be difficult to interpret customer responses. To avoid this problem, a customer satisfaction questionnaire should use more specific statements that leave less room for varying interpretations. The following statements could more clearly describe *availability*:

1. The merchant was available to schedule me at a good time.

2. I could get an appointment with the merchant at a time I desired.

3. My appointment was at a convenient time.

Availability is now defined more precisely in terms of scheduling and appointment time. Thus, responses to these items are more definitive than responses to the previous items. In addition, all three of these items still reflect the customer requirement of availability of service.

When we use more specific statements, the questionnaire provides specific feedback concerning organizational and staff performance. For example, a questionnaire using the word *availability* may discover that customers are not satisfied with the availability of service. Knowing that the customers are not satisfied, however, does little to help the organization pinpoint how to accomplish improvements. If the organization used more specific items (as in the second example), it would know precisely how to increase customers' level of satisfaction with the customer requirement of availability of service.

In summary, when developing questionnaires to assess customer satisfaction with a given product or service, we must ensure that our questions are not ambiguous. Using specific statements in questionnaires will enhance the information gained, because responses mean the same thing for all customers (no differing definitions) and responses will provide more specific feedback on ways to improve the service or product.

Satisfaction Items Revisited

Because we want the questions in our questionnaire to be specific, the next step would be to determine which questions or statements to include. Recall, from Chapter 2, that the critical incident technique includes the creation of satisfaction items. These can be used as items in the questionnaire. Satisfaction items related to the banking industry from Figure 2.1 are presented in Figure 4.1.

---

1. I waited a short period of time before I was helped.

2. The service started promptly when I arrived.

3. The teller handled transactions in a short period of time.

4. The teller took a long time to complete my transaction.

5. The financial consultant was available to schedule me at a good time.

6. My appointment with the financial consultant was at a convenient time.

7. The teller talked to me in a pleasant way.

8. The teller was very personable.

9. The teller carefully listened to me when I was requesting a transaction.

10. The teller knew how to handle the transactions.

11. The quality of the way the teller treated me was high.

12. The way the teller treated me met my expectations.

13. I am satisfied with the way the merchant treated me.

Figure 4.1   Satisfaction items from Figure 2.1.

Satisfaction items can also provide indirect help by aiding the generation of new items for the questionnaire. This process entails rewriting the satisfaction items to reflect a neutral statement (neither positive nor negative) rather than a declarative statement. These items, however, are still specific in their content. These items (using the banking industry) appear in Figure 4.2.

The items, either satisfaction items or items generated from them, are specific enough to be of value for feedback purposes. Instead of indicating only that customers are satisfied or dissatisfied with the level of professionalism of the service, these items can specify exactly *why* customers are satisfied or dissatisfied (items 7 through 10). After studying the specific feedback these satisfaction items offer, we can then calculate a general index of the professionalism customer requirement by combining the responses of items 7 through 10. We can also calculate indices for other quality dimensions or customer requirements using specific satisfaction items: responsiveness (items 1 and 2), speed of transaction (items 3 and 4), availability (items 5 and 6), and overall satisfaction with service (items 11 through 13). We can then determine the reliability of these summary scores using the reliability estimate formulae in Chapter 3.

1. Period of time waited before I was helped

2. Promptness of service when I arrived

3. Length of time of the transaction

4. Time to complete my transaction

5. Availability of financial consultant to schedule me for an appointment

6. Convenience of my appointment with the financial consultant

7. Way in which the teller talked to me

8. Way in which the teller conducted the transaction

9. Way in which the teller listened to me when I was requesting a transaction

10. Knowledge of teller in handling the transactions

11. The quality of the way the teller treated me

12. Overall quality of the visit

13. The way I was treated

Figure 4.2 New items generated from original satisfaction items.

The quality dimension development process also resulted in statements that could be included in the questionnaire. Recall that these statements also describe specific instances of the service or product that defined their respective quality dimensions. These statements are similar to the satisfaction items that result from the critical incident approach. Consequently, these statements can also be used directly in the customer satisfaction questionnaire.

CHARACTERISTICS OF GOOD ITEMS

It is important that items in the questionnaire possess certain characteristics, and writing them can be difficult. They should appear relevant to what you are trying to measure, assessing customer requirements established earlier in the process. Items that do not appear to measure anything relevant to the service or product might confuse respondents, especially if the instructions indicate that the questionnaire is designed to assess the quality of the service or product.

Items should also be concise. Items that are too long can make the questionnaire too long and difficult to read. Discard superfluous words. The following is an example of a long item:

The service person seemed to act in a very personable manner to me when I asked for service.

This concise version reflects the same content:

The service person was very personable.

Items should be unambiguous. The respondent should be able to understand precisely what the items are asking. Any ambiguity in the items can lead to equivocal responses. Try to avoid items that are vague and imprecise, such as this example:

The transaction with the service provider was good.

This item does not reflect precisely why the service was good. Some respondents might interpret the item as assessing the promptness of the transaction, while others might think it assesses the service provider's professionalism. To avoid this confusion, we can write two items:

The transaction took a short period of time.
The service provider talked to me in a pleasant way.

Each of these items reflects an unambiguous thought, each representing one customer requirement.

A good item will contain only one thought. That is, the item should ask only a single question. If an item asks more than one question, the respondent may be frustrated trying to respond affirmatively to one part of the question and negatively to the other part. A positive response to this type of item would indicate that the respondent agrees to both parts of the item. A negative response might indicate either that the respondent disagrees with one part of the item or that the respondent disagrees with both parts of the item. This is an example of a poor item:

The provider listened to me and took a short time to handle the transaction.

This item contains two parts, one dealing with how the provider listened to the customer and the other with how much time was needed to handle the transaction. This item can be divided into two separate items:

The provider listened to me.
The provider took a short time to handle the transaction.

The fifth characteristic of a good item is that it should not contain a double negative. This is an example of an item with a double negative:

The clerk was never not there when he or she was needed.

This is a better way to write this item:

The clerk was there when he or she was needed.

In summary, a good item should appear relevant, should be concise and unambiguous, should contain only one thought, and should not contain double negatives. Items with these characteristics offer respondents clear and simple questions for response. They contribute to a questionnaire that is easy to read and easy to complete.

Although the items are an important part of the questionnaire, the response format of the items can also influence the quality of the responses obtained. The following section discusses response formats.

RESPONSE FORMATS

The second step in scale construction is to select a response format for the questionnaire that determines how customers will respond to the items. The choice of response format is an extremely important step in the development process since it determines how the data from the questionnaire can be used.

There are several possible response formats or scaling methods for questionnaires. These scaling methods include Thurstone's method of equal-appearing intervals (Thurstone 1929), Guttman's scalogram approach (Guttman 1950), and the Likert scaling method (Likert 1932), to name a few. Questionnaire development using either the Thurstone or Guttman approach is more laborious than the Likert method. In addition, scales developed using the Likert method yield higher reliability coefficients with fewer items than scales developed using the Thurstone method (Edwards and Kenney 1946). Therefore, for the sake of simplicity and utility, I will not present the Thurstone or Guttman approaches. I will limit this discussion of response formats to two approaches: the checklist format and the Likert-type format. Several books discuss the other types of scaling procedures that are not presented here (Dawes 1972; Fishbein 1967; and Reckase 1990).

Checklist Format

The quality of a service or product can be quantified by the number of positive things said about it. The more positive things said about a service (or the fewer negative things said about it), the better the service. For each item in the questionnaire, customers will be allowed to respond either "yes" or "no." Customers are asked to respond "yes" if the satisfaction item reflects the service or product they received and "no" if the item does not reflect the service or product they received. An example of a checklist format appears in Figure 4.3. The checklist format should be used only when the satisfaction items are being used as the items in the questionnaire. The benefit of the checklist method is the ease with which customers can respond to the items. Customers can easily indicate whether or not the item describes the service they received.

Likert-Type Format

The quality of the service or product can also be indexed by the strength of response toward each satisfaction item. The Likert-type format is designed to allow customers to respond in varying degrees to each item that describes the service or product. For example, although two customers may say that a particular item describes the service, one customer may want to indicate that the item describes the service to a greater extent than does the other customer.

To allow customers to respond in varying degrees to each item, a Likert-type response format can be used. R. A. Likert (1932) developed a scaling procedure in which the scale represents a bipolar continuum. The low end

---

Please indicate whether or not each statement describes the service you received. Check "Yes" if the statement describes the service or "No" if the statement does not describe the service.

	Yes	No
1. I could get an appointment with the merchant at a time I desired.	____	____
2. The merchant was available to schedule me at a good time.	____	____
3. My appointment was at a convenient time for me.	____	____
4. The merchant was quick to respond when I arrived for my appointment.	____	____
5. The merchant immediately helped me when I entered the premises.	____	____
6. My appointment started promptly at the scheduled time.	____	____

Figure 4.3 Example questionnaire using a checklist response format.

represents a negative response while the high end represents a positive response. Some Likert-type formats, each representing a bipolar continuum, appear in Figure 4.4.

We can use these response formats for a particular type of item. The first response format in Figure 4.4 (the agree-disagree continuum) is used with satisfaction items. Recall that satisfaction items are declarative items that reflect specific good or bad aspects of the service or product. The response scale, therefore, should reflect whether the satisfaction item describes the service. Customers respond to each item in terms of how well that particular item describes the service they received. The quality of the service is then indexed by the extent to which the items describe the service received. An example of a questionnaire using this rating format appears in Figure 4.5.

The second and third response formats in Figure 4.4 (dissatisfied-satisfied or poor-good continua) can be used for items like those found in Figure 4.2. Although these items still reflect specific aspects of the service, they are somewhat neutral. The response scale, therefore, should reflect the degree to which the items (aspects of service) are satisfying (or good) versus dissatisfying (or poor). The quality of the service is indexed by the degree to which people say they are satisfied with the service or the degree to which the service is rated as good. Examples of questionnaires using these rating formats appear in Figures 4.6 and 4.7.

Advantage of Likert-Type Format

The advantage of using the Likert-type format rather than the checklist format is reflected in the variability of scores that result from the scale. With the quality dimension represented in our questionnaire, we allow customers

Strongly Disagree	Disagree	Neither Agree nor Disagree	Agree	Strongly Agree
1	2	3	4	5
Very Dissatisfied	Dissatisfied	Neither Satisfied nor Dissatisfied	Satisfied	Very Satisfied
1	2	3	4	5
Very Poor	Poor	Neither Poor nor Good	Good	Very Good
1	2	3	4	5

Figure 4.4   Examples of Likert-type response formats.

Please indicate the extent to which you agree or disagree with the following statements about the service you received from [company name]. Circle the appropriate number using the scale below.

1—I Strongly Disagree with this statement (SD).
2—I Disagree with this statement (D).
3—I Neither agree nor disagree with this statement (N).
4—I Agree with this statement (A).
5—I Strongly Agree with this statement (SA).

	SD	D	N	A	SA
1. I could get an appointment with the merchant at a time I desired.	1	2	3	4	5
2. The merchant was available to schedule me at a good time.	1	2	3	4	5
3. My appointment was at a convenient time for me.	1	2	3	4	5
4. The merchant was quick to respond when I arrived for my appointment.	1	2	3	4	5
5. The merchant immediately helped me when I entered the premises.	1	2	3	4	5
6. My appointment started promptly at the scheduled time.	1	2	3	4	5

Figure 4.5 Questionnaire using a Likert-type response format.

to express the degree of their opinion in the service or product they received rather than restricting them to a "yes" or "no" answer. From a statistical perspective, scales with two response options have less reliability than scales with five response options (Lissitz and Green 1975). In addition, reliability seems to level off after five scale points, suggesting minimal incremental utility using more than five scale points.

In addition, using the Likert-type format will still allow you to determine the percentage of positive and negative responses for a given item. You may do this by combining the responses on the ends of the scale (for example, combining Strongly Disagree with Disagree and combining Strongly Agree with Agree). A response of 1 or 2 is now considered to be a response of 1, a response of 3 is considered to be a response of 2, and a response of 4 or 5 is now considered to be response of 3. We have transformed our five-point scale into a three-point scale. A score of 1 represents a negative response, while a score of 3 represents a positive response. This transformation, therefore, creates somewhat of a checklist format.

Please indicate the extent to which you are satisfied or dissatisfied with the following aspects of the service you received from [company name]. Circle the appropriate number using the scale below

1—I am Very Dissatisfied with this aspect (VD).
2—I am Dissatisfied with this aspect (D).
3—I am Neither satisfied nor dissatisfied with this aspect (N).
4—I am Satisfied with this aspect (S).
5—I am Very Satisfied with this aspect (VS).

	VD	D	N	S	VS
1. Appointment time with the merchant	1	2	3	4	5
2. Availability of merchant to schedule me at a good time	1	2	3	4	5
3. Convenience of my appointment	1	2	3	4	5
4. Responsiveness of the merchant when I arrived for my appointment	1	2	3	4	5
5. Promptness of the start time of my appointment	1	2	3	4	5

Figure 4.6 Questionnaire using a Likert-type response format of the satisfaction continuum.

INTRODUCTIONS TO CUSTOMER SATISFACTION QUESTIONNAIRES

The next step is to write the introduction to the questionnaire. The introduction should be brief. It should explain the purpose of the questionnaire and provide instructions for completing the questionnaire.

Also, you might explain how the data will be used. Keep this in simple terms that are easily understood. Usually the questionnaire is designed to assess the customers' level of satisfaction. In some circumstances, however, a questionnaire may be designed for a special research project. To the extent that customer knowledge of the purpose of the project does not influence their responses, you might explain the purpose in the instructions. Inclusion of the purpose could increase customer perceptions that their responses are highly valued, thus making them more likely to complete the questionnaire.

The introduction should tell responders how to complete the items and should explain the scale to be used. These instructions must be consistent with the type of response format in the questionnaire. When you use the agree-disagree continuum as the response format, the instructions should

Please rate the extent to which the aspect of the service from [company name] was good or bad. Circle the appropriate number using the scale below.

1—Aspect of service was Very Poor (VP).
2—Aspect of service was Poor (P).
3—Aspect of service was Neither poor nor good (N).
4—Aspect of service was Good (G).
5—Aspect of service was Very Good (VG).

	VP	P	N	G	VG
1. Appointment time with the merchant	1	2	3	4	5
2. Availability of merchant to schedule me at a good time	1	2	3	4	5
3. Convenience of my appointment	1	2	3	4	5
4. Responsiveness of the merchant when I arrived for my appointment	1	2	3	4	5
5. Promptness of the start time of my appointment	1	2	3	4	5

Figure 4.7 Questionnaire using a Likert-type response format.

ask respondents to indicate the extent to which they agree or disagree with the statements in the questionnaire. When you use the satisfaction continuum as the response format, the instructions should ask respondents to indicate the extent to which they are satisfied.

I have been asked why some of the items in the questionnaires seem redundant. Because some customers become irritated when they feel they are answering the same question over and over again, you may want to include the reason for the similarity of some items. Explain that the questionnaire was designed to include multiple items in order to obtain a more accurate assessment of your customers' opinion. This may not be necessary if the items in the questionnaire are not highly similar. You could pilot test the questionnaire to see whether respondents comment about the apparent redundancy of items.

Here is an example of an introduction for a questionnaire using the agree-disagree continuum:

To help us better serve you, we would like to know your opinion of the quality of service you recently received at [name of company or department]. Please indicate the extent to which you agree or disagree with the following statements about the service you received from the staff. Circle the appropriate number using the scale below. Some statements are similar to others; this will ensure that we accurately determine your opinion concerning our service.

1—I Strongly Disagree with this statement (SD).
2—I Disagree with this statement (D).
3—I Neither agree nor disagree with this statement (N).
4—I Agree with this statement (A).
5—I Strongly Agree with this statement (SA).

This introduction includes the purpose of the questionnaire and instructions for completing the questions. Also, the introduction explains the purpose of using multiple items that are similar.

ITEM SELECTION

Step four in the construction process involves selecting the items to be used in the final questionnaire. Item selection might be warranted if the critical incidents technique resulted in a large number of satisfaction items. For example, if the critical incidents technique resulted in four quality dimensions each containing 10 items, it might not be practical to use all of the items because it could be difficult to get customers to complete a 40-item questionnaire. In this situation, we might want to select the best items from the original set in order to create a smaller, yet equally effective, customer satisfaction questionnaire. If the ratio of satisfaction items to quality dimensions is small (2:1 or less), we may not need to conduct any item selection procedure. Excluding items from an already small set could result in a customer satisfaction questionnaire with low reliability.

I will present two methods that will help you select the best satisfaction items to include in the customer satisfaction questionnaire. The first method is based on human judgment, the second on mathematical indices.

Judgmental Item Selection

One way to select items is to use your best judgment. For your final customer satisfaction questionnaire, try to include items that best represent customers' requirements. The most critical element of this process is to examine the similarity of items within a given quality dimension or customer requirement. Because the goal is to select items that best represent a particular dimension (customer satisfaction or various dimensions of customer requirements), these items should be somewhat similar to each other. If the items obtained from the critical incidents technique are all good, however, selecting the best items might be difficult.

One way to select the best satisfaction items—those that clearly reflect the quality dimension—is to have two people independently select a specified number of items from the total list. Those chosen by both people will be retained. If there is low agreement, it is possible that all satisfaction items are equally good indicators of the underlying quality dimension; if people cannot easily make a distinction between the items, the low agreement may be due to chance factors.

If there is no agreement in selected items, if all the satisfaction items are judged to be equally good indicators of the quality dimensions, then another method must be tried. In the random selection process, any randomly selected set of satisfaction items from the original list will be a representative sample of items from the entire list. A version of random selection is to select either every odd or every even numbered satisfaction item from the full list.

Mathematical Item Selection

Another method of selecting items is to administer all items generated from the critical incidents approach to some actual customers. After these customers complete the questionnaire, conduct item analysis on the data. Item analysis is a catch-all phrase that includes such processes as correlational analysis and factor analysis. You may conduct these statistical techniques to select the best items (those that have equal means and are highly interrelated). These statistical procedures require the help of an expert in questionnaire development. The following section of this chapter illustrates one approach that can be used in item selection.

Statistical procedures such as these will allow you to select which items to retain for your final measure of customer satisfaction. Although this approach is more complex than judgmental item selection, you achieve the invaluable payback of knowing your final questionnaire is statistically reliable; items retained as a result of the item analysis will be, by design, mathematically sound. The general goal in the selection of items is to retain those that differentiate between customers who are dissatisfied and those who are satisfied and drop those items that do not. That is, the items should be able to discriminate between varying levels of customer satisfaction. Items on which highly satisfied and highly dissatisfied customers score the same are not very useful. Item analysis will allow us to identify those items that can discriminate between varying levels of satisfaction.

Item-total correlations. Item-total correlations are correlations between an item and the overall dimension score to which that item belongs (not including the one item being correlated). For example, if we had three items, each measuring the same quality dimension, we would calculate three item-total correlations: (1) item 1 correlated with the composite of items 2 and 3, (2) item 2 correlated with the composite of items 1 and 3, and (3) item 3 correlated with the composite of items 1 and 2. This type of correlation will tell you the extent to which each item is linked to the overall dimension score with which it should be highly linked. The criterion for a cutoff for a correlation coefficient varies depending on the purpose of the measure being developed. When developing a general type of measure, you would use less stringent criteria compared to a measure designed to assess a more specific attitude (Likert 1932). An important requirement is that the overall score of the measure be reliable.

As an example, we might have five items we want to combine into an overall score of professionalism. We must ensure that combining the five items makes sense. If all the items are designed to measure the same dimension (perception of professionalism), then all items for that dimension should be positively related to each other; we would expect to see high item-total correlations. Let's say we used the questionnaire on 100 customers and calculated five item-total correlation coefficients, one for each item. The results of a hypothetical item-total correlation analysis appear in Figure 4.8. We see that item 3 is not highly correlated with a composite of the remaining four items; it might be dropped from the questionnaire. The remaining items show relatively high item-total correlations with the composite score of the remaining items. The results suggest that it would make sense to combine items 1, 2, 4, and 5 to obtain an overall score of professionalism.

The low correlation between item 3 and the remaining items could be due to several things. One possibility of why an item demonstrates a low correlation with its subscale might be that it is poorly written. For example, it might include more than a single thought, causing some respondents to want to respond favorably to one part of the item and unfavorably to the other part. It might be necessary to rewrite the item to reflect only one thought or divide it into two separate items.

Overall score (minus item being correlated)	
Item 1	$r = .67$
Item 2	$r = .55$
Item 3	$r = .23$
Item 4	$r = .59$
Item 5	$r = .77$

Figure 4.8   Hypothetical results of item-total correlations of items designed to measure perception of professionalism.

Another possibility is that a particular item measures some other customer requirement than what was originally thought. For the previous example, we could calculate a correlation between item 3 and the other customer requirements. If item 3 does show a high correlation with another customer requirement, perhaps it should not be dropped from the questionnaire but, instead, included in the summary score for that particular customer requirement to which it is highly linked.

Another possibility is that the item represents a different customer requirement than those included in the questionnaire. An item may not correlate highly with any of the customer requirements. It could be that we failed to establish an important customer requirement in our clustering of critical incidents. This correlational approach could address such errors of omission. When this situation arises, perhaps we could write more items to reflect the content of that particular item. Subsequently, we could re-administer the revised questionnaire (with the new items) to conduct additional item analysis. If the new items are representative of that lone item, then that lone item should now correlate highly with the new items, thus forming a new customer requirement scale.

Group differences. Another mathematical item selection strategy employs the comparison of two groups of respondents (Likert 1932). This procedure is also conducted after respondents have completed the questionnaire. Within each subscale (for example, availability or timeliness), we select two groups of people, each group representing the extreme of the attitude measured by a particular scale. Usually, the top and bottom 10 percent are selected, based on their overall score for the particular subscale. Next, for each group, we calculate means for each item. Then we calculate a difference score for each item, subtracting the mean of the lower extreme group from the mean of the higher extreme group.

For each item we obtain a difference score. This difference score reflects how much a particular item was able to discriminate between the two groups on an attitude the item was designed to measure. The higher the difference score, the higher the discrimination. If an item does not differentiate between the two groups, then we would obtain a difference score of 0. These items are dropped from the questionnaire. For items that are positively phrased (higher score means higher level of the attitude), we select items that have a large positive difference score. For those items that are negatively phrased (higher score means lower level of the attitude), we select items that have a large negative difference score.

The indices used in the item-total correlation procedure (item-total correlation) and the group differences procedure (difference score) have been shown to be highly correlated (Likert 1932). This suggests that both procedures will result in similar outcomes with respect to the inclusion of items in the final form of the questionnaire.

Factor analysis. Another statistical technique of item selection, often used in conjunction with item-total correlations, is factor analysis. This technique (see Appendix K) will demonstrate which items are more highly related to the underlying dimension they are designed to measure.

Factor analysis is a highly specialized form of analysis. It is beyond the scope of this book to provide you with exact procedures for the selection of items. However, here are some general guidelines. It is essential that items within each scale load on a single factor if the items are to be used in a composite score. When an item loads highly on a different factor than the one for which it was intended, this suggests that the item might best be combined with items with which it is highly related. When an item does not load highly on any factor, this suggests that the item does not discriminate between high and low groups on the attitudes that are measured with the items in the current questionnaire.

An advantage of using factor analysis is the identification of underlying constructs (customer requirements) being measured by the items in the questionnaire. Also, factor analysis allows us to determine which customer requirement each item is measuring. A disadvantage of factor analysis is that it requires a large number of questionnaire respondents if the results are to be reliable. The number of respondents should be five to 10 times the number of items in the questionnaire. For example, if the questionnaire contains 20 items, the factor analysis should be conducted using the responses of 100 to 200 people.

Factor analysis has been used in applied research. For example, Parasuraman, Zeithaml, and Berry (1988) used factor analysis in developing a service quality questionnaire. The goal of the research was to develop a reliable scale that assesses various components of service quality. The authors present the results of the exploratory factor analysis of responses to 97 items.

On the basis of the factor analysis, the authors selected items that were good indicators of underlying dimensions. They also presented the results of the factor analysis, which included the number of factors as well as the factor pattern matrix (after rotation). This article presents an excellent example of the use of factor analysis in developing customer satisfaction questionnaires.

Mathematical item selection is usually used in the initial stages of questionnaire development. Even if you use the judgmental item selection process, you may conduct item analysis on the retained items (after customers have completed them) to determine whether the items chosen constitute a reliable scale. Figure 4.9 presents the chronological use of item analysis in the selection of items when using either the mathematical item selection or the judgmental item selection process.

Judgmental Item Selection	Mathematical Item Selection
1. Select small set of items using judgmental criteria or random selection.	1. Place all satisfaction items in the questionnaire.
2. Place this set of satisfaction items in the questionnaire.	2. Use questionnaire on customers.
3. Use questionnaire on customers.	3. Conduct item analysis to determine which items to retain for final questionnaire (need sufficient sample size of approximately five people per item if factor analysis will be used).
4. Conduct item analysis to determine if these items measure quality dimensions.	4. Examine outcome of item analysis and select good items for final version of questionnaire.
5. Examine outcome of item analysis to retain good items.	5. Use final version of the questionnaire.
6. Results may indicate entire questionnaire revision (if items do not measure the underlying dimensions).	

Figure 4.9 The use of item analysis in judgmental item selection and mathematical item selection.

SUMMARY OF ITEM SELECTION

Items in the customer satisfaction questionnaire should be relevant, concise, and unambiguous. They should also be written clearly to avoid double negatives and to reflect only a single thought. A well-written introduction describes the purpose of the questionnaire and provides instructions for completing it.

This chapter presented two response formats that can be used in questionnaires. A checklist format allows customers to indicate whether a particular item represents the service or product. A Likert-type format allows customers to further distinguish their responses beyond what is allowed by the checklist format. The choice between these two types of format depends on the type of data desired from the questionnaire.

Also, this chapter outlined two procedures used when selecting items for the customer satisfaction questionnaire. The judgmental procedure can be useful when the initial items are all good items. If you are using the mathematical approach, consult somebody conversant in these mathematical procedures when you attempt to select items. Mathematical item selection is designed to select items that are statistically sound.

Figure 4.10 outlines the general steps to follow in questionnaire development. Each step is accompanied by various methods that are used for that step and by other important issues for consideration. This figure is designed to summarize and highlight the important points in the chapter and can be used as a checklist when developing the questionnaire.

WEB-BASED CUSTOMER SURVEYS

Web-based surveys are popular for collecting customer feedback data. According to a recent survey (Hayes, 2008), 68 percent of customer feedback professionals indicated that their company uses web-based surveys to collect customer feedback data. This web-based platform for collecting these data was as popular as or more popular than other traditional methods, including telephone (66 percent), paper-pencil (47 percent), and interviews (47 percent).

In Web-based surveys, respondents are typically invited via email containing a hyperlink that takes them directly to the survey. An example of an email introduction and survey appears in Figure 4.11.

Survey invitations have an embedded hyperlink that directs respondents to the hosted survey. Some companies use surveys that provide a unique hyperlink to each respondent, the hyperlink identifying the respondent. In these cases, existing customer data (for example, product owned, service warranty levels, region, and age) can be matched to each respondent's survey responses for later segmentation. The existing customer data can be used to personalize the email invitation and can help to deliver the appropriate customer survey to the right people (for example, customers in the sales cycle receive the sales survey; customers in the service cycle receive the service survey). Additionally, the existing data helps reduce the number of survey questions asked of the respondent.

The hyperlink sends the respondents to a survey in which they can provide feedback about the company. (See Figure 4.12 for an example of a web-based survey.)

Steps	Important Issues
1. Generate items for questionnaire.	• Select items from satisfaction item list. • Write items based on satisfaction items.
2. Ensure items are written appropriately.	• Items should appear relevant to what you are trying to measure. • Items should be concise. • Items should be unambiguous. • Items should contain only one thought (items ask only one question). • Items should not contain double negatives.
3. Select response format for items.	• Checklist format. • Likert-type format.
4. Write introduction to questionnaire.	• State the purpose of the question-naire. • State instructions on how to com-plete the questionnaire.

5. Select representative sample of items.
  a. Using judgmental item selection
  b. Using mathematical item selection
	• Items within each quality dimension should be similar in content.
	
	• Use multiple judges to select the items.
	
	• Use item-total correlations or group differences approach in selecting items.
	
	• Could also use factor analysis.

6. Evaluate the retained items.	• Calculate reliability of the scales within questionnaire using split-half method or Cronbach's estimate.

Figure 4.10   Guidelines in the development of questionnaires.

We are conducting a survey to help us understand your opinions about our products and services. To that end, we have developed a survey enabling you to provide specific feedback on how you feel about our company. Your feedback will help us make improvements to ensure we deliver the best products and services to you.

Survey Company is conducting this survey for Business Over Broadway; we invite you to connect to the survey site and complete your response. To access the survey, please click on the URL below. The survey will take approximately 10 minutes to complete. It will remain open until <CLOSE DATE>.

http://www.surveyhyperlinkgoeshere.com

Individual responses to this survey will remain strictly confidential. Results will be reported in aggregate form only.

Thank you for your time and feedback.

Sincerely,

Bob E. Hayes, Ph.D.
President, Business Over Broadway
bob@businessoverbroadway.com
www.businessoverbroadway.com

Figure 4.11 Sample email invitation to Web-based survey.

Benefits of Web-Based Surveys

There are a few benefits of collecting customer feedback using Web-based surveys, compared to other traditional methods. First, Web-based surveys are relatively inexpensive to conduct. Unlike paper-pencil methods, there are no costs associated with printing, stuffing envelopes, postage, or data entry. Additionally, no interviewer is needed with Web-based surveys.

Response rates for Web-based surveys are typically higher than for other methods because they are easier to complete and respondents can respond at their own convenience.

Dillman (2000) has listed other advantages of web surveys, which are related to faster response rate, ease of sending reminders to participants, and ease of data processing because survey responses can be downloaded to a spreadsheet, data analysis package, or database without the need for manual data entry.

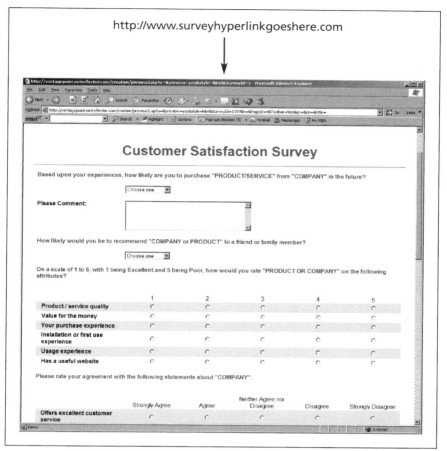

Figure 4.12 Hyperlink takes respondent directly to the web-based survey.

Survey presentation and completion are greatly facilitated with the use of Web-based surveys compared to other survey methods. Specifically, survey questions can be sorted randomly or in any other desired order. Dynamic error checking (that is, verifying that responses are appropriate or valid) is also an advantage of Web-based surveys. Additionally, skip patterns for survey questions are facilitated with Web-based surveys where a response to a given question dictates future survey questions which are asked. (For example, respondents are asked whether they received technical support. If yes, they are asked additional questions about technical support. If no, they are not asked these additional questions.). Web surveys allow for the inclusion of pop-up instructions for selected questions as well as multiple methods for answering questions (for example, check-box, drop-down boxes, and so on).

Principles for Designing Web-based Surveys

Dillman et al. (1998) outlines several principles to consider when designing Web surveys:

1. Introduce the questionnaire with a welcome screen that is motivational, that emphasizes the ease of responding, and that instructs respondents on the action needed for proceeding to the next page.

2. Begin with a question that is fully visible on the first screen of the questionnaire, one that will be easily comprehended and answered by all respondents.

3. Present each question in a conventional format similar to that normally used on paper questionnaires.

4. Limit line length to decrease the likelihood of a long line of prose extending across the screen of the respondent's browser.

5. Provide specific instructions on how to take each necessary computer action for responding to questionnaires.

6. Provide computer operation instructions as part of each question for which action is to be taken, not in a separate section prior to the beginning of the questionnaire.

7. Do not require respondents to provide an answer to every question before being allowed to proceed to subsequent questions.

8. Construct questionnaires that scroll from question to question unless sequence is a major concern, a large number of questions must be skipped, or a mixed-mode survey is being done for which telephone interview and web results will be combined.

9. When the number of answer choices exceeds the number that can be displayed on one screen, consider double-banking; be sure to include appropriate navigational instructions.

10. Use graphical symbols or words that convey a sense of where the respondent is in completing the survey.

Tips for Conducting Web-Based Surveys

1. Shorten the timing between notice and reminders and the total duration of the response period. Most of the time, 8-10 working days or less is sufficient.

2. Shorten the length of invitation and reminder messages.

3. Keep the questionnaires short.

4. Simplify the questions even more so than in paper surveys.

5. Think of the survey as an outline version of a conversation. Build in a natural flow, with appropriate transitions between one thought and the next.

6. Pilot test each survey with a variety of people using different browsers.

7. Avoid undeliverable e-mail invitations by developing accurate potential respondent e-mail lists.

8. Extract narrative text responses from data before importing into the numerical data analysis program SPSS. Extraneous commas and other characters will require "cleaning" the data.

CUSTOMER LOYALTY MEASUREMENT

The concept of customer loyalty is as broad as the fields to which it is applied. Marketing departments create customer loyalty programs to ensure that customers purchase more frequently and exclusively at their company. Companies add new features to increase the "stickiness" of their Web sites so customers stay longer, increasing the opportunity that customers will make a transaction. While these areas of customer loyalty are beyond the scope (or intent) of this discussion, this section will focus on the measurement of customer loyalty as it applies to customer survey research. Please see the bibliography for useful books on these topics.

Customer Loyalty and Financial Performance

Customer loyalty has been shown to be a leading indicator of business performance metrics. Researchers have demonstrated a link between customer loyalty and financial success and growth. For example, Reichheld et al. (1990) demonstrated that decreasing customer defections by 5 percent increases profits from 25 percent to 85 percent across a variety of industries. While they focused on defection rates, there are several objective measures of customer loyalty that show a relationship with financial performance:

- Number of referrals
- Word of mouth / word of mouse
- Purchase again
- Purchase additional products
- Increase purchase size
- Customer retention / defection rates

Based on the objective measures of customer loyalty, we can see how company financial growth can occur through the increase in customer loyalty. Through the referral process, companies can grow through the acquisition of new customers. The idea is that the customer acquisition process relies on existing customers to promote and recommend the company to their friends; these friends, in turn, become customers. Another way to strengthen the financial growth of a company is to affect the purchasing behavior (that is, increase the number of purchases or stimulate the purchase of additional products or services) of existing customers. Finally, company growth is dependent on its ability to not lose existing customers at a rate faster than they are acquired. For example, customer defection rate is an important metric in the wireless service industry, where customer defections not uncommon.

MEASUREMENT OF CUSTOMER LOYALTY

Customer loyalty, when measured through surveys, is typically assessed through the use of standard questions or items, mirroring the objective measures listed above. For each item, customers are asked to rate their level of affinity for, endorsement of, and approval of a company. The items usually ask for a rating that reflects the likelihood that the customer will exhibit future positive behaviors toward a company. Commonly used customer loyalty survey questions include the following items:

- Overall satisfaction

- Likelihood to choose again

- Likelihood to recommend

- Likelihood to continue purchasing the same products and services

- Likelihood to purchase additional products and services

- Likelihood to increase frequency of purchasing

- Likelihood to switch to a different provider

The first question is rated on a scale (for example, 0 = Extremely dissatisfied to 10 = Extremely satisfied). The remaining questions allow respondents to indicate their likelihood of behaving in different ways toward the company (for example, 0 = Not at all likely to 10 = Extremely likely). Higher ratings reflect higher levels of customer loyalty.

Customer loyalty questions should appear at the start of the survey, before business attribute questions are presented. Presenting loyalty questions at the start of the survey ensures that responses to those loyalty questions reflect the respondents' general perceptions regarding their relationship with the company. When loyalty questions follow other business attribute questions, respondents' rating of the loyalty questions is affected.

Standardized Loyalty Questions

The loyalty questions mentioned previously have been used in many research studies across a variety of industries; results have shown that these loyalty questions are reliable, valid, and useful measures of customer loyalty (see Chapter 6 for detailed research behind these questions).

Additionally, these loyalty questions are both theoretically and empirically linked to financial growth of companies across a variety of consumer groups. Responses to these loyalty questions help organizations understand their expected growth.

The loyalty questions presented have merit. However, my intent is not to discourage you from developing your own loyalty questions for your particular organizational needs. Nevertheless, your time might be better spent developing specific business attribute questions for your particular needs rather than developing loyalty questions.

CUSTOMER SURVEYS AND CUSTOMER LOYALTY

While many objective measures of customer loyalty exist (for example, defection rate, number of referrals), customer surveys remain a frequently used way to assess customer loyalty. There are valid reasons for the popularity of customer surveys in customer experience management. First, customer surveys allow companies to quickly and easily gauge levels of customer loyalty. Companies may not have easy access to objective customer loyalty data; they may simply not gather such data. Second, results from customer surveys can be easily used to change organizational business process. Customer surveys commonly include questions about customer loyalty as well as the customer experience relative to product, service, and support. Used jointly, both business attribute items and loyalty indices (driver analysis, segmentation analysis) can be used to identify reasons why customers are loyal or disloyal. Finally, objective measures of customer loyalty (for example, defection rates and repurchase rates) provide a backward look into customer loyalty levels. Customer surveys allow companies to examine customer loyalty in real time. Surveys ask about expected levels of loyalty-related behavior and let companies "look into the future" regarding customer loyalty.

Customer Relationship Management and Customer Experience Management

While there has been a change in business nomenclature around the application of customer surveys, from "customer relationship management" to "customer experience management," the analytical techniques used to understand the survey data (for example, segmentation analysis and driver analysis) remain exactly the same. The ultimate goal of customer loyalty survey analyses, no matter what business nomenclature you use, is to identify the reasons why customers are loyal or disloyal. You might think of customer loyalty as the ultimate criterion in customer relationship and experience management.

The use of customer loyalty survey data to help manage customer relationships has benefited from technological innovation over the past decade. Web-based surveys provide an easy vehicle for customers to provide feedback. For example, in B2B uses of customer loyalty surveys, individual customer concerns are addressed by means of automated prompts (typically in the form of emails) to account team members who are responsible for quickly resolving specific issues. Additionally, organization-wide customer loyalty issues are identified through automated analyses (for example, driver analysis) that highlight common causes of customer loyalty and disloyalty. Furthermore, customer survey results are accessible 24x7 by all employees through Web-based reporting tools. Finally, companies even link customer survey data to their CRM systems in order to enhance day-to-day account management with both attitudinal data and operational data. It is clear that efforts in the field of customer loyalty have simplified the process of data collection, analysis, reporting, and integration with existing business systems.

Chapter 7 will discuss in more detail how customer surveys can be used in customer relationship and experience strategies to improve customer loyalty.

5

Sampling Methods

Sometimes it is not possible to administer surveys to all your customers. Organizations with tens of thousands of customers may not have the resources to conduct a large-scale project. In fact, it may not be necessary to survey all of a company's clients in order to get a reliable picture regarding levels of customer satisfaction. This chapter will cover sampling methods and related topics: determining sample size, determining confidence levels, and increasing response rates to written surveys.

STATISTICAL SAMPLING

We often make judgments about a large group of "things" based on our observations of a smaller subset of those "things." For example, we talk to a few customers in order to learn about the quality of service we provide to all of our customers. In quality improvement organizations, someone checks a selection of products in order to determine whether there may be major problems with the entire lot. To determine the quality of coffee beans from a roaster, the tester tastes a small handful of beans taken from that roaster. When preparing a stew, the chef might taste a small spoonful from the pot in which the stew is cooking in order to determine whether the entire pot is ready. In these examples, people have drawn conclusions about something in its entirety (such as all the soup or all the coffee beans) from a small subset of its content (a spoonful of soup or a handful of beans). We typically refer to the large group as the *population* and the small subset of that group as the *sample*. (See Appendix F for a more detailed description of the characteristics of populations and samples.)

When conducting a customer satisfaction survey, we typically cannot administer the survey to the entire customer base. We may not have the financial resources, or we may need the results of the survey immediately, which would preclude the time-consuming task of measuring all customers' attitudes. In these and other cases, we administer the customer survey to a smaller set of customers, a sample. The process of selecting a sample from the larger population is referred to as *sampling*.

A major goal in sampling is to ensure that the results of the client satisfaction questionnaire are representative of the larger population of customers. This chapter will discuss various methods of statistical sampling that will help you determine your sampling plan. It is assumed that readers have a basic knowledge of statistics. For a quick review, refer to the appendices before reading this chapter. After reading this chapter, you should have a better understanding of the intricacies of sampling methods and should be able to conduct simple statistical sampling.

TYPES OF SAMPLING: CENSUS, JUDGMENT, AND STATISTICAL

We are the owners of a newspaper and we would like to know the satisfaction level of our customers, the readers of our newspaper. In order to accomplish this, we must first determine the population of our customers. The determination of our population was done, in part, early on in our questionnaire development phase. We tailored the questionnaire with a specific customer base in mind. Using sampling terminology to define our population of customers, a question to ask ourselves is, "To whom do we want the customer survey results to generalize?" To generalize the results to the population, we must first ensure that the sample of respondents of our survey is representative of that larger population. In our newspaper study, all readers of our newspaper are our population. To determine the customers' satisfaction levels from a sample of readers, we could take one of three general approaches to obtain a sample from this population. The three broad sampling approaches are: census, judgment, and statistical.

Census Sampling

One approach to sampling is to gather information from all customers. This is referred to as *census sampling,* essentially sampling all possible cases in our population. We know the sample is representative of the population because the sample *is* the population.

A census approach can be used in various circumstances when, due to the nature of the product, a company might want input from all of its customers. For example, the manufacturer of a new and specialized surgical device might want feedback from all of the surgeons who use its product. If each surgeon is a potential source of critical information, it may warrant census sampling. Companies also use census sampling when a customer base is small enough that sampling the entire population is financially feasible. Manufacturers of an expensive bone-cutting device may have only a few customers (say, 100) that use these devices. In this case, a census approach to sampling would be appropriate. Finally, when all necessary information regarding customers is already available electronically, computers can quickly and easily include all customers in the data analysis. The major drawback to using census sampling is the high cost associated with measuring all cases in the population.

Judgmental Sampling

Another approach to sampling is to use judgment in the selection of customers to be measured. Using our example of the newspaper publisher, we might want to select a sample from the population based on readers' ages in order to ensure that all age categories are represented. We might also take steps to ensure that both genders are represented in our sample. In judgmental sampling, the decision about which cases from the population to include in the sample is solely at the discretion of the person conducting the sampling procedure.

Judgmental sampling is useful for case studies in which few cases are needed to illustrate a researcher's major points. The business consultant Tom Peters uses this method, illustrating his theories with a discussion of several companies. One major drawback to judgmental sampling is the inability to generalize to a population. Conclusions drawn from such case studies can be used as a great starting point for understanding business processes, but making generalizations to the population is not possible. A statistical approach to sampling is a better option when a researcher wishes to make strong conclusions regarding the population.

Statistical Sampling

The third approach to sampling is based on statistical probability, on the use of chance to determine selection. In statistical sampling we use random selection in the inclusion of the cases into the sample, we can statistically determine an appropriate sample size, and we can statistically determine the probability that our sample is not representative of the population.

A major advantage of the statistical sampling approach, especially when compared to judgmental sampling, is that it permits generalizing of results to the population from which the sample was drawn. Someone conducting a judgmental sampling may be confident in his or her own judgment, but others may question whether the final sample is representative of the entire population. The person creating the sample might have unrecognized biases that influence the selection of cases into the sample.

At a certain level, the results of a customer survey tell us the satisfaction level of the sample of customers. At another level, the results of a well done customer survey tell us about the satisfaction level of the entire population of customers. If the sample is somehow not representative of the population, the survey may have been a waste of time and resources. The effect of bias in judgmental sampling may be quite apparent in the outcome of a study. For example, if the results of a customer satisfaction survey determine financial bonuses, an office manager might administer the customer survey to only those customers he thinks are satisfied. Conclusions based on such a sample might not reflect the true level of satisfaction of all customers. In this case, this sample is referred to as a *biased sample,* one that is not representative of the population. Statistical sampling increases the chances that the sample is representative of the population.

Table 5.1 defines and details important points of the three sampling methods just explained. Census sampling is relatively expensive and judgmental sampling carries the potential for unintended bias; these methods are less often used than statistical sampling. Statistical sampling is the most reliable method of gathering data and providing useful information about the population. The next section will focus on the different statistical

Table 5.1 Sampling methods.

Method	Definition	Important Points
Census	Select all cases from the population	• Sample is representative of the population because it *is* the population
		• Could be used when feedback from *all* customers is important
		• Could be used if all data are easily accessible (data are already on computer)
		• Cost may be high
Judgment	Select subset of cases based on discretion of person creating the sample	• Degree to which results from sample can generalize to population is questionable
		• Easy approach
Statistical	Select subset of cases based on chance	• Can calculate probability that our sample is not representative of the population
		• Can generalize results to the population

sampling methods: simple random sampling, stratified sampling, and cluster sampling.

Simple random sampling. This is the simplest approach to determining which cases are to be included in the sample. In simple random sampling, every case in the population has an equal chance of being included. In our newspaper scenario, we may be interested in the overall satisfaction level of all readers (subscribers and those buying the paper at a newsstand), but we want to survey only 100 customers. To generate a random sample from our population of customers, we start with a list of all readers ($N = 9000$). Next, we randomly select 100 readers as our sample and measure their level of satisfaction with the newspaper. From this sample, we make generalizations about the satisfaction level of the entire customer base (the population).

Stratified sampling. Stratified sampling refers to the approach in which the population is first divided into two or more groups (strata). After stratification, simple random sampling is conducted within each group. When determining the various strata to be used in the study, it is important that the strata be mutually exclusive. That is, membership in one stratum precludes membership in the other strata.

For stratified sampling, each stratum is treated as if it were a separate population. From each of these strata, cases are selected for inclusion in the sample. For example, we may divide the population of readers into strata based on such variables as annual income, gender, and location. Looking at the annual income of readers, we might divide our population into the following five strata:

- $20,000 or less
- Greater than $20,000 and less than $40,000
- Greater than $40,000 and less than $60,000
- Greater than $60,000 and less than $80,000
- Greater than $80,000

For gender, the identification of the two strata is obvious:

- Female
- Male

For the location of the reader, we might identify five districts (strata) where our newspapers are distributed:

- Wallingford
- Eastside
- Ballard
- West Seattle
- Auburn

When using a stratified random sampling procedure, we would first divide the population of customers into the strata that were identified. Using the gender strata, we would divide the population into subgroups, male and female, and then randomly select readers from each. Using the districts strata, we would first divide readers into the five subgroups (Wallingford, Eastside, Ballard, West Seattle, and Auburn) and then randomly select the readers. It is also possible to overlap the variables and create more strata. For example, we could use gender and district variables to create the 10-level strata illustrated in Table 5.2 and then conduct random selection.

A stratified sampling method has several advantages compared to a simple random sampling:

1. We can obtain better precision with the same overall sample size or obtain the same level of precision with a smaller sample size.

2. We can obtain estimates of customer satisfaction levels for each stratum. This is particularly valuable when we want to make comparisons across different strata. Although we can make comparisons across different groups using simple random sampling, stratified random sampling ensures that we have enough customers within each stratum to make these comparisons meaningful and useful.

3. We can focus on a particular stratum. For example, we might focus on male Wallingford readers in order to determine why male readership is so low in that district.

Under what conditions might we want to conduct stratified random sampling? The division of the population into various strata might be useful if we believe that there are differences in these various strata and if one contains a relatively smaller number of cases compared to the others. For example, the content of our newspaper might be aimed at people involved in childrearing. Typically, these types of newspapers have more female readers than male. We might want to see whether the female readers are

Table 5.2   Strata for stratified sampling.

	Districts				
Gender	**Wallingford**	**Eastside**	**Ballard**	**West Seattle**	**Auburn**
Female					
Male					

more satisfied with our newspaper than our male readers. Given that we have a limited number of males who read our paper, a simple random selection of readers from the entire population might result in only a few males in our sample and, consequently, lead to a poor estimate of the satisfaction level of the entire population of male readers. To obtain a better estimate of the level of satisfaction of male readers, we could first divide our population into two strata, male and female, and randomly select a given number of males from our male stratum to ensure we have a high number of males in our final overall sample. This method would lead to a more reliable comparison between the two genders on levels of customer satisfaction.

Cluster sampling. The previous two sampling methods created samples by selecting individual cases (customers) to be included in the sample. Cluster sampling, on the other hand, is a sampling approach in which the selection process is conducted at the group level rather than at the individual level. That is, the individual cases within the population are clustered into groups such as office or store locations, product line, or physician specialty. These groups are the level at which random selection is conducted, resulting in a small subset of offices, products, or types of physician, respectively.

For example, we might have 200,000 customers throughout our 200-office location. These 200 offices would constitute our clusters. In cluster sampling, we would think of our 200 offices as our population and then randomly select our clusters to form our sample from this 200-office population. We could randomly select, say, 40 offices (clusters) to be included in our sample. We would use the customer surveys from these 40 offices in our statistical analysis.

If the clusters are large (if, for example, there are many cases within the clusters), it is possible to conduct random sampling from the selected clusters. Within each of the selected clusters, we would conduct a random sampling of the individual cases. This is referred to as *two-stage cluster sampling*. In our previous example, even though we have only 40 offices as a result of our cluster sampling procedure, each of these clusters may be quite large. On the average, each office surveys 1000 clients. Consequently, we would have 40,000 customer surveys in our sample. If this number is too large to handle, we could conduct random sampling from these 40,000 clients to obtain a smaller sample.

Summary

We have covered three different types of sampling methods: simple random sampling, stratified random sampling, and cluster sampling. These methods are presented in Table 5.3. For random sampling, each customer has an equal chance of being selected from the overall population. In

Table 5.3 Statistical sampling methods.

Method	Definition	Steps	Important Points
Simple random	Each customer has an equal chance of being selected	• Obtain list of all customers (population) • Randomly select customers from this list	• Simple method • Assume there is some variability in the characteristic being measured
Stratified	Within each stratum, each customer has an equal chance of being selected	• Divide customers into strata (or groups) • Conduct simple random selection within each group	• Each level of the groupings must be mutually exclusive from the others • Each stratum should be treated as if it were a population • Can obtain better precision with same sample size • Obtain estimates for each stratum • Can target specific strata to ensure they are included in the final overall sample
Cluster	Each cluster (or group) has an equal chance of being selected	• Customers are already "naturally" clustered into groups • Conduct simple random sampling of the clusters	• Clusters must already be formed • Can conduct random sampling within the selected clusters

stratified random sampling, the population is divided into strata or groups and random sampling is conducted within each stratum or group. All customers within a group have an equal chance of being selected. In cluster sampling, random sampling is conducted at the group level. Each group, rather than each customer, has an equal chance of being selected.

The next part of the chapter will discuss the determination of sample size. Toward this end, we need an understanding of statistics, parameters, and sampling error. Although these concepts are discussed in Appendix F, they will be presented here to assist in your understanding of the determination of sample sizes.

SAMPLE SIZE AND SAMPLING ERROR

Recall that statistical sampling leads to a sample of cases are were randomly drawn from the population. As a result of statistical sampling, we end up with a sample from which we can make generalizations about the population. Numbers calculated from the sample are referred to as *statistics*. Numbers calculated from the entire population are referred to as *parameters*. Statistics are denoted by the following symbols: The mean is $\bar{x}$, the variance is s^2, and the standard deviation is s. Parameters are usually denoted by Greek symbols. The population mean is μ, the variance is σ^2, and the standard deviation is σ. We use statistics as estimators of the parameters. For example, we can measure the level of customer satisfaction from the sample and conclude, based on this sample, the level of satisfaction of the population.

So, in terms of generalizing from the sample of customers to the population of customers, we use the statistics calculated from the sample as estimators for the parameters calculated from the population of customers.

Sampling Error

Suppose we have a customer base of 500 customers (population). It would be possible to draw random samples of some size from this population. For illustrative purposes, let's set our sample size to equal 10. For each sample we select from this population, we calculate the mean level of satisfaction. This statistic (the sample mean of customer satisfaction) would be our estimator of the parameter (the population mean of customer satisfaction). If we randomly select a sample of size 10 many times, we would probably get different results each time we calculate the mean of that particular sample. This variation from sample to sample is referred to as *sampling error*. In any given sample, the satisfaction level of the 10 customers would be a little bit higher or lower than the satisfaction level for all 500 customers. This type of error is expected and is considered to be random.

Let's look at an example to illustrate the concept of sampling error. For the sake of argument, let's say the level of satisfaction of our population of customers might be 4.5 (of course, we might never know this, but it helps me to explain this concept). In our company, we have several teams working on the measurement of customer satisfaction, each team responsible for measuring the satisfaction level of 10 customers. In one randomly selected sample of 10 customers, Team A finds the level of customer satisfaction to be 4.0. Team B finds the level of customer satisfaction for its 10 randomly selected customers to be 4.7. Yet another team, Team C, finds that its randomly selected sample of 10 customers results in a satisfaction level of 4.9. Are two of the teams wrong? No, of course not. The error in the estimation of the true population parameter of 4.5 is expected and is a result of the use of a sample.

Standard Error of the Mean

In the previous example, we observed sampling error; the means varied from sample to sample. Because we do not know the exact population mean, we cannot calculate the exact amount of error associated with any one sample mean. We can determine, however, the degree of error we would expect for any given sample size. I know this all sounds magical, but it is really quite simple. In theory, we could randomly select an infinite number of samples of size 10 and calculate the mean for each. As a result of this process, we would get an infinite number of means (each based on a sample size of 10). Next, we could plot these means to form a distribution. This distribution of sample means is, in turn, described by a mean and a standard deviation. This distribution of means is referred to as a *sampling distribution of the mean.* The mean of this sampling distribution would be our best estimate of the population mean and the standard deviation of this distribution would be our standard error of the mean (sem). The sem would be the degree of error we would expect in our sample mean. OK. That was not the simple method. As you might have guessed, it is impossible to randomly select an infinite number of samples in order to calculate the standard error of the mean. The simple method of determining the standard error of the mean involves a simple formula. The standard error of the mean can be calculated if we know the population standard deviation. The formula for the standard error of the mean is

$$\text{Standard error of the mean} = \sigma / \sqrt{n}$$

where n is the sample size and σ is the population standard deviation. If we do not know σ, we can calculate the standard error of the mean using the sample standard deviation as an estimate of the population standard deviation.

The sem essentially is a measure of the degree of sampling error. From this formula, you can see the relationship between the sem (sampling error) and sample size. As sample size increases, sampling error decreases.

The relationship between sampling error and sample size is quite intuitive. (I always hated when my statistics professor said that phrase in class, but now I understand what he was saying.) It is clear if we look at an example we used earlier. From our population of 1,000,000 customers, we randomly select five customers and calculate the mean satisfaction level. We place that sample of customers back into the population and randomly select another sample of five customers. We do this again and again. Do you think the sampling distribution of these means would reflect wide variability? You bet. We know that we need more customers to get a good estimate of the population mean.

Now, from our population of 1,000,000 customers we randomly select 500 customers and calculate the mean satisfaction level. We place that sample of customers back into the population and randomly select another sample of 500 customers. We do this again and again. Do you think the sampling distribution of these sample means would reflect wide variability? Probably not.

Let's use numbers now to illustrate this point. Let's say we calculate the sample standard deviation (to be used as our estimate of our population standard deviation) and it equals 1.01. Now, using our formula for the sem, we can calculate the sem for various sample sizes. In our former case with the sample size of five, the sem would be .45 $(1.01/\sqrt{5})$. In the latter case with the sample size of 500, the sem would be .045 $(1.01/\sqrt{500})$. The larger the sample size, the smaller the sem (sampling error).

Calculating Sample Size

Statistical sampling helps us ensure that we can make generalizations from our sample to the population from which the sample was drawn. An important characteristic regarding our sample is the degree of precision of our generalizations. We can define precision as the degree of sampling error (the amount our sample statistics vary from the population parameter). The greater the sampling error, the less precision we have in our estimate of the population parameter. We can use our knowledge of sampling error to help us calculate the precision of our estimate of the population parameter. Additionally, we can use our knowledge of sampling error (and its relationship to sample size) to help us determine the sample size we need for a given level of precision of our estimate.

When considering the determination of the sample size *(n)*, we must consider three variables:

- Standard deviation of the characteristic being measured *(s)*
- Confidence level *(t)*
- Tolerable error (TE)

Standard deviation reflects the degree of variability of the characteristic being measured. We denote this value with an *s*.

The *confidence level* reflects the degree of confidence we have that the sample statistic we obtain from our sample is close to the population parameter. The degree of confidence is operationalized by a *t*-value (found in any statistics textbook). If a 95 percent confidence level is desired, we can set *t* to equal roughly 2.0.

Table 5.4 lists *t*-values for some commonly used confidence levels.

These *t*-values are used to calculate the *confidence interval*. The confidence interval describes the interval that surrounds the sample statistic. The confidence interval is calculated by first multiplying the sem by the *t*-value. Next, this value is subtracted from the mean (estimate) to get the lower bound of the confidence interval and added to the mean to get the upper bound of the confidence interval. The formula for the confidence interval is

$$\text{Confidence interval} \;=\; \bar{x} \;\pm\; (s/\sqrt{n})\, t$$

For example, we could conduct a survey on a sample of 300 customers and calculate a mean of 4.5 and a standard error of .04. To calculate a 95 percent confidence level, we would multiply .04 by 2.0. The lower confidence interval would be 4.42 and the upper confidence interval would be 4.58.

So, how do we interpret these results? Someone could hand you a report with a confidence interval of 4.5 and 4.9 with a 95 percent confidence level using a sample size of 300. What does that mean? If you were to conduct this sort of study 100 times, each of these 100 studies would result in slightly different confidence intervals (perhaps 4.4 to 4.8 or 4.45 to 4.85). Based on statistical theory, given a 95 percent confidence interval, out of the 100 studies you could conduct, 95 studies would result in a confidence interval that would encompass the true population mean.

Tolerable error reflects the desired level of precision. Tolerable error is essentially the sampling error at a specified level of confidence.

Table 5.4 *t*-values for commonly used confidence levels.

Confidence level (as a percent)	*t*-value
50	0.6745
80	1.282
90	1.645
95	1.960 (2.0)
98	2.326
99	2.578
99.5	2.810

Next, we will use this information to determine the appropriate sample size to attain a given level of confidence and tolerable error. To calculate the needed sample size, the survey team sets two factors: the confidence level and the amount of tolerable error. The standard deviation of the characteristic being measured is estimated with existing data.

Let's look again at the formula for the sem: $s/\sqrt{n}$. Recall that the tolerable error is the degree of sampling error given a specified level of confidence. Therefore, the formula for tolerable error is very similar to the formula for the sem.

$$\text{Tolerable error} = \text{TE} = (t \times s)/\sqrt{n}$$

We add the *t*-value in the formula to specify a given level of confidence. Given that the other values of the equation remain the same, the greater the confidence we want, the greater the tolerable error must be.

Given this formula, we can now solve for the sample size, *n*. This results in the following formula:

$$n = (t^2 \times s^2)/\text{TE}^2$$

So, we see how these variables are related to sample size *(n)*. As your desired level of confidence increases *(t)*, sample size must increase. If the variability of the characteristic increases *(s)*, the sample size increases. If tolerable error (TE) decreases, sample size increases.

Let's look at a real example. For a major insurance company, we want to determine the needed sample size for a given level of confidence *(t)* and a given level of tolerable error (TE). The survey team wanted to have a confidence level of 95 percent *(t* = 2.0) and a tolerable error (TE) = .20. (Using a five-point scale as our response format, this amount of error was acceptable.) Using previous survey research conducted at this insurance company and other survey research, we have found that *s* for survey items, on the average, equals 1.0.

Given the formula to calculate sample size, we solve for *n* and see that we need a sample size of 100 = $(2^2 \times 1.0^2)/.20^2$ to obtain a tolerable error of .20 with a 95 percent confidence level.

Next, we set up different scenarios given a level of tolerable error at a 95 percent confidence level. Table 5.5 contains this information.

Summary

From a basic formula, we were able to determine sample size for a given level of precision. When conducting customer surveys, we need to ensure that the results from our sample of customers are good estimates of our population parameters. By using these formulae, we can determine a satisfactory level of precision. These formulae are useful when planning a customer satisfaction survey. Before any surveys have been administered,

Table 5.5 Tolerable error at a 95 percent confidence level.

If $s = 1.0$

TE	n
.20	100
.30	44
.40	25
.50	16

we could estimate the number of surveys we need. This would greatly help us in the budgeting process when estimating the cost to conduct our customer satisfaction study (for example, printing costs, mailing costs, labor hours). We would have the financial numbers in hand to help us convince management of the cost/benefit of conducting a customer survey.

RANDOM SELECTION PROCEDURES

The three sampling procedures discussed previously involve a method of random selection, each in a slightly different form. The difference among the various sampling procedures (random, stratified, and cluster) is represented by the unit that is selected. In the simple random sampling procedure, the unit of selection is the individual customer from the entire population. In the stratified sampling procedure, the unit of selection is the individual customer from each stratum. In the cluster sampling procedure, the unit of selection is not the individual customer but the group of customers. In each of the sampling procedures, random selection procedures are used to select the units.

Next, we will discuss two types of random selection procedure: systematic selection with a random start and random number sampling.

Systematic Selection with a Random Start

In this procedure, the sample is selected based on a fixed interval between the sampling units (typically the customers) after establishing a random starting point. The fixed interval is calculated by dividing the population size by the sample size. The random start point is typically determined by selecting a random number between 1 and the sampling interval (usually with a computer).

For example, we may want to sample 100 of our customers from our population of 14,210 customers. First, we need the list of 14,210 customers in some form, either on computer or in some format where they can be counted by hand. Next, we divide 100 into 14,210 to obtain our sampling interval. This is calculated to be 142.1. Rounding down to the nearest whole number, our sampling interval is 142. Next, we establish a starting point by randomly selecting a number between 1 and 142, inclusive. This is done by arbitrarily picking a number from Appendix L. If our random starting point were calculated to be 90, we would first survey customer 90 and then every 142nd customer thereafter. We would survey customer 90, 232, 375, 517, and so on until we reach our criteria of 100 customers.

Random Number Sampling

The next method of random selection procedures is best illustrated by an example. Say we have 20,000 customers and we want to obtain a random sample consisting of 100 customers. The chance of selecting one person from the population would be 1 in 200 (or .5 percent). We could select these customers by writing their names on slips of paper, placing those 20,000 slips into a barrel, and then blindly selecting 100 slips. With this method, each person has an equal chance of being selected. (Actually, each customer's chance of being selected increases slightly if we do not return the previously selected customers to the population.)

If the population is small enough, this paper-in-a-barrel method would be possible. With large populations, however, this method is not practical. Instead, we would use a computer program to randomly select 100 customers from a list of the population of customers (given that the list is available electronically).

Another method would be to use a random number table. Let's say we have 200 customers and we want to sample 100 of them. We would assign each customer a number ranging from 1 to 200. Next, we would use a random number table to determine which customer is selected into the sample. A random number table is presented in Appendix L. You should note that the numbers in this random number table have five digits. Since we are interested in 200 customers, we need to look at only the first digits in each of the five-digit random numbers. First, close your eyes and arbitrarily put your finger somewhere on the table. This is your starting point. Let's say your finger falls on the number 06476 (column 7, row 4). The three-digit number is 064, so we would select customer 64 to be included in our sample. Go to the next number in the table (70782). Since the first three digits of this number are larger than 200, we go on down until we find a number in which the first three digits are 200 or less (12159); customer 121 is selected into the sample. Once a number has been used in the selection, all subsequent encounters of that number are ignored. This procedure is done until 100 customers have been selected for the sample.

As is evident even in this simplistic example, the random number table method is not practical when our population is very large (thousands) or our sample is large. Typically, the selection of a sample is conducted with the aid of a computer. This method of the random number table is useful, nonetheless, to illustrate the concept that behind the random selection of a sample from the population.

Table 5.6 summarizes the two random selection procedures. The specific steps for each selection procedure are presented in this table.

Summary

The various sampling methods and random selection procedures just discussed illustrate how important it is that the sample be representative when we're making generalizations about the population. As we can see, the precision with which we make an estimation of the population parameters is dependent, in part, on the results of the sampling methods. The next section will discuss the effect of response rates on the sampling process and various methods of increasing response rates.

Table 5.6   Random selection procedures.

Method	Definition	Steps
Systematic selection with a random start	Selection procedure is conducted by selecting the sample based on a fixed interval between the sampling units after establishing a random starting point	• Acquire complete list of the unit (typically customers) • Divide sample size into population size to obtain interval (z) • Establish random starting point to select unit • Select every zth unit from the list
Random number sampling	Random number table (or comparable computer program) used to select customers	• Assign all units (typically customer) a unique number • Use random number table to select unit into the sample

RESPONSE RATES

When conducting a customer survey, it is unlikely that all customers will respond. For our purposes, response rate is defined as the percent of returned, completed surveys of all the surveys that were administered. For example, if we mail out 1000 surveys and only 300 written surveys are returned, we have a response rate of 30 percent. For written, mail surveys, response rates can be very low. Due to apathy, interest level, and various other factors, customers may not complete a survey. A low response rate does affect the outcome of the sampling procedure. We saw earlier in this chapter the relationship between sample size and tolerable error. Here are the formulas again:

$$n = (t^2 \times s^2)/\text{TE}^2$$

$$\text{Tolerable error} = \text{TE} = (t \times s)/\sqrt{n}$$

If a survey team is relying on a given number of surveys to establish a given level of precision, a low response rate from customers will lead to a wider confidence interval. Recall that the confidence level and tolerable error are affected by the sample size. As sample size decreases, the confidence interval increases and tolerable error increases.

Consequently, when planning our sampling procedures, we must take into account the response rate. To obtain a given sample size, in the end our sampling procedure will require administering more customer surveys than we will ultimately need for analysis. For example, we may have concluded that we need a sample size of 200 for a given level of confidence. If we expect a response rate of 30 percent for our survey, how many surveys should we administer (mail)? The formula to calculate the distribution sample size is

$$\text{Distribution size} = \text{Needed sample size}/\text{Response rate}$$

where distribution size is the number of surveys we should administer; needed sample size is the sample size we determined we needed for a given level of confidence and tolerable error; and response rate is the actual or expected number of returned surveys from our satisfaction study.

For our example, we would need to administer about 670 surveys (200/.30) to our customers. A survey distribution of this size would ensure that we have enough customers in our final sample to maintain the given level of confidence and tolerable error that were established earlier in the sampling process.

Establishing Response Rates

The key factor in the previous equation is the response rate. Our distribution sample size is determined by this factor. Response rates can vary from study to study and we really have little control over them. In my experience, I have seen response rates as low as 7 percent and as high as 50 percent. We can, however, estimate what our response rate will be for our study. We could determine whether a survey had been conducted in the past and use that information to estimate a response rate for our study. Another method would be to conduct a literature search in our specific industry to learn what other researchers have found regarding response rates of similar customer groups. If these methods are not feasible, it is always possible to conduct our satisfaction survey, monitor the response rates throughout the process, and adjust our mailing list (increase the distribution list size) in order to obtain more customers in our final sample.

The factors that tend to affect response rates are related to the ease with which the subjects can return the surveys. Basically, if the return process is made simple for customers, the response rate will go up. Some research regarding the factors that affect response rates for mail surveys are presented next.

Methods of Increasing Response Rates of Mail Surveys

Although we mail out a given number of customer surveys, we invariably get only a portion mailed back to us. Here are some suggestions that have been shown to increase response rates of mail surveys:

- Repeated contacts in the form of preliminary notification and follow-ups. If possible, notify customers that they will be part of a satisfaction survey. Once the customers are included in the sample, contact them again requesting completion of their surveys.

- Appeals. Customers want to know how their input will be used and whether their opinions are making a difference in the organization. Informing the recipients of mail surveys about the use of their information will increase response rates. In the survey, tell your customers why their opinions are valued and how the information will be used throughout the company.

- Inclusion of a return envelope. Always include an envelope for the return of the survey. Relying on the customer to provide his or her own envelope reduces response. The cost of envelopes might be less than the cost of additional mailings if the initial response rate is low. Some companies format the survey in such a way that it becomes a return mailer. Customers need only fold the survey to expose the return address and then drop it in a mailbox.

- Postage. Providing postage makes the return process easier for customers and increases the likelihood that they will respond.

- Monetary incentives. Providing incentive in the form of monetary reward has been shown to increase response rates to mail surveys. This might take the form of a simple lottery. From all the returned surveys, one is randomly chosen to receive a monetary reward. Some companies donate to a charity for every returned survey. While monetary incentives work, other studies have shown that non-monetary incentives do not increase response rates.

- First-class outgoing postage. Research has shown that first-class outgoing postage increases the response rates of mail surveys. Using first-class postage indicates to the recipient the importance of the survey; customers assume that companies wouldn't use first-class postage if the results were not important.

- Sponsorship. Finally, research has shown that mail survey response rates increase when the study is sponsored by a third party such as a survey research firm or a university. The sponsoring organization, acting as an independent party, is perceived to lend credibility to the entire survey process. Customers may feel that their responses will be treated with more care and honesty by an unbiased party who is organizing the data.

Summary

The use of these methods to increase response rates does not guarantee that all surveys will be returned. These methods do, however, increase your chances for an acceptable response. The extent to which these methods are used will depend on your resources. Some companies might not be able to provide monetary incentives to customers or might not be able to provide first-class outgoing postage. Although these methods are presented separately, some methods might be used in conjunction with others to increase response rates. At a minimum, you should provide postage and a means by which to have the surveys returned.

6
Customer Loyalty 2.0: Beyond the Ultimate Question

The Net Promoter Score (NPS) is used by many of today's top businesses to monitor and manage customer relationships. Fred Reichheld and his co-developers of the NPS say that a single survey question, "How likely are you to recommend Company Name to a friend or colleague?," on which the NPS is based, is the only loyalty metric a company needs with which to grow its business. Despite its widespread adoption by such companies as General Electric, Intuit, T-Mobile, Charles Schwab, and Enterprise, the NPS is now at the center of a debate regarding its merits.

I will summarize the NPS methodology, including its developers' claims and opponents' criticisms. Additionally, I will discuss and study the meaning of customer loyalty as it is measured through survey questions. Finally, I will illustrate how the predictability of business performance measures can be improved when the specificity in the loyalty question and business performance measure is the same.

NPS METHODOLOGY

The NPS is calculated from a single loyalty question, "How likely are you to recommend us to your friends / colleagues?" Based on their rating of this question using a 0 to 10 likelihood scale where 0 means "Not at all Likely" and 10 means "Extremely Likely," customers are segmented into three groups: (1) Detractors (ratings of 0 to 6), (2) Passives (ratings of 7 and 8) and (3) Promoters (ratings of 9 and 10). A company can calculate its Net Promoter Score by simply subtracting the proportion of Detractors from the proportion of Promoters.

$$NPS = prop(Promoters) - prop(Detractors)$$

NPS CLAIMS

Fred Reichheld (along with NPS co-developers Satmetrix and Bain & Company) has made strong claims about the advantage of the NPS over other loyalty metrics. Specifically, they have said:

1. The NPS is "the best predictor of growth" (Reichheld 2003)

2. The NPS is "the single most reliable indicator of a company's ability to grow" (Netpromoter.com 2007)

3. "Satisfaction lacks a consistently demonstrable connection to... growth" (Reichheld 2003)

Reichheld supports these claims with research displaying the relationship of NPS to revenue growth. In compelling graphs, Reichheld (2006) illustrates that companies with higher Net Promoter Scores show better revenue growth compared to companies with lower Net Promoter Scores. (See top graph in Figure 6.1.) Reichheld cites only one study conducted by Bain & Associates showing the relationship between satisfaction and growth to be 0.00.[1]

Recent Scientific Challenges to NPS Claims

Researchers, pointing out that NPS claims are supported only by Reichheld and his co-developers, have conducted rigorous scientific research on the NPS with startling results. For example, Keiningham et al. (2007), using the same technique employed by Reichheld to show the relationship between NPS and growth, used survey results from the American Customer Satisfaction Index (ACSI) to create scatterplots to show the relationship between satisfaction and growth. Looking at the personal computer industry, they found that satisfaction is just as good as the NPS at predicting growth (see Figure 6.1). Keiningham et al. (2007) found the same pattern of results in other industries (for example, insurance, airline, ISP). In all cases, satisfaction and NPS were comparable in predicting growth.

Still other researchers (Morgan & Rego 2006) have shown that other conventional loyalty measures (for example, overall satisfaction, likelihood to repurchase) are comparable to NPS in predicting business performance measures such as market share and cash flow.

Contrary to Reichheld, other researchers, in fact, have found that customer satisfaction is consistently correlated with growth (Anderson, et al. 2004; Fornell, et al. 2006; Gruca & Rego 2005).

Problems with NPS Research

Recent scientific, peer-reviewed studies cast a shadow on the claims put forth by Reichheld and his cohorts. In fact, as of this writing, this author knows of no published empirical studies supporting the superiority of the NPS over other conventional loyalty metrics.

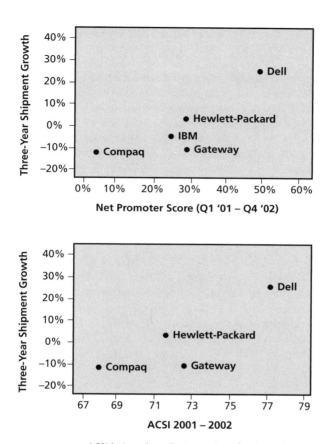

Figure 6.1 Predicting shipment growth using NPS and satisfaction (ACSI).

Keiningham et al. (2007) aptly point out that there may be research bias by the NPS developers. There seems to be a lack of full disclosure from the Net Promoter camp with regard to their research. The Net Promoter developers, like any research scientists, should present their analysis to back up their claims and refute the current scientific research that brings their methodological rigor into question. To date, they have not done so. Instead, the Net Promoter camp only points to the simplicity of this single metric, which allows companies to become more customer-centric. That is not a scientific rebuttal. That is marketing.

MEASUREMENT AND
MEANING OF CUSTOMER LOYALTY

Why do commonly used loyalty questions show a similar pattern of relationship to revenue growth? The measurement process behind the loyalty questions plays a key role in understanding the meaning of customer loyalty. First, let's look at objective measures of loyalty. These metrics have minimal measurement error associated with them. Because these objective loyalty metrics are not subject to interpretation, they have unambiguous meaning. The number of recommendations a customer makes is clearly distinct from the number of repeat purchases that customer makes.

Let us now look at the use of surveys to gauge customer loyalty. Customers' ratings of each loyalty question (that is, likelihood to recommend, satisfaction, likelihood to repurchase) become the metric of customer loyalty. Even though we are able to calculate separate loyalty scores from each loyalty question (for example, NPS, Overall Satisfaction, Likelihood to Repurchase), the distinction among the loyalty questions may not be as clear as we think. Because of the way customers interpret survey questions and the inherent error associated with measuring psychological constructs (yes, measured in surveys, customer loyalty is a psychological construct), ratings must be critically evaluated in order to ensure that we understand the meaning behind the them (American Educational Research Association, American Psychological Association, and National Council on Measurement in Education, 1985). Psychological measurement principles and analyses (for example, correlational analysis, factor analysis, and reliability analysis) are used to help identify the meaning behind the customers' ratings.

I set out to compare four commonly used loyalty questions and study the differences, if any, among the questions. The four loyalty questions were:

1. Overall, how satisfied are you with COMPANY ABC?

2. How likely are you to recommend COMPANY ABC to friends or colleagues?

3. How likely are you to continue purchasing the same product and or service from COMPANY ABC?

4. If you were selecting a company (within the industry) for the first time, how likely is it that you would choose COMPANY ABC?

An 11-point rating scale was used for each question. Question 1 was rated on a scale of 0 (Extremely Dissatisfied) to 10 (Extremely Satisfied). The remaining questions were rated on a scale of 0 (Not at all Likely) to 10 (Extremely Likely). With the help of GMI (Global Market Insite, Inc., www.gmi-mr.com), which provided online data collection and consumer panels, I surveyed about 1000 respondents (general consumers in the United States ages 18 and older) who were asked to identify and then rate their wireless service provider on the four questions. I obtained objective business metrics, when available, for each wireless service provider; these were annual revenue (2005 and 2006) and defection rates (Q2 2007).

I applied standard statistical analyses that are commonly used to evaluate survey questions. First, the average correlation among the four loyalty questions was very high ($r = .87$). This finding reveals that customers respond to the four questions in a consistent manner. That is, customers who are highly likely to recommend the company are also highly likely to be satisfied with the company; conversely, customers who are not likely to recommend the company are also not likely to be satisfied with the company. The same pattern is seen across all pairings of the loyalty questions. Second, a factor analysis of the four questions showed a clear one-factor solution. Factor loadings, essentially representing the correlation between each question and its underlying factor, were all .90 or higher. This pattern of results clearly shows that all four questions, including the "likelihood to recommend" question, measure one underlying construct, customer loyalty.[2]

Supported by the analyses above, the four loyalty questions can be averaged to get a more reliable measure of loyalty, what I refer to as the Advocacy Loyalty Index (ALI). The high reliability of the ALI (Cronbach's alpha = .96, quite high by psychological measurement standards) indicates that there is little measurement error when all four questions are used together. Using the ALI in customer loyalty management is better than using any single question because the ALI provides a more precise measure of loyalty than any of the four questions used alone.

Figure 6.2 shows that the NPS and the ALI are similarly related to revenue growth.[3] T-Mobile, Alltel, and Verizon, all with high ALI or Net Promoter scores, have faster revenue growth compared to Sprint, which has a lower ALI and NPS.

Specificity vs. Generality of Measurement

Predictability is improved when the specificity in the predictor and outcome are the same (see Figure 6.3). That is, specific outcomes are best predicted by specific measures. As an example, an employee's intention to quit his or her job is a better predictor of whether or not that employee actually quits compared to general measures of employee satisfaction. Conversely, general outcomes are best predicted by general measures.

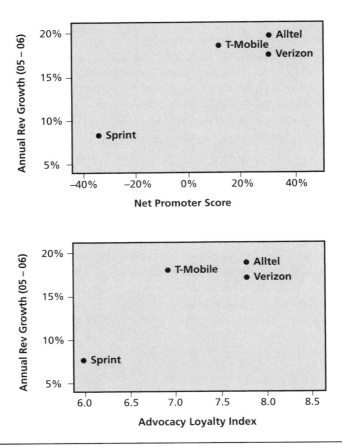

Figure 6.2   Predicting revenue growth using the NPS and the Advocacy Loyalty Index.

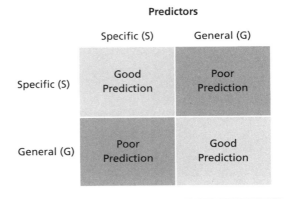

Figure 6.3   Specificity of predictors and outcomes and the quality of prediction.

In the survey, I included another loyalty question, "How likely are you to switch to a different provider in the next 12 months?" When predicting revenue growth, we see that the Advocacy Loyalty Index (general predictor) is better than Likelihood to Switch (specific predictor) in predicting Revenue Growth (general outcome) (see Figure 6.4). Revenue growth is impacted by more than just customers' likelihood to switch. Advocacy loyalty, however, predicts growth better because of its general nature.

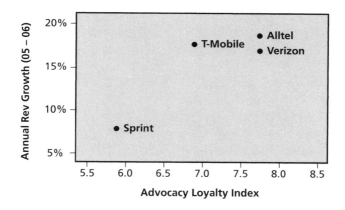

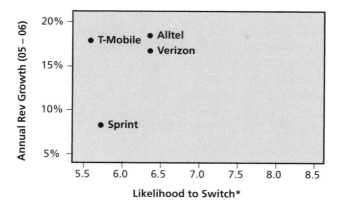

* How likely are you to switch to a different wireless service provider within the next 12 months? Ratings are indicated on a scale ranging from 0 (Not at all Likely) to 10 (Extremely Likely). For analysis purposes, ratings are reverse coded; higher scores indicate lower likelihood to switch.

Figure 6.4   Predicting a general outcome with general and specific predictors.

When we predict a more specific outcome, we see a different pattern of results (see Figure 6.5). Likelihood to Switch (specific predictor) is better than Advocacy Loyalty Index (general predictor) in predicting Defection Rate (specific outcome). Likelihood to switch is a better predictor because it is specific and targeted to the outcome of interest.

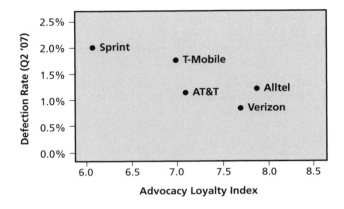

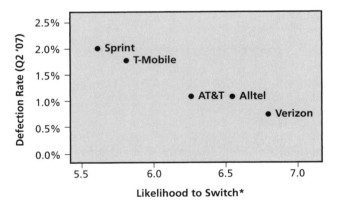

* How likely are you to switch to a different wireless
   service provider within the next 12 months? Ratings
   on a scale from 0 (Not at all Likely) to 10 (Extremely
   Likely). For analysis purposes, ratings are reverse coded;
   higher scores indicate lower likelihood to switch.

Figure 6.5   Predicting a specific outcome with general and specific predictors.

Advocacy loyalty, however, encompasses aspects that are not related to whether customers stay or leave. Companies need to examine their business metrics closely and then select the appropriate loyalty metrics that best match them. Managing important customer outcomes goes far beyond a single, ultimate question.

Potential Loss of Revenue when using the NPS: An Example

A company, relying solely on the NPS as the ultimate metric, may overlook disloyal customers defined in other ways. In the wireless service provider study, I found that, of the customers who are non-detractors (those scoring 7 or above), *31 percent* are still likely to switch to a different wireless service provider. As a predictor to manage customer relationships in order to minimize customer defections, the NPS falls short.

Relying solely on NPS to manage customers would result in missed opportunities to save a large number of at-risk customers from defecting. This mismanagement of customer relationships in the wireless industry, where defection rate is a key business metric, can be detrimental to revenue growth. Using Q2 2007 data for T-Mobile USA (see Figure 6.6), it is estimated

Recommend (NPS)	Percent of T-Mobile Customers	Number of T-Mobile Customers	Percent Highly Likely to Switch to Another Provider*	Number of T-Mobile Customers Highly Likely to Switch*
0	2%	637,795	59%	375,174
1	3%	850,394	52%	445,444
2	1%	212,598	39%	82,677
3	3%	850,394	11%	94,488
4	1%	212,598	8%	17,008
5	11%	2,976,378	4%	127,196
6	5%	1,275,591	4%	57,116
7	18%	4,889,764	4%	175,891
8	19%	5,102,362	5%	259,442
9	17%	4,464,567	7%	325,233
10	20%	5,527,559	3%	167,502
TOTAL	**100%**	**27,000,000**	**8%**	**2,266,321**

* How likely are you to switch to a different wireless service provider within the next 12 months? Highly Likely reflects ratings of 9 or 10 on a 0 (Not at all Likely) to 10 (Extremely Likely) scale.

Figure 6.6   T-Mobile USA example using NPS methodology.

that, of non-detractors, more than 900,000 T-Mobile USA customers are still likely to switch to another provider, with a potential annual revenue loss of more than $29 million!

Summary and Conclusions

The NPS is not the best predictor of business performance measures. Other conventional loyalty questions are equally good at predicting revenue growth. Reichheld's claims are grossly overstated with regard to the merits of the Net Promoter Score. The developers do not address these criticisms about the quality of the research (or lack thereof) behind their claims.

General loyalty questions, including "likely to recommend," measure one general construct, customer loyalty. Consequently, it not surprising that many researchers find similar results across these loyalty questions when predicting revenue growth. Because individual survey questions have inherent measurement error, aggregating responses across general loyalty questions (for example, overall satisfaction, recommend, repurchase, choose again) is a useful way to create reliable loyalty metrics.

Companies should use a variety of loyalty questions to ensure that at-risk customers are identified in a variety of ways. How well we are able to predict business performance measures depends on the match between the business metric and the loyalty questions. Specific loyalty questions are useful for predicting specific business outcomes (for example, defection rate). General loyalty questions are useful for predicting general business outcomes (for example, revenue). Companies need to do their research to fully understand how different loyalty measures correspond to specific business outcomes. Single, simple metrics are fraught with potential for error and can lead to the mismanagement of customers and, ultimately, loss of revenue.

Objective vs. Subjective Measures of Loyalty and Measurement Error

In psychological measurement terms, the loyalty questions are simply observable indicators of a single underlying construct (see Figure 6.7). Specifically, customers' rating of each of the questions (loyalty items) is simply a function of an underlying construct (loyalty). That is, customers respond consistently across all the loyalty questions. A customer who is loyal will rate each loyalty question high and a customer who is disloyal will tend to rate each loyalty question low.

What Loyalty Questions are Measuring: A Factor Analytic View

To determine the extent of commonality across the loyalty items, a set of loyalty questions was subjected to a series of analyses using responses from

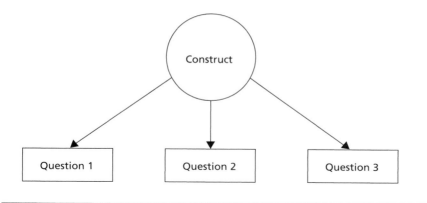

Figure 6.7　Relationship between a construct and its questions.

actual customers. Two separate studies were conducted, each within a specific industry: 1) wireless service providers, and 2) personal computer manufacturers. For each study, surveys were fielded in June and July of 2007, respectively, asking a sample of about 1000 general consumers in the United States ages 18 and older about their attitudes toward their wireless service provider or personal computer manufacturer. All respondents were interviewed to ensure they met correct profiling criteria, and were rewarded with an incentive for filling out the survey. The survey data for this study were collected by GMI (Global Market Insite, Inc.).

The seven loyalty items listed earlier in Chapter 4 (page 80) were included in the wireless service provider sample. For the PC manufacturer sample, the first six questions were used with an additional question added (likelihood to increase frequency of purchasing). For each study, a factor analysis was conducted on the set of loyalty questions.

Factor analysis, in statistical terms, is a data reduction technique that explains the statistical relationships among a given set of variables using fewer unobserved variables (factors). In simpler terms, a factor analysis tells us two things: 1) the number of factors (constructs) that are being measured by the set of questions and 2) which questions are related to which factors.

Specifically, for our problem, a factor analysis will help us determine whether the seven original loyalty questions are actually measuring fewer constructs (factors). It is important to note that an exploratory factor analysis involves some form of judgment when determining the number of factors as well as which variables are related to the smaller set of factors. A full discussion is beyond the scope of this work, but the interested reader can find more about this topic in Appendix K.

The elements in the factor pattern matrix are called factor loading; they essentially reflect the correlation between each item and the three factors. Higher factor loadings indicate a stronger relationship between the item and the underlying factor.

The results of the factor analysis suggest that there is considerable overlap among some of the loyalty items. In fact, the results suggest that the seven items measure fewer constructs (three constructs for the wireless sample and two for the PC sample). Figures 6.8 and 6.9 represent the factor pattern matrices.

Advocacy, Purchasing, and Retention Loyalty

The labeling of the factors involves examining the content of the items that have high factor loadings. The naming of factors in a factor analysis involves some level of creativity and subjectivity. Other researchers might label the factors with different (but probably similar) words; the underlying construct being measured, however, remains the same.

The items that load on the first factor appear to have a strong emotional component to them, reflecting the extent to which customers advocate the company. Consequently, this factor is labeled advocacy loyalty. The items that load on the second factor reflect specific purchasing behaviors. This second factor is labeled purchasing loyalty. For the wireless service provider sample, the item that represents the third factor reflects retention (opposite of switching) and is, therefore, labeled retention loyalty.

Results suggest that there are three types of customer loyalty: advocacy, purchasing, and retention. Loyalty indices for each can be calculated by averaging the loyalty items that load highly on the same factor:

- **Advocacy Loyalty Index (ALI):** Reflects the degree to which customers will be advocates of the company (average across satisfaction, recommend, choose again, purchase same)

- **Purchasing Loyalty Index (PLI):** Reflects the degree to which customers will increase their purchasing behavior (average across purchase different, purchase increase, purchase frequency)

- **Retention Loyalty Index (RLI):** Reflects the degree to which customers will remain with a given company (single defection item, reverse coded)

Reliability of Loyalty Indices

Reliability estimates were calculated for each of the loyalty indices. Reliability deals with the extent to which measurement is free from random error. For the wireless service provider example, the reliability (Cronbach's alpha) of the Advocacy Loyalty Index (ALI) was .92. The reliability estimate

Questions (Items)	Factors*		
	1 (Advocacy)	2 (Purchasing)	3 (Retention)
Overall satisfaction	.79	.34	.35
Choose again	.71	.41	.43
Recommend	.78	.40	.39
Purchase same	.61	.37	.58
Purchase different	.29	.75	.09
Purchase increase	.26	.76	.09
Likelihood to switch to another provider[1]	.32	.12	.68

Based on a factor analysis with Varimax rotation.
[1] *Reverse coded so higher scores mean lower likelihood of switching.*

Figure 6.8   Factor pattern matrix of the seven loyalty questions for the wireless service provider study.

Questions (Items)	Factors*	
	1 (Advocacy)	2 (Purchasing)
Overall satisfaction	.77	.32
Choose again	.71	.41
Recommend	.78	.40
Purchase same	.61	.37
Purchase different	.29	.75
Purchase increase	.26	.76
Purchase frequency	.32	.79

Based on a factor analysis with Varimax rotation.

Figure 6.9   Factor pattern matrix of the seven loyalty questions for the PC manufacturer study.

(Cronbach's alpha) for the purchasing loyalty index (PLI) was .82. For the personal computer manufacturer sample, the reliability of the ALI was .94. The reliability of the PLI was .87. These levels of reliability are considered very good for attitude research (Nunnally, 1978; 0 = no reliability, 1 = perfect reliability).

Net Promoter Score vs. Satisfaction vs. Purchase Same

Of particular interest are three specific loyalty items that load on Factor 1 in each study: (1) Satisfaction, (2) Recommend, and (3) Purchase same. The Net Promoter Score (NPS) developers state that the "recommend" question is the best predictor of business growth (Reichheld 2003, 2006). This conclusion has come under recent attack from other researchers who have found that the "satisfaction" and "purchase same" questions are just as good as the "recommend" question in predicting business growth (Fornell, et al. 2006; Keiningham, et al. 2007; Morgan & Rego 2006).

The current factor-analytic findings cast additional doubt on the conclusions by the NPS camp. The recommend question appears to measure the same underlying construct as these other two loyalty questions. There is no scientific evidence that the "recommend" question (NPS) is, or should be, a better predictor of business growth compared to other loyalty questions.

Single-Item Measures or Aggregated Metrics

The NPS developers support the use of a single question to understand customer loyalty. This single-item approach is not supported with the present study findings. There is nothing unique and special about the "recommend" question. Furthermore, single-item measures are less reliable (contain more measurement error) than multiple-item measures. Measuring loyalty with a single question is akin to measuring math skills with a single-item math test. An answer to the single-item test would be a less reliable reflection of math skills compared to the combined answers to a 50-item math test. Would you want your child's SAT score to be determined by a single question or by the entire set of questions on the test? Using the loyalty indices in customer loyalty management is statistically better than using any single question because the indices provide a more precise measure of loyalty than any of the items used alone.

Ranking Companies on Loyalty

For each study, the loyalty indices were calculated for each company. Figures 6.10 and 6.11 illustrate the average loyalty indices for the PC manufacturers and the wireless service providers, respectively. The results show that the loyalty indices were able to detect meaningful difference across the companies.

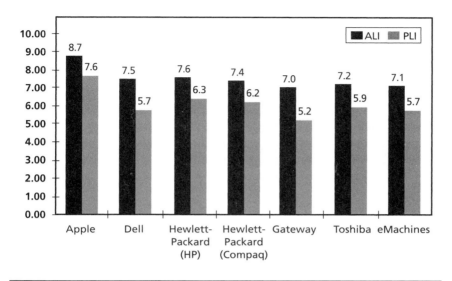

Figure 6.10   Bar graph of loyalty scores for PC manufacturers.

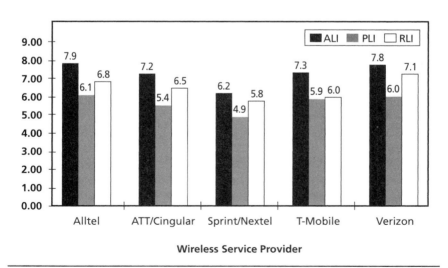

Figure 6.11   Bar graph of loyalty scores for wireless service providers.

The analyses show that the loyalty indices, ALI and PLI, are sensitive enough to detect differences across the different companies; it appears that the measurement precision of each of the loyalty scales is able to detect meaningful differences across different companies, thus allowing researchers and practitioners the ability to reliably study different types of loyalty across different groups of customers.

ALI, PLI, and RLI Predict Business Growth

To understand how well the ALI and PLI predict future growth, objective loyalty measures for the wireless service providers were collected for Q3 2007 (fiercewireless.com and quarterly reports from provider's respective Web sites).

Each of the loyalty indices was correlated with each of the following objective loyalty measures that were collected in Q3 2007 (see Table 6.1 for values):

- Average revenue per user (ARPU) growth (Q2-Q3 2007)

- Churn for Q3 2007 (reverse coded so higher scores reflected better retention)

- Percent total of new customer growth (Q2-Q3 2007) estimated from churn rate and net new customers

The correlations for each of the loyalty indices with each of the objective loyalty measures are located in Figure 6.12. As we can see, all of the loyalty indices (Q2 2007) were differentially related to the objective loyalty measures (Q3 2007).

The ALI shows its greatest impact on new customer growth; companies that had higher ALI scores experienced greater new customer growth compared to companies that had lower ALI scores. Figure 6.13 illustrates the relationship between the ALI and new customer growth.

Table 6.1   Objective loyalty measures for wireless service providers.

	ARPU Growth (Q2-Q3 '07)	Churn Q3 2007	Percent Total New Customer Growth (Q2–Q3 '07)
Alltel	$1.86	1.9%	3.7%
AT&T	$0.19	1.7%	4.7%
Sprint/Nextel	−$1.00	2.3%	2.3%
T-Mobile	$2.60	2.9%	5.9%
Verizon	$0.33	1.2%	6.8%

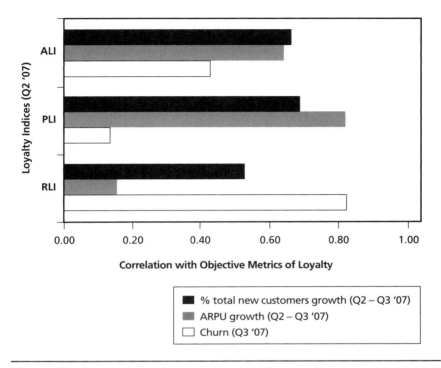

Figure 6.12 Impact of each loyalty index on objective loyalty measures.

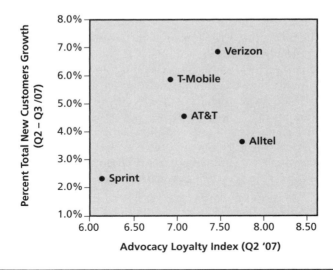

Figure 6.13 Relationship between Advocacy Loyalty Index and new customer growth.

The PLI, however, was highly predictive of average revenue per user (ARPU) growth; companies that had higher PLI scores also experienced greater ARPU growth compared to companies that had lower PLI scores. Figure 6.14 illustrates the relationship between the Purchasing Loyalty Index and ARPU growth.

Finally, the retention loyalty index was the best predictor of actual churn rates for wireless service providers; companies that had higher RLI scores had lower churn rates compared to companies that had lower RLI scores. Figure 6.15 illustrates the relationship between the Retention Loyalty Index and churn rate.

The results show that loyalty indices are predictive of future business growth through new customers (new customer growth) and existing customers (ARPU), suggesting that the ALI, PLI, and RLI are useful measurement instruments in managing customer loyalty and business growth. While the present results are only based on the wireless industry, the findings showing the predictive power of the ALI and PLI are compelling. Future research in other industries can help verify and extend the current findings.

Hayes Loyalty Grid

The two loyalty indices, ALI and PLI, assess the types of potential business growth that companies are likely to experience in the future. The ALI assesses new customer growth while the PLI assesses purchasing growth. The Hayes Loyalty Grid charts the ALI and PLI, helping companies understand where they rank in the competitive landscape with respect to predicted business growth. Two examples of the Hayes Loyalty Grid appear in Figures 6.16 and 6.17. Figure 6.16 represents the Hayes Loyalty Grid for the PC industry and Figure 6.17 represents the Hayes Loyalty Grid for the wireless service provider industry.

As is seen in Figure 6.16, there is considerable variability across PC manufacturers with respect to their growth potential. Clearly, Apple has high levels of both advocacy loyalty and purchasing loyalty. Compared to other PC manufacturers, Apple should expect to see faster growth with respect to acquiring new customers and increasing the purchase behavior of existing customers.

HP (HP) and Apple appear in the upper right quadrant, suggesting that both PC manufacturers are poised to experience faster growth with respect to customer acquisition and increased purchases from existing customers. HP (Compaq) and Dell's growth potential are on par with the industry average. Located in the lower left quadrant, Gateway, Toshiba and eMachines, relative to their competitors, are expected to experience slower growth in both customer acquisition and increased purchases from existing customers.

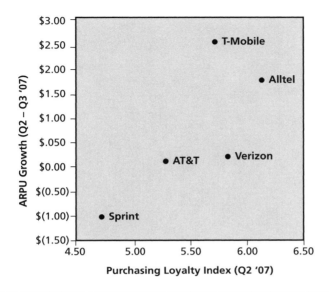

Figure 6.14 Relationship between Purchasing Loyalty Index and ARPU growth.

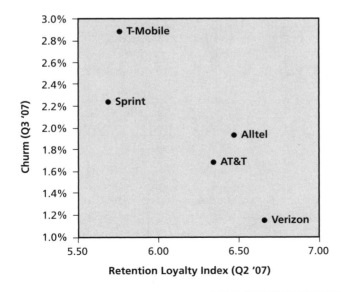

Figure 6.15 Relationship between Retention Loyalty Index and Churn.

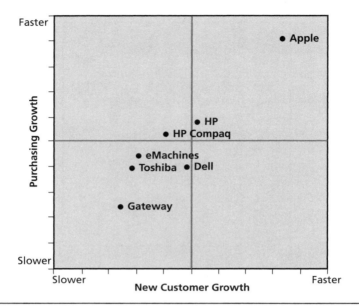

Figure 6.16 Hayes Loyalty Grid for the PC industry.

As you can see in Figure 6.17, Alltel and Verizon appear in the upper right quadrant, suggesting that they are poised to experience faster growth with respect to customer acquisition and increased purchases from existing customers. Additionally, T-Mobile customers indicate that they are likely to increase their purchase behavior at the rate comparable to the customers of Alltel and Verizon.

AT&T's new customer growth potential is on par with its industry average. Located in the lower left quadrant, Sprint/Nextel, relative to its competitors, will experience slower growth in both customer acquisition and increased purchases from existing customers.

Summary

Customer loyalty is not a unidimensional construct. Results of two studies show that there are three general types of customer loyalty: advocacy loyalty, purchasing loyalty, and retention loyalty. These can be reliably measured, and each provides unique and useful information regarding the quality of the customer relationship. Each of the loyalty indices was predictive of actual future growth (that is, business outcomes). Customer Loyalty 2.0 is aimed at helping companies to effectively measure and manage the different types of customer loyalty. By measuring advocacy, purchasing, and retention loyalty, companies will be better able to manage their customer relationships to maximize growth.

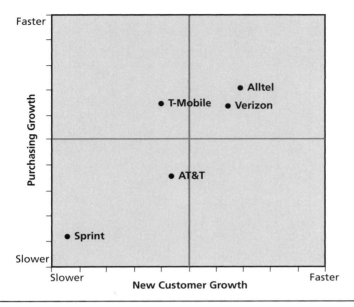

Figure 6.17 Hayes Loyalty Grid for the wireless industry.

ENDNOTES

1. http://resultsbrief.bain.com/videos/0402/main.html
2. A more detailed factor analysis of loyalty questions is presented later in the chapter.
3. When examining each of the four loyalty questions individually, researchers found the relationship to revenue growth to be the same.

7

Using Customer Satisfaction Questionnaires

T his chapter will present five examples of customer satisfaction questionnaires and outline some specific things you can do with data derived from them. I will demonstrate how you can present and summarize data and determine which of the customer requirements is most important in determining customer satisfaction. Also, I will demonstrate how the data can be applied to traditional quality improvement methodologies, including control charting techniques.

EXAMPLES OF CUSTOMER SATISFACTION QUESTIONNAIRES

Previous chapters outlined some guidelines and issues to address when developing customer satisfaction questionnaires. This section will present five customer satisfaction questionnaires: one based on the results of the quality dimension development process applied to the software industry, another based on the general quality dimensions applied to a facilities organization within a company, and three based on the results of the critical incident technique applied to the banking and automobile industries and the internal statistical department discussed in Chapter 2. These will allow you to see the structure of a questionnaire that was designed following the guidelines presented in earlier chapters.

Software Quality

The response format for each questionnaire is the Likert-type format using the agree-disagree continuum. (The checklist format could have been used also.) The questionnaire for the software industry appears in Figure 7.1. Although there are 20 items in the questionnaire, this questionnaire was designed to represent 10 dimensions of software quality. Therefore, we could conceivably derive 10 scores, each score representing the quality for a particular dimension.

The dimensions and their items are:

1. Correctness (items 1 and 2)
2. Reliability (items 3 and 4)
3. Usability (items 5 and 6)
4. Maintainability (items 7 and 8)
5. Testability (items 9 and 10)
6. Portability (items 11 and 12)
7. Interoperability (items 13 and 14)
8. Intra-operability (items 15 and 16)
9. Flexibility (items 17 and 18)
10. Overall satisfaction (items 19 and 20)

Additional analysis (factor analysis) might reveal a smaller subset of dimensions after customers complete the questionnaire. Customers may not be able to distinguish between nine separate dimensions of software quality.

To better serve you, we would like to know your opinion of the quality of our software. Please indicate the extent to which you agree or disagree with the following statements about the software [name of software]. Circle the appropriate number using the scale below. Some of the statements are similar to others in order to ensure that we accurately determine your opinion concerning the software.

  1—I Strongly Disagree with this statement (SD).
  2—I Disagree with this statement (D).
  3—I Neither agree nor disagree with this statement (N).
  4—I Agree with this statement (A).
  5—I Strongly Agree with this statement (SA).

	SD	D	N	A	SA
1. I am able to complete my job with this software.	1	2	3	4	5
2. The software meets my specifications in getting my job done.	1	2	3	4	5
3. I am able to perform functions with precision.	1	2	3	4	5
4. The software allows me to perform functions accurately.	1	2	3	4	5

Figure 7.1 Example of a customer satisfaction questionnaire for the software industry. *(Continued)*

(Continued)

	SD	D	N	A	SA
5. I was able to learn about the output from programs in a short amount of time.	1	2	3	4	5
6. The output of the programs is easy to understand.	1	2	3	4	5
7. Fixing an error in the operational program is easy.	1	2	3	4	5
8. Locating an error in the operational program is easy.	1	2	3	4	5
9. The testing of the program required a short amount of time.	1	2	3	4	5
10. Testing the program to ensure it performed functions was easy.	1	2	3	4	5
11. Transferring the program between different hardware configurations is easy.	1	2	3	4	5
12. I am able to transfer programs between different software environments with little problem.	1	2	3	4	5
13. Coupling one system to another is easy.	1	2	3	4	5
14. The software allows for simple coupling between systems.	1	2	3	4	5
15. Communicating between software components is simple.	1	2	3	4	5
16. I am able to communicate between software components easily.	1	2	3	4	5
17. I am able to modify the operational program with little effort.	1	2	3	4	5
18. Changing the operational program is easy to do.	1	2	3	4	5
19. I am very happy with the software.	1	2	3	4	5
20. The software meets my expectations.	1	2	3	4	5

Additional comments:

Figure 7.1   Example of a customer satisfaction questionnaire for the software industry.

Facilities Department

The next questionnaire is presented in Figure 7.2. This example illustrates the use of customer satisfaction questionnaires for internal customers (customers within the same company as the provider). The questionnaire was based on the general service quality dimensions presented by Kennedy and Young (1989). The items reflect each of the quality dimensions. The quality dimensions and their respective items are:

1. Availability of service (items 1 through 3)

2. Responsiveness of service (items 4 through 6)

3. Timeliness of service (items 7 through 9)

4. Professionalism of service (items 10 through 12)

5. Overall satisfaction with service (items 13 through 15)

6. Overall satisfaction with product (items 16 through 18)

To better serve you, we would like to know your opinion of the quality of our services and products. You recently received help from the Facilities department. Please indicate the extent to which you agree or disagree with the following statements about the service you received from the staff. Circle the appropriate number using the scale below. Some of the statements are similar to others in order to ensure that we accurately determine your opinion concerning our service.

1—I Strongly Disagree with this statement (SD).
2—I Disagree with this statement (D).
3—I Neither agree nor disagree with this statement (N).
4—I Agree with this statement (A).
5—I Strongly Agree with this statement (SA).

	SD	D	N	A	SA
1. I could get help from Facilities when I needed.	1	2	3	4	5
2. The Facilities staff was there when they were needed.	1	2	3	4	5
3. I could arrange convenient meeting times with the staff.	1	2	3	4	5
4. Facilities was quick to respond when I asked for help.	1	2	3	4	5

Figure 7.2   Example of a customer satisfaction questionnaire for a facilities organization.   *(Continued)*

Although this questionnaire might represent a comprehensive examination of the general service quality dimensions, there still may be other quality dimensions specific to any one facilities organization that should be included in the questionnaire. Therefore, more items might be needed in order to more fully represent the entire range of possible quality dimensions.

(Continued)

	SD	D	N	A	SA
5. Facilities immediately helped me if needed.	1	2	3	4	5
6. I waited a short period of time to get help after I asked for it.	1	2	3	4	5
7. Facilities completed the job when expected.	1	2	3	4	5
8. Facilities did not meet my deadline(s).	1	2	3	4	5
9. Facilities staff finished their responsibilities within the stated time frame.	1	2	3	4	5
10. The staff conducted themselves in a professional manner.	1	2	3	4	5
11. The staff was courteous.	1	2	3	4	5
12. The staff cared about what I had to say.	1	2	3	4	5
13. The quality of the way Facilities treated me is high.	1	2	3	4	5
14. The way Facilities treated me met my expectations.	1	2	3	4	5
15. I am satisfied with the way Facilities treated me.	1	2	3	4	5
16. The quality of the final job Facilities provided is high.	1	2	3	4	5
17. The job met my expectations.	1	2	3	4	5
18. I am satisfied with the job that Facilities provided.	1	2	3	4	5
Additional Comments:					

Figure 7.2 Example of a customer satisfaction questionnaire for a facilities organization.

Banking Industry

The next questionnaire is presented in Figure 7.3; it represents the banking industry. One of its statements has a negative connotation (item 4). It is possible that some items in a questionnaire will be phrased negatively. In such cases, a score of 5 for a negative statement reflects poor service while a score of 1 reflects good service. Thus, adding the scores from a negative statement (item 4) to scores from item 3 would be incorrect. Due to the negativity of item 4, we would reverse the scores for this statement so that a score of 1 on the original scale becomes 5, 2 on the original scale becomes 4, 4 on the original scale becomes 2, and 1 on the original scale becomes 5. Once we have completed the transformation, averaging the response of items 3 and 4 is appropriate.

You could conceivably derive 13 scores for each customer based on this questionnaire (one score for each of the 13 items). This questionnaire, however, was designed to assess four quality dimensions and one dimension labeled *overall customer satisfaction*. Therefore, some items would be combined to measure customers' perception of various quality dimensions. The dimensions and their corresponding items are:

1. Responsiveness of service (items 1 and 2)

2. Speed of transaction (items 3 and 4)

3. Availability of service (items 5 and 6)

4. Professionalism (items 7 through 10)

5. Overall satisfaction with service (items 11 through 13)

Automobile Industry

The next customer satisfaction questionnaire is presented in Figure 7.4; it represents the automobile industry. The introduction to this questionnaire is addressed to the person who just drove a particular car. It demonstrates a particular use of customer satisfaction questionnaires: the comparison of cars from different automobile manufacturers. This questionnaire might be used by an independent customer research group conducting a study comparing different cars. The full experimental design of the study would be complex and will not be presented here. The general design of the study, however, would be to allow customers to drive all the cars being studied. After each drive, the person would be asked to complete the questionnaire to indicate his or her perception of the car's quality. Subsequently, the data can be used to make direct comparisons between the automobiles.

To better serve you, we would like to know your opinion of the quality of our services and products. Please indicate the extent to which you agree or disagree with the following statements about the service you received from [company name]. Circle the appropriate number using the scale below. Some of the statements are similar to others in order to ensure that we accurately determine your opinion concerning our service.

1—I Strongly Disagree with this statement (SD).
2—I Disagree with this statement (D).
3—I Neither agree nor disagree with this statement (N).
4—I Agree with this statement (A).
5—I Strongly Agree with this statement (SA).

	SD	D	N	A	SA
1. I waited a short period of time before I was helped.	1	2	3	4	5
2. The service started immediately when I arrived.	1	2	3	4	5
3. The teller handled transactions in a short period of time.	1	2	3	4	5
4. The teller took a long time to complete my transaction.	1	2	3	4	5
5. The financial consultant was available to schedule me at a good time.	1	2	3	4	5
6. My appointment with the financial consultant was at a convenient time.	1	2	3	4	5
7. The teller talked to me in a pleasant way.	1	2	3	4	5
8. The teller was very personable.	1	2	3	4	5
9. The teller carefully listened to me when I was requesting a transaction.	1	2	3	4	5
10. The teller knew how to handle the transactions.	1	2	3	4	5
11. The quality of the way the teller treated me was high.	1	2	3	4	5
12. The way the teller treated me met my expectations.	1	2	3	4	5
13. I am satisfied with the way the teller treated me.	1	2	3	4	5

Additional comments:

Figure 7.3 Example of a customer satisfaction questionnaire for the banking industry.

We would like to know your opinion of the quality of the automobile you just drove. Please indicate the extent to which you agree or disagree with the following statements. Circle the appropriate number using the scale below. Some of the statements are similar to others in order to ensure that we accurately determine your opinion concerning the automobile.

> 1—I Strongly Disagree with this statement (SD).
> 2—I Disagree with this statement (D).
> 3—I Neither agree nor disagree with this statement (N).
> 4—I Agree with this statement (A).
> 5—I Strongly Agree with this statement (SA).

	SD	D	N	A	SA
1. The seating position was very comfortable.	1	2	3	4	5
2. The visibility through the window was good.					
3. The inside of the car was noisy.	1	2	3	4	5
4. The instrumentation panel was simple to understand.	1	2	3	4	5
5. The instrumentation panel was clearly visible from the driving seat.	1	2	3	4	5
6. The car stopped smoothly when I applied the brakes.	1	2	3	4	5
7. The car vibrated at high speeds.	1	2	3	4	5
8. The car handled corners well.	1	2	3	4	5
9. I enjoyed driving the car.	1	2	3	4	5
10. I liked the overall driving experience of the car.	1	2	3	4	5
11. The drive was excellent.	1	2	3	4	5

Additional comments:

Figure 7.4   Example of a customer satisfaction questionnaire for the automobile industry.

Again, scores derived from this questionnaire should reflect dimensions being measured by the various items. The dimensions and their corresponding items are:

1. Interior quality (items 1 through 3)

2. Instrumentation (items 4 and 5)

3. Drivability (items 6 through 8)

4. Overall satisfaction with auto (items 9 through 11)

Statistical Support Department

The questionnaire for the statistical support department is presented in Figure 7.5. This questionnaire would likely be distributed to internal customers after the completion of a project and customers would answer the questionnaire with respect to that particular project. This questionnaire was designed to assess five customer requirements as well as overall customer satisfaction:

1. Statistical support (items 1 through 3)

2. Enthusiasm (items 4 and 5)

3. Final written report (items 6 and 7)

4. Responsiveness (items 8 and 9)

5. Project management (items 10 and 11)

6. Overall satisfaction with service (items 12 and 13)

USES OF CUSTOMER SATISFACTION QUESTIONNAIRES

Next, I will present four uses of customer satisfaction questionnaires: (1) summarizing data with descriptive statistics, (2) determining the most important customer requirement, (3) tracking the quality of the product or service over time by means of control chart techniques, and (4) the comparison of customer satisfaction between companies.

SUMMARY INDICES

The presentation of data is an important issue. The quality of the data obtained from the customer satisfaction questionnaire can be affected by the way in which the data are summarized and presented. A reliable questionnaire will be of little practical use if the data cannot be understood. This part of the chapter will demonstrate how data can be presented.

To better serve you, we would like to know your opinion of the quality of our services and products. You recently received help from the statistical support department. Please indicate the extent to which you agree or disagree with the following statements about the service you received from the staff. Circle the appropriate number using the scale below. Some of the statements are similar to others in order to ensure that we accurately determine your opinion concerning our service.

    1—I Strongly Disagree with this statement (SD).
    2—I Disagree with this statement (D).
    3—I Neither agree nor disagree with this statement (N).
    4—I Agree with this statement (A).
    5—I Strongly Agree with this statement (SA).

	SD	D	N	A	SA
1. The staff person explained the statistical tests in understandable words.	1	2	3	4	5
2. The statistical analyses were thorough.	1	2	3	4	5
3. The staff understood my software requirements.	1	2	3	4	5
4. The staff person was always willing to help.	1	2	3	4	5
5. The staff person went out of his or her way to help.	1	2	3	4	5
6. The written report was sufficiently detailed.	1	2	3	4	5
7. The written report contained what I needed.	1	2	3	4	5
8. The staff person completed the job quickly.	1	2	3	4	5
9. The staff person finished the project in the stated time frame.	1	2	3	4	5
10. The staff person planned out the entire project through its completion.	1	2	3	4	5
11. The staff person understood how much time the project required.	1	2	3	4	5
12. I am satisfied with the service I received.	1	2	3	4	5
13. The quality of the service met my expectations.	1	2	3	4	5

Additional comments:

Figure 7.5 Example of a customer satisfaction questionnaire for an internal statistical support department.

One way to summarize the data is to use summary indices that describe important aspects of it. Summary indices that describe a sample of data are called *statistics* (Appendix E).

The statistics that summarize the elements in a data set reflect the central tendency of the data and the dispersion of the data. Three statistics are the *arithmetic average* or *mean*, the *variance*, and the *standard deviation*. The mean indicates the central tendency of data, while the latter two describe the spread of the data. The formula for the arithmetic average is $(\Sigma x_i)/n$. The Σ notation (called *sigma*) indicates summation of the variables, and n equals the number of elements in the data set. For the present equation, sigma indicates that all the observations going into the calculation of the mean will be added together. This sum is then divided by the number of observations. The resulting number is the mean. The equation for the mean can also be expressed as

$$\bar{x} = \frac{x_1 + x_2 + \ldots + x_n}{n}$$

where n equals the number of elements in the data set.

The formula for the variance is

$$s^2 = \frac{\sum_{i=1}^{n}(x_1 - \bar{x})^2}{n - 1}$$

where n equals the number of elements in the sample.

The sample standard deviation, which is also a measure of variability, is the square root of the sample variance.

Presentation of Data

I will use a hypothetical example to illustrate how data can be presented. A company used a customer satisfaction questionnaire to gauge the level of service it provided. This questionnaire was designed to measure several customer requirements and overall customer satisfaction. A portion of these items appear in Figure 7.6. Items 1 through 3 measure availability of service, items 4 through 6 measure responsiveness of service, and items 7 through 9 measure overall customer satisfaction.

The company solicited responses from customers. Data for 20 customers are presented in Table 7.1. It is apparent, even from this small set of data, that examination of the raw data does not reveal much information. The table looks like a series of unrelated numbers. We need to summarize the data in a clear, concise format in order to interpret the important findings. To do so, we must calculate the average and standard deviation for each item.

Also, summary scores for the two customer requirement categories are calculated, as well as a summary score for overall customer satisfaction. These scores are the average of the items within that given dimension. These summary scores can provide a more general measure of service quality; they are particularly useful for presentations to upper management. We have calculated reliability estimates (Cronbach's alpha estimate) for each dimension. These estimates are essential because they indicate the quality of the summary scores.

Please indicate the extent to which you agree or disagree with the following statements concerning the service you received. Please circle your response for each question using the following scale.

       1—I Strongly Disagree with this statement (SD).
       2—I Disagree with this statement (D).
       3—I Neither agree nor disagree with this statement (N).
       4—I Agree with this statement (A).
       5—I Strongly Agree with this statement (SA).

	SD	D	N	A	SA
1. I could get an appointment with the merchant at a time I desired.	1	2	3	4	5
2. The merchant was available to schedule me at a good time.	1	2	3	4	5
3. My appointment was at a convenient time for me.	1	2	3	4	5
4. The merchant was quick to respond when I arrived for my appointment.	1	2	3	4	5
5. The merchant immediately helped me when I entered the premises.	1	2	3	4	5
6. My appointment started promptly at the scheduled time.	1	2	3	4	5
7. The quality of the way the merchant treated me was high.	1	2	3	4	5
8. The way the merchant treated me met my expectations.	1	2	3	4	5
9. Overall, I am satisfied with the service.	1	2	3	4	5

Figure 7.6 Example of satisfaction items measuring two customer requirements and overall customer satisfaction.

Table 7.1   Example data from 20 customers responding to a customer satisfaction questionnaire.

Satisfaction items

Customer	1	2	3	4	5	6	7	8	9
1	5	4	5	3	4	4	3	4	3
2	3	2	3	5	4	5	4	4	4
3	4	5	5	3	2	2	3	3	4
4	3	2	3	4	3	4	4	5	4
5	3	3	3	4	4	4	3	3	3
6	4	4	5	4	5	4	4	5	4
7	3	4	2	4	3	3	3	2	3
8	5	4	5	4	4	4	5	4	5
9	3	2	3	4	3	4	4	4	3
10	3	4	3	4	4	4	3	4	3
11	5	5	5	5	5	5	5	5	5
12	4	4	4	3	3	4	4	4	4
13	4	4	5	5	5	4	4	4	5
14	2	2	3	4	4	5	3	3	2
15	4	5	5	4	4	3	4	3	3
16	5	4	5	5	5	5	4	4	4
17	3	4	3	5	4	4	4	4	4
18	3	2	4	3	3	4	2	2	2
19	5	4	3	4	5	4	3	3	4
20	3	3	3	4	3	3	4	4	4
Mean =	3.70	3.55	3.83	4.05	3.85	3.95	3.65	3.70	3.65
Standard deviation =	0.92	1.05	1.04	0.69	0.88	0.76	0.75	0.87	0.88

Summary scores for customer requirements (reliability estimates in parentheses)

	Availability of service (.85)	*Responsiveness of service* (.81)	*Overall satisfaction* (.88)
Mean =	3.70	3.95	3.67
Standard deviation =	.88	.66	.74

Summary

It is important that data from questionnaires be summarized in an understandable format. Often, the mean and standard deviations are used to summarize information in the data set. Summary scores for each dimension can provide general measures of the quality of the service or product.

IDENTIFY IMPORTANT
CUSTOMER REQUIREMENTS

Suppose our service organization has developed a customer satisfaction questionnaire that assesses five quality dimensions and overall customer satisfaction, and we solicit responses from our customers. Also, suppose that the questionnaire results indicate that the average score for the five quality dimensions and the overall customer satisfaction score are roughly the same. In addition, our supervisor has given us the resources to increase service quality. Given this information, to which of the five quality dimensions should we apply the resources?

For this situation (and possibly for all situations), examining the satisfaction level for each dimension would be of little use, since the satisfaction levels are (or could be) the same across all dimensions. A better method would be to determine which quality dimensions are most highly related to overall customer satisfaction. If our goal is to increase overall customer satisfaction, we should direct resources toward those dimensions.

To determine which dimensions are closely linked with overall customer satisfaction, we could determine the extent to which each dimension is correlated with overall customer satisfaction. One way to determine which quality dimension is most important would be simply to ask customers the extent to which each quality dimension is important in making them satisfied with the service. For example, customers could rate the importance of each quality dimension in their satisfaction. For each dimension, we would calculate an average score of these ratings. This average would indicate the level of importance of that particular dimension in satisfying the customers.

Research on human judgment, however, suggests that people are poor judges about what information they think they use. A statistical model is better at predicting outcomes compared to judgmental models. One statistical approach is correlation analysis (see Appendix J).

After customers complete the customer satisfaction questionnaire, we would calculate scores for each quality dimension. Therefore, each customer would get a score on each of the quality dimensions represented on the customer satisfaction questionnaire, as well as a score for overall satisfaction.

After calculating scores, the next step would be to correlate each quality dimension with the overall satisfaction score. The correlations between each of the quality dimensions and overall customer satisfaction scores reflect the importance of each quality dimension in predicting overall customer satisfaction. The higher the correlation, the more important the quality dimension is in satisfying customers.

Here is an illustration of this method using quality dimensions associated with the banking industry. Suppose I calculated the correlations between each of the quality dimensions and overall customer satisfaction and found them to be $r = .50$ for responsiveness of service, $r = .15$ for speed of transaction, $r = .25$ for availability of service, and $r = .40$ for professionalism. These results reveal that both responsiveness and professionalism are important in determining overall customer satisfaction. As a result, resources would probably have their greatest affect on overall customer satisfaction if applied in these two areas.

Determination of important quality dimensions need not be confined to a single point in time. Even though current results indicate that the most important quality dimensions are responsiveness and professionalism, other quality dimensions may come to the fore later. The relative ordering of customers' requirements or expectations may change over time. Thus, a continual determination of important customer requirements is necessary. Also, it is important to consider the affect of reliability on the correlation between variables (see Chapter 3). Recall that a statistically nonsignificant correlation between two variables might result from the unreliability of the scales. Therefore, you must determine the reliability of the scales.

Summary

Recall that all of the quality dimensions being assessed by the customer satisfaction questionnaire are, by design, important to customers. It is beneficial to understand which of these quality dimensions is most highly linked with overall customer satisfaction. This information is essential when determining where to direct company resources. The best method is to collect data with the questionnaire and determine, through correlational analysis, the most important quality dimensions.

Interpretation of the correlations is reserved for those knowledgeable in statistics. Factors such as restriction in range of scores and colinearity of quality dimensions should be considered when determining which quality characteristic is most important in determining overall customer satisfaction. Also, calculation of correlation coefficients is only one way of determining the important dimensions. Another approach involves multiple regression analysis, which is a more sophisticated method of determining relationships between variables. For interested readers, several statistics textbooks include these topics (Neter, Wasserman, and Kutner 1985; Pedhazur 1982).

Once we have identified these important quality dimensions, the next step is to track their levels of quality. This is often done with the help of control charts. Next, I will present an overview of control chart techniques and discuss specific uses of these charts. A more comprehensive discussion of control charts and statistical process control methodologies is available elsewhere (Montgomery 1985).

CONTROL CHARTS

Control charts represent various ways data can be charted. An example of a control chart appears in Figure 7.7. The control chart is a visual display of the overall service or product quality. In addition, control charts can display each of the quality characteristics. The ordinate (vertical axis) of the control chart represents the measurement of the overall quality of a particular quality dimension. The abscissa (horizontal axis) represents either the sample number or time. The control chart includes a center line representing the average value of the quality dimensions over the entire range of samples. The chart also contains an upper control limit (UCL) and lower control limit (LCL) that run parallel with the center line.

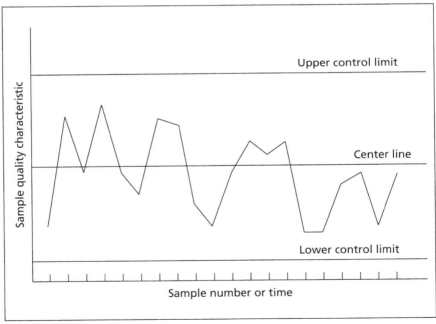

Figure 7.7   Example of satisfaction items measuring two customer requirements and overall customer satisfaction.

There are general formulae for the control chart's center line, UCL, and LCL. Let's use Q to represent the sample statistic of the quality characteristic we are measuring. Let's indicate the mean of Q as $\bar{x}_Q$ and the variance of Q as $s^2_{(Q)}$. With these labels, the general formulae for the control charts are

$$\text{UCL} = \bar{x}_Q + k\sqrt{s^2_{(Q)}}$$
$$\text{Center line} = \bar{x}_Q$$
$$\text{LCL} = \bar{x}_Q - k\sqrt{s^2_{(Q)}}$$

where k represents a constant used to determine the distance of the UCL and LCL from the center line. It is standard that k equal 3.0; therefore, 3 will be used in the remaining equations.

Interpretation of the Control Chart

Control charts can monitor the business processes that generate the data in the chart. Each data point in the control chart indicates how the process is running at a given time. Over time, because of natural variability inherent in the process, we expect that not all data points will fall on the center line. This natural variability is due to random causes referred to as *uncontrollable factors*. Under these conditions, we expect the data points will fall somewhere between the UCL and the LCL. When this pattern occurs, the process is said to be in *statistical control*.

There are additional sources of variability that will influence the output of the process. The variability from these other sources is usually larger than the natural variability and is due to events that represent a potential problem in the process when they occur. The sources of this extreme variability are referred to as *assignable causes*. Their presence is indicated by a data point falling outside the control limits (either above the UCL or below the LCL). When this pattern occurs, the process is said to be out of control. Using control charts helps us remove the source of this type of variability. Specific uses of control charts will be presented in examples later in the chapter.

Types of Data

Quality dimension data can be categorized as *attribute data* and *variable data*. Attribute data are usually categorical. Measurements of quality characteristics are classified as either conforming to specifications or not conforming to specifications; these divide occurrences into nondefective or defective categories, respectively.

Variable data are numerical. We can apply a unit of measurement (for example, inches or minutes) to quality characteristics. Not only can we determine the number of nonconforming occurrences, we can also determine the degree to which an occurrence is not conforming to specifications.

The type of data that is gathered is often a function of the process being measured or the measurement tool used. As will be apparent later, data from customer satisfaction questionnaires can be used as either categorical data or variable data. We can apply either of the two types of data (attribute or variable) to control charts. Next, I will present some ways in which we can apply data from customer satisfaction questionnaires to control chart techniques.

CONTROL CHARTS FOR ATTRIBUTE DATA

Recall that we can allocate attribute data into categories (for example, categories of defective and nondefective). Two attribute control charts that apply are the p chart and the c chart.

The p Chart

Quality of a service could be evident in the percentage of people who volunteer at least one negative response. A decrease in the percentage of these people indicates an increase in the quality of service. For any given sample of customers completing our questionnaire, we can calculate the percentage of people who gave at least one negative response. In a sense, this percentage represents the number of defects in our sample. The formula for this percentage is

$$p_i = D_i / n_i$$

where D_i is the number of people who gave at least one negative response for a given sample (i) and n_i is the sample size.

The percentage, p, is calculated for every sample. Given that the sample size is constant, we can create the control chart using the average of all ps. The formulae for the UCL, center line, and LCL are

$$UCL = \bar{p} + 3 \sqrt{\frac{\bar{p}(1 - \bar{p})}{n}}$$

$$Center\ line = \bar{p}$$

$$LCL = \bar{p} - 3 \sqrt{\frac{\bar{p}(1 - \bar{p})}{n}}$$

Example of the p Chart

Using the customer satisfaction questionnaire for the banking industry (see Figure 7.3), a bank receiving a high number of complaints would like to determine the percentage of customers who give at least one negative response about service they received from banking personnel. A negative response occurs when the customer indicates he or she either disagrees or strongly disagrees to a positively phrased satisfaction item (for example, questions 2 and 3) or agrees or strongly agrees to a negative satisfaction item (for example, question 4). Data collected over 20 weeks appear in Table 7.2. Sample size for each of the 20 samples is 50.

The calculations of the UCL, center line, and LCL are

$$UCL = .213 + 3(.0579) = .3867$$

$$Center\ line = .213$$

$$LCL = .213 - 3(.0579) = .0393$$

Table 7.2 Data for the *p* control chart example (note *n* = 50).

Sample	Number of customers who gave at least one negative response (D_i)	Percentage of customers who gave at least one negative response (p_i)
1	5	.10
2	20	.40
3	15	.30
4	16	.32
5	10	.20
6	8	.16
7	15	.30
8	20	.40
9	7	.14
10	2	.04
11	10	.20
12	13	.26
13	20	.40
14	13	.26
15	4	.08
16	4	.08
17	9	.18
18	11	.22
19	5	.10
20	6	.12
	total = 213	$\bar{p}$ = .213

The resulting control chart appears in Figure 7.8. The plotted numbers for each sample represent the percentage of people who gave at least one negative response on the customer satisfaction questionnaire. The control chart indicates that several points lie outside the control points. This could indicate that an event (assignable cause) occurred during the week in which those points fell outside the UCL. Perhaps during those weeks new staff members were being trained on the job or some employees resigned, leaving the bank understaffed. If we can identify assignable causes for these points, we should exclude these samples when calculating the control limits and center line. We do this because the control limits and center line are calculated to reflect how the process typically functions. If no assignable causes are apparent, then the current control limits and center line are appropriate.

The *c* Chart

The *p* chart allowed us to display the percentage of customers who gave at least one negative response. We may, however, want to get an indication of how many negative responses there were among a given sample of customers. A customer may have many negative responses about the service he or she received. The *c* chart is a way of graphing this type of data,

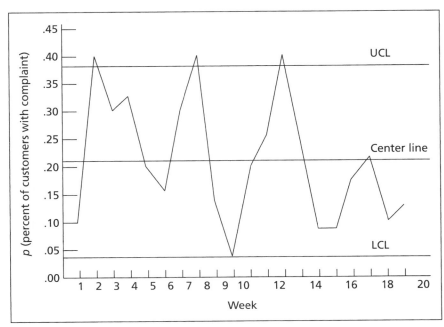

Figure 7.8 The *p* control chart using data from Table 7.2.

where c is the total number of negative responses indicated by the customers. The formulae for the UCL, center line, and LCL are

$$UCL = \bar{c} + 3\sqrt{\bar{c}}$$
$$\text{Center line} = \bar{c}$$
$$LCL = \bar{c} - 3\sqrt{\bar{c}}$$

where c is the number of negative responses per sample.

Example of the c Chart

I will use the banking example again to illustrate the c chart. We would now like to monitor the total number of negative responses from customers. We collect data for 20 weeks (see Table 7.3). After examining the data, we decide to create a control chart. The control limits and the center line are calculated to be

$$UCL = 31.61$$
$$\text{Center line} = 18.65$$
$$LCL = 15.69$$

The c control chart is presented in Figure 7.9. The figure demonstrates that no points fall outside the control limits, suggesting that the process is in control. This indicates that the average number of negative responses per sample is approximately 19. Even though the process is in statistical control, the data indicate a high number of negative responses from customers. To change this situation requires a change in the banking personnel's contact with customers. This type of process change requires action from management and might include additional training for banking personnel, providing more tellers, or increasing the number of banking windows.

Additional data presented in Table 7.3 illustrate other methods of control charting based on the original information for the c control chart. The two additional variables, u and $p(tot)$, are calculated from c. The u variable reflects the average number of negative responses per person and is calculated by dividing c by the number of customers per sample. For our example, the variable u will be calculated by dividing c by 50. We can also plot this variable in a control chart called the u chart. The formulae for the control limits and the center line are

$$UCL = \bar{u} + 3\sqrt{\frac{\bar{u}}{n}}$$
$$\text{Center line} = \bar{u}$$
$$LCL = \bar{u} - 3\sqrt{\frac{\bar{u}}{n}}$$

where u is the average number of negative responses per person for a given sample and n is the number of customers per sample.

Also, $p(tot)$ reflects the percent of negative responses out of all the possible responses for a given sample. Since our questionnaire had 13 questions, we calculate $p(tot)$ by dividing u by 13. Again, the $p(tot)$ variable can be incorporated into a control chart with its corresponding control limits and center line. The formulae are

$$\text{UCL} = \bar{p}(tot) + 3\sqrt{\frac{\bar{p}(tot) - \bar{p}(tot)}{n(tot)}}$$

$$\text{Center line} = \bar{p}(tot)$$

$$\text{LCL} = \bar{p}(tot) - 3\sqrt{\frac{\bar{p}(tot) - \bar{p}(tot)}{n(tot)}}$$

Table 7.3 Data for the c control chart example (note $n = 50$).

Sample (week)	Number of negative responses (c_i)	Average number of negative responses per person (u_i)	Percentage of negative responses out of all possible responses $[p_i(tot)]$
1	15	.30	.023
2	20	.40	.038
3	14	.28	.022
4	25	.50	.038
5	24	.48	.037
6	18	.36	.028
7	26	.52	.040
8	28	.56	.043
9	15	.30	.023
10	8	.16	.012
11	17	.34	.026
12	20	.40	.038
13	28	.56	.043
14	21	.42	.032
15	13	.26	.020
16	16	.32	.025
17	18	.36	.028
18	22	.44	.034
19	10	.20	.015
20	15	.30	.023
	$\bar{c} = 18.65$	$\bar{u} = .373$	$\bar{p}(tot) = .029$

where $p(tot)$ represents the percentage of negative responses for a given sample and $n(tot)$ represents the total possible number of responses for a given sample ($n(tot)$ = number of items × sample size).

It is important to note that the variables c and u might be misinterpreted, either indicating a product/service problem that does not actually exist or indicating no problem when a problem actually does exist. It should be apparent that the number of negative responses from customers depends on the number of items on the questionnaire. A high number of questionnaire items creates a greater potential for negative responses.

For example, c (the number of negative responses) may equal 40 for a sample of 50 people responding to a 100-item questionnaire, while c equals 20 for a sample of 50 people responding to a two-item questionnaire. By using the c chart or u chart, we might conclude that customers from the first sample are more dissatisfied than customers from the second sample, since the number of negative responses is larger in the first sample. A closer look indicates that this conclusion is not warranted.

We should look at the number of possible responses that could have been made by the sample. For the first sample, 5000 negative responses are possible (100 items × 50 customers). For the second sample, 100 negative responses are possible (two items × 50 customers). In the first sample, negative responses constitute .8 percent of all possible responses, while in the second sample negative responses make up 20 percent of all possible responses.

Therefore, when using the c and u chart, we must consider the number of items on the questionnaire when making conclusions. One way to avoid this problem is to use the $p(tot)$ chart, since it takes into account the number of items on the questionnaire.

Summary

Customer satisfaction questionnaires provide attribute data that we can subsequently incorporate into control charts for attribute data. There are several types of control charts used with attribute type data. The p chart monitors the percentage of customers who give at least one negative response to the customer satisfaction questionnaire. The c chart monitors the total number of negative responses. From the c chart data, we can calculate other statistics (u and $p(tot)$) with corresponding control charts. Although we can apply data from customer satisfaction questionnaires to attribute control charts, the data are probably best suited for variable control charts.

CONTROL CHARTS FOR VARIABLE DATA

Recall that variable data represent measurements of quality characteristics. We can develop customer satisfaction questionnaires that provide scores reflecting units of measurement: the higher the score, the higher the quality of the service or product.

Because variable data are quantified in units of measurement, the distribution of scores can be represented by two statistics: the average and the standard deviation. The average represents the center of the distribution, and the standard deviation represents the variability of scores around the average. The larger the standard deviation, the wider the variability. In quality improvement efforts, it is customary to control both the average of the quality characteristics and the variability. Control of the average is accomplished with a control chart for means, the $\bar{x}$ chart. Control of the variability of the process can be accomplished with a control chart for the standard deviation, the s chart.

The $\bar{x}$ and s Control Charts

The $\bar{x}$ chart plots the means of a quality characteristic for each sample, while the s chart plots the standard deviations of the quality characteristic for each sample. For a given sample, we calculate the mean of the quality characteristic by adding the scores for the quality characteristic and dividing by the sample size, n. The formula for sample average was presented earlier. If we have a sample that consists of three observations where $x_1 = 5$, $x_2 = 4$, and $x_3 = 2$, then the mean for this sample equals

$$\bar{x} = (5 + 4 + 2)/3 = 3.67$$

We can also calculate the average value of the sample averages. If we have a number of samples, it is possible to calculate averages for each sample and obtain an average of the sample averages. The formula for this overall average is

$$\bar{\bar{x}} = \frac{\bar{x}_1 + \bar{x}_2 + \ldots + \bar{x}_m}{m}$$

where m equals the number of samples.

This overall sample average provides the center line for the control chart. Also, recall that the distribution for each of the samples can be represented by an index of variability called the *sample standard deviation*. To calculate the standard deviation, we will first calculate the sample variance. The formula for the sample variance was presented earlier in the chapter. After calculating the sample variance, we can calculate the standard deviation by taking the square root of this variance. Again, if we have multiple samples, we can calculate a sample standard deviation for each sample.

We can now calculate the average standard deviation for all the samples. This formula is

$$\bar{s} = \frac{1}{m} \Sigma s_i$$

where m equals the number of samples, and Σs_i is the sum of all sample standard deviations.

We calculate the UCL and LCL for the $\bar{x}$ chart using the average standard deviation. The calculation of the control limits also involves a constant, c_4, that depends on the sample size. A full explanation of this constant is presented in Montgomery (1996) and will not be discussed here. The upper and lower control limits for the s chart also depend upon two constants, B_4 and B_3, respectively. These constants are also discussed in Montgomery (1996).

Knowing the sample averages and the average standard deviation, we can now calculate the parameters for the $\bar{x}$ chart. The formulae for the center line and upper and lower control limits are

$$\text{UCL} = \bar{\bar{x}} + \frac{3\bar{s}}{c_4 \sqrt{n}}$$

$$\text{Center line} = \bar{\bar{x}}$$

$$\text{LCL} = \bar{\bar{x}} - \frac{3\bar{s}}{c_4 \sqrt{n}}$$

where n equals the sample size.

The formulae for the parameters of the s chart are

$$\text{UCL} = B_4 \bar{s}$$

$$\text{Center line} = \bar{s}$$

$$\text{LCL} = B_3 \bar{s}$$

Example of $\bar{x}$ and s Charts

A bank would like to determine its customers' level of satisfaction. The bank collects data over 20 weeks using the customer satisfaction questionnaire in Figure 7.3. Each week the bank collects data from 25 customers. The bank decides that, of the four quality characteristics, the most important is the speed of transaction dimension (items 3 and 4). As a result, the bank examines only this dimension. The data appear in Table 7.4.

Table 7.4 Data for the $\bar{x}$ and s control chart example (note $n = 25$).

Sample	Score for speed of transaction dimension (average of items 3 and 4)	Sample standard deviation for speed of transaction dimension
1	2.5	1.20
2	3.0	1.10
3	3.4	1.15
4	3.2	1.22
5	3.7	1.10
6	3.0	1.00
7	2.7	1.21
8	3.2	1.15
9	3.2	1.10
10	3.4	1.20
11	3.0	1.25
12	2.9	1.18
13	2.8	1.20
14	3.1	1.15
15	3.6	1.18
16	3.2	1.23
17	2.9	1.20
18	2.9	1.17
19	2.4	1.21
20	2.5	1.20
	total = 60.6	total = 23.4

The center line and the upper and lower control limits for the $\bar{x}$ chart are

$$\text{UCL} = 3.739$$
$$\text{Center line} = 3.03$$
$$\text{LCL} = 2.321$$

where the constant for the UCL and LCL are $c_4 = .9896$.

The center line and the upper and lower control limits for the s chart are

$$\text{UCL} = 1.679$$
$$\text{Center line} = 1.17$$
$$\text{LCL} = 0.661$$

where the constants for the UCL and LCL are $B_4 = 1.435$ and $B_3 = .565$. The control charts appear in Figure 7.10.

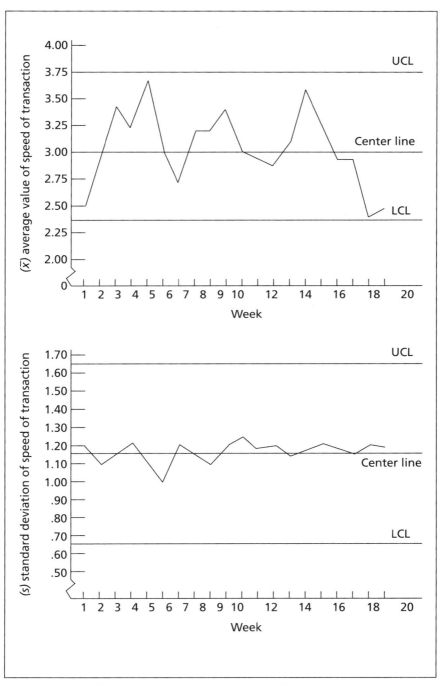

Figure 7.10 The $\bar{x}$ and s control chart using the data from Table 7.4.

These two control charts indicate that the process is in statistical control. The $\bar{x}$ chart, however, indicates that there is considerable room for improvement. Since the scores can range from 1 to 5, the average score of 3.03 indicates that speed of transaction should be improved. Management intervention will improve first speed of transaction and ultimately customer's perceptions.

Once management implements changes, we can calculate differences between pre- and post-intervention and conduct statistical tests to see whether these differences are substantial. The mathematical formula for testing differences in data is available in various statistics textbooks (Loftus and Loftus 1988).

Charting and presenting the data can provide a feedback mechanism for employees who are in direct contact with customers and who may directly influence customers' perceptions. Charting techniques such as these have been effective in increasing organizational productivity (Pritchard, et al. 1988). Goal setting, used in conjunction with this feedback method, can increase performance even more (Locke, et al. 1981).

ORGANIZATIONAL COMPARISONS

Customer satisfaction data can be used not only to make comparisons within a single organization across time, it can also be used to make comparisons between organizations (see Appendices F through I). Comparisons between organizations can help identify areas for improvement for organizations with lower satisfaction scores on certain dimensions. An organization can first determine dimensions on which it is poorly serving its customers and then determine how other companies serve their customers on that particular dimension.

Organizations can also compare satisfaction with products. For example, some automobile manufacturers are designing their cars to make the driver "feel" better. A direct comparison between these cars and other cars could determine whether these automobiles do, in fact, make the driver feel better. A company could use the customer satisfaction questionnaire in Figure 7.4 for comparison.

Organizations making comparisons with other organizations would be taking some risk, since their scores may indicate that they are the lowest among all organizations in the comparison. However, the Baldrige Award dictates that companies make these comparisons. With these types of data, organizations that score low will identify the dimensions on which they should focus their resources. Better organizational decisions based on actual data will allow these organizations to make improvements in appropriate areas.

DETERMINE EFFECTIVENESS OF INTERVENTION PROGRAMS

Companies spend millions of dollars on intervention programs designed to increase the quality of their services and products. Intervention often takes the form of formal employee training programs as well as new business processes to facilitate work flow. In either case, customer satisfaction questionnaires can determine the effectiveness of these programs (see Appendices F through I).

Training Programs

Companies implement training programs to enable employees to better fulfill their job duties. A company might have determined through a customer satisfaction questionnaire that its customers are not satisfied with the service they received. The company might, therefore, implement a program to improve employees' communication and interpersonal skills in hopes that this will lead to better employee-customer interactions.

The company might determine the effectiveness of such a training program by comparing customer satisfaction results before and after training. If customer satisfaction scores are higher after training than before, this provides evidence of the program's effectiveness. Statistical analyses will determine whether differences are meaningful. There are various methods for determining the effectiveness of intervention programs (Campbell and Stanley 1966).

Benchmarking

Benchmarking is the search for an industry's best practices that lead to excellent performance. Camp (1989) outlined a process of benchmarking that includes identifying premier companies and determining their business practices. Once a company identifies these superior business practices, it may incorporate them into its own practices or change existing processes to conform to the ones identified. This change is designed to increase the organization's effectiveness in meeting its customers' requirements.

It is important to determine whether these changes have, in fact, led to increases in performance. Customer satisfaction questionnaires can index the effectiveness of this benchmarking process in changing customers' perceptions. This is done by examining the difference between customer satisfaction before and after benchmarking has been implemented.

ADDITIONAL QUESTIONS

Other questions might also be included in a customer satisfaction questionnaire. Some could solicit information about the time the customer received the service. This might reveal whether differences in customer perception are due to factors present only at certain times of the day. A question about the location of the service might provide useful information. For instance, a bank could determine whether certain branches are better than others at satisfying customers. Once identified, successful business processes from one location can be adopted by another. Also, a question asking for information on the type of product might determine whether certain products are more appealing than others.

Additional questions could be included to obtain more information for comparisons. Companies should carefully choose questions that represent variables that would provide potentially rich information. Questions should have a specified purpose. If certain patterns are suspected (differences between branches, time of day, and so on), an additional question could help substantiate such predictions and lead to insights about possible improvements.

CUSTOMER LOYALTY MANAGEMENT

Companies are not static entities; they make business decisions in hopes to increase customer loyalty and grow their business. The key to business growth is to make correct decisions that will improve customer loyalty. Customer loyalty management is the process by which companies identify decisions to be made in order to increase customer loyalty. To understand how improvements in customer loyalty will improve business growth, we need to first understand the value of customers to the organization.

Customer Lifetime Value (CLV)

Customer lifetime value reflects the present total value of a customer to the company over his or her lifetime. The concept of CLV implies that each customer (or customer segment) differs with respect to its value to the company. When we discuss CLV, we typically refer to the value of a single customer, whether that customer represents the typical customer overall or the average customer within a customer segment (for example, West coast customer vs. East coast customer).

The generic model of CLV can be broken down as a function of four elements:

- NC: Number of customers

- NP: Number of times the average customer makes a purchase each year

- CL: Average customer life (in years)
- PPS: Average profit per sale (total sales revenue – costs)/number of sales

While there are other elements included in the calculation of the equation (for example, future value of the dollar and risk factors), these four elements are at the core of understanding how customer loyalty and customer value relate to each other. Using these elements, we can calculate the customer lifetime value for the entire customer base (or customer segment):

$$\text{CLV} = \text{NC} \times \text{NP} \times \text{CL} \times \text{PPS}$$

Increasing the Lifetime Value of the Customers

Using this CLV model, organizations can now view customers as assets with a specified value that, in turn, becomes the basis for making business decisions. The goal for management, then, is to maximize the CLV to the company. To increase the lifetime value of its customers, organizations can do one or more of the following four things:

- Increase size of the customer base (or customer segments)
- Increase the number of purchases each customer makes
- Increase the average customer life
- Increase profits per sale

We see that higher CLV equates to greater financial growth with respect to profits and a greater likelihood of long-term business success. It is important to note that, because the CLV is a multiplicative function of four elements, a negative value of profits (costs are greater than revenue) results in a negative CLV no matter how large the other elements of the CLV become. Therefore, before trying to manage the loyalty of a particular customer segment, it is important to know whether the customer segment is worth growing or even worth having. This step involves calculating the profits per sale.

Determining a value for profit is oftentimes a game of guesswork when companies lack an understanding of costs associated with a given customer relationship. Costs may be difficult to quantify due to the lack of available data needed to make such precise calculations; costs may be overlooked due to a lack of understanding of the company resources necessary to maintain relationships with customers. The procedure for estimating the profit value of a customer should be transparent and should be shared across the organization in order to ensure that assumptions about its calculation are reviewed by all interested parties.

While the concept of CLV traditionally has been applied in sales and marketing fields to understand the cost of attracting new customers, more comprehensive CLV models include costs associated with other phases of the customer lifecycle. Consider the customer lifecycle model in Figure 7.11. We see that a customer's tenure with the company involves three general phases: attraction (marketing), acquisition (sales), and service (service). Within each customer lifecycle phase, company resources are required to maintain a relationship. Accordingly, to get a more accurate estimation of the customer lifetime value, organizations are now including the costs to service the customers. Extending beyond the costs of attracting and acquiring customers, servicing costs expend organizational resources such as customer service staff costs and employee training costs, just to name a few. These service costs, along with sales and marketing costs, should be included in the estimation of profit per sale.

Once the costs associated with a given customer group are established, the lifetime value of that customer group can be determined. While some customer segments could be very profitable, other customer segments might not be profitable at all.

After identifying the extent to which a customer segment is profitable or not, the organization now must make a choice as to whether or not they want to invest in that customer segment in order to increase the lifetime value of its customers. Clearly, a customer segment that is costing more to maintain than the revenue it generates should raise red flags across the organization. In this situation, the organization can either attempt to decrease the costs of maintaining these relationships or simply attrite the relationships. For a customer segment that is profitable, the organization can determine how best to increase the lifetime value of that segment through loyalty management.

In the next step, the organization needs to understand how to increase the lifetime value of customers in the profitable customer segments. From the remaining elements of the CLV, the organization can improve the CLV

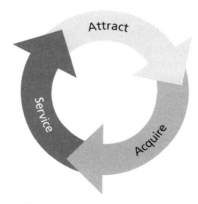

Figure 7.11   Customer lifecycle.

by focusing on one or more of the customer-focused elements of the CLV model. Specifically, a company can increase the size of the customer base, increase the purchasing behaviors of the customer base, and increase the tenure of individuals within the customer base.

Each of the customer-centric elements of the CLV corresponds directly to a facet of customer loyalty identified through our research. As we will see later, the management of customers is simply a matter of managing the three types of customer loyalty: advocacy loyalty, purchasing loyalty, and retention loyalty.

Business Model and Customer Lifetime Value

For large organizations, customer surveys can result in hundreds of thousands of data points. Consider one high-tech company that surveys its customer base bi-annually with a survey that contains roughly 50 questions (both loyalty questions and business attribute questions). Given a sample size of 14,000 respondents per survey period, this company has 1.4 million pieces of customer feedback data annually with which to help them manage their customer relationship! While most companies might not have this magnitude of customer feedback data, even smaller amounts of data (20,000 data points from 20 questions and 1000 respondents) can overwhelm a company trying to use its data intelligently to manage its customer relationships.

Business Model. To help us understand how to use the data, we can employ models that put the data in context. There are many different types of models regarding customer satisfaction and loyalty (ACSI 2008; Heskett, Sasser & Schlesinger 1997), but they all have elements in common. A basic model incorporating common elements of each of these models appears in Figure 7.12.

This business model illustrates the interrelatedness of the organizational variables that ultimately affect the company's financial performance. Empirical research shows that business growth is stimulated primarily by customer loyalty. Loyalty is a direct result of customer satisfaction, and satisfaction is largely influenced by the value of services provided to customers. Value is created by satisfied, loyal, and productive employees. Employee satisfaction, in turn, is influenced by the business strategies and internal systems that enable employees to deliver results to customers. Partners also provide products and services to joint customers and help to increase customer loyalty to the partnering company.

There are two major differences between this model and other models: (1) expansion of the business ecosystem to include partner relationships, and (2) inclusion of facets of customer loyalty.

Because employees and partners provide direct front-line marketing, sales, and support to customers, companies must ensure that they effectively manage those employee and partner relationships. Consequently, companies are now expanding their loyalty management efforts to other constituencies,

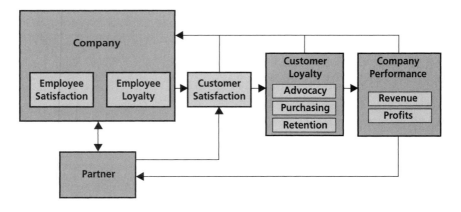

Figure 7.12 Marketing/sales/service business model and the relationship among key organizational variables. (Adapted from Heskett, Sasser & Schlesinger 1997 and ACSI 2008.)

including employees and partners. Although not discussed in this chapter, the methodology of loyalty management presented here applies to the management of employee relationships and partner relationships.

Customer Lifetime Value. Older models examining the relationships among organizational variables, whether purposefully or not, do not make the distinction among the different facets of customer loyalty. Chapter 6 included research that shows that customer loyalty can be conceptualized as three distinct types: advocacy loyalty, purchasing loyalty, and retention loyalty. Additionally, each of these dimensions of loyalty can be reliably and validly measured. The distinction of the facets of customer loyalty goes beyond conventional thinking regarding the simplistic notions of customer relationship management. In fact, three of the elements of the CLV, not surprisingly, correspond exactly with the three facets of customer loyalty found in Chapter 6. No longer should we assume that loyalty can be measured with a single question.

Increasing the lifetime value of customers requires the management of all three types of loyalty in the customer base (or segment). By measuring and examining each type of customer loyalty, executives can more effectively manage their customer relationships. To improve the CLV, the loyalty management process encourages companies to address customer growth, purchase behavior, and customer retention. Business decisions can now be targeted to address specific types of loyalty concerns. The following section will outline how a company can manage its customers using the different types of loyalty measures. First, we will discuss loyalty management in general. Then, we will apply loyalty management to each of the loyalty measures.

CUSTOMER LOYALTY MANAGEMENT

There are two general approaches to customer loyalty management: 1) the micro or individual approach, and 2) the macro or organizational approach.

Micro (Individual) Approach to Loyalty Management

The micro approach examines the customer relationship for a specific customer or survey respondent. In this approach, the organization identifies customers who are disloyal and intervenes to address the specific customer's concerns. This approach addresses special causes of disloyalty (those that fall outside of normal variations) and is a short-term solution to customer concerns. Rather than focusing on improving the business process that caused this customer to become at risk, the organization's main goal is to address this at-risk customer's concerns. Improvements are targeted at disloyal customers in order to immediately address their specific needs.

In this approach, timely handling of unhappy, disloyal customers is key to ensuring that their attitudes regarding the company do not ultimately result in disloyal behaviors (for example, to defect or discontinue buying). Web-based surveys are an important ingredient in the micro approach to handling disloyal customers. The Web-based survey utilizes the power of the Internet to notify the organization regarding the specific customer's negative response(s). Trigger email alerts are often used to alert employees of unhappy, disloyal customers.

During the development of the customer survey administration process, survey questions should be assigned to a given individual or department responsible for those particular results. The decision to assign a survey question to a specific department should be based on whether that department has the ability to change customers' ratings on that question. A survey question regarding the sales process, for example, should be assigned to the sales department. A survey question regarding technical support quality should be assigned to the technical support department. These two departments influence the quality of the sales process and technical support process, respectively; they are in the best position to address problems from these areas.

The trigger emails are keyed off of customer's response to these satisfaction and loyalty questions. For example, an organization may set up an automatic email trigger to notify an Account team member when his or her customer responds to an overall satisfaction question with a rating of 5 or below on a 0 to 10-point scale. Such a low rating is an indication that this customer is at risk for exhibiting disloyal behavior. The email alert is sent to the Account team member immediately after the respondent submits the survey responses.

The trigger email alert should include information the recipient needs in order to immediately contact the respondent to address concerns identified in the email. Typical information in a trigger email includes the respondent's name, company name, product information, and the ratings on the key questions used as criteria to trigger the alert. An example of a trigger email alert appears in Figure 7.13.

This micro approach to loyalty management requires that the respondent be identified during the completion of the survey. The trigger email approach is not uncommon in B2B customer surveys. Most surveys of large-scale vendors possess this sort of sophisticated survey approach, allowing companies to identify respondents in order to address their individual concerns.

Macro (Organizational) Approach to Loyalty Management

The macro approach examines the customer relationship across all customers (or customer segments) in which data are analyzed as a whole. In doing so, the organization attempts to identify systemic factors causing loyalty and disloyalty. As such, this approach addresses common causes of disloyalty and focuses on improving systemic issues responsible for it. Organizational improvements are targeted across a large group of customers (or, at least, large customer segments) and are aimed at improving the service delivery system that will have long-term effects on customer loyalty.

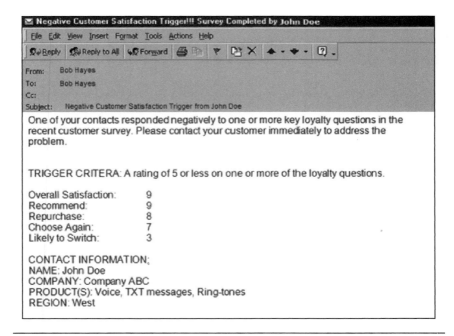

Figure 7.13 Trigger email indicating an at-risk customer. (Likely to switch < 6, indicating defection is likely.)

The macro or organizational approach to loyalty management begins with loyalty driver analysis. Loyalty driver analysis essentially identifies business areas that, when improved, would have a substantial impact on increasing customer loyalty.

LOYALTY DRIVER ANALYSIS

Loyalty driver analysis is a process by which we identify how best to improve customer loyalty. Two pieces of information are examined: 1) derived importance, the degree of impact of each business attribute on customer loyalty, and 2) performance, the level of performance of each business attribute.

Derived Importance

The derived importance of a business attribute is the correlation coefficient between satisfaction ratings for that business attribute and the measure of customer loyalty (see Appendix J for a description of correlation coefficients). The correlation between the satisfaction scores of a business attribute and loyalty indicates the degree to which performance on the business attribute has an impact on customer loyalty behavior.

Performance

Performance of a given business attribute is the average rating for that particular attribute.

Loyalty Matrix

Each business attribute has a derived importance and a performance score associated with it. Using both the derived importance of each business attribute and the performance (that is, rating) of each business attribute, we can create a loyalty matrix (see Figure 7.14) that allows us to visually examine all business attributes at one time and understand how each business attribute affects customer loyalty.

The abscissa (x-axis) of the loyalty matrix is the performance rating (agreement, performance, satisfaction) of the business attributes. The ordinate (y-axis) of the loyalty matrix is the impact (derived importance) of the business attribute on customer loyalty. The loyalty matrix is divided into quadrants using the average score for each of the axes. Each of the business attributes will fall into one of the four quadrants. Loyalty management at the macro (organizational) level is a process of understanding this matrix and the types of business decisions that should be made to maximize customer loyalty.

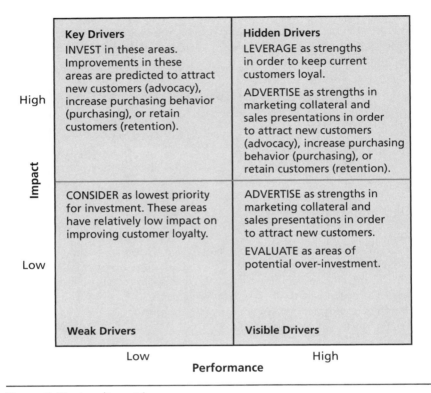

Figure 7.14   Loyalty matrix.

Let us take a look at the loyalty matrix using the Advocacy Loyalty Index. Using the PC manufacturing study, we can set up a loyalty matrix. This matrix appears in Figure 7.15. Based on this loyalty matrix, the organization can make business decisions that will have a positive impact on advocacy loyalty.

Key Drivers. Business attributes that appear in the upper left quadrant are often referred to as key drivers. Key drivers reflect business attributes that have both a large impact on advocacy loyalty and low performance ratings relative to the other business attributes. Business attributes that are key drivers reflect areas for potential improvement that should affect the advocacy of their customers. Improving advocacy will improve new customer growth.

To see improvements in advocacy loyalty, the results of the driver analysis suggest this organization should improve technical support excellence.

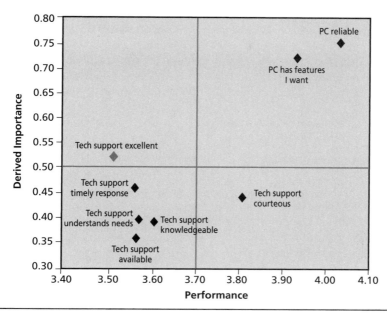

Figure 7.15   Advocacy loyalty driver analysis—PC manufacturer.

Hidden Drivers. Business attributes that appear in the upper right quadrant are referred to as hidden drivers. Hidden drivers reflect business attributes that have a large impact on advocacy loyalty and high performance ratings relative to other business attributes. These reflect the strengths that keep the customer base advocating the company's product. These areas should be monitored regularly in order to ensure that they remain high. These attributes could also be used in marketing material designed to attract new customers.

The company's strengths are:

- Product is reliable

- Product has features I want

Weak Drivers. Business attributes that appear in the lower left quadrant are referred to as weak drivers. Weak drivers reflect business attributes that have a small impact on advocacy loyalty and low performance ratings relative to other business attributes. Business attributes that are weak drivers reflect areas that are lowest priorities for investment. These areas are of low priority because improvement would not have a substantial impact on whether or not customers will advocate the product or company.

The following areas do not have a large impact on whether your customers will advocate the product/company. If your resources are limited, improvement in these areas might take a back seat to improvements to your key drivers above. The weak drivers are:

- Tech support understands needs

- Tech support offers timely response

- Tech support is available

- Tech support is knowledgeable

Visible Drivers. Business attributes that appear in the lower right quadrant are referred to as visible drivers. Visible drivers reflect business attributes that have a low impact on advocacy loyalty and high performance ratings relative to other business attributes. Business attributes that are visible drivers reflect the company's strengths. These areas may not be responsible for encouraging customers to be advocates, but they do reflect high performance. These business attributes can be advertised as strengths in marketing collateral and sales presentations in order to attract new customers.

The following area does not have a large impact on advocacy loyalty but performance is good. The company might consider featuring this area in sales and marketing materials to attract new customers:

- Tech support is courteous

Because we have two customer loyalty indices, we can calculate multiple

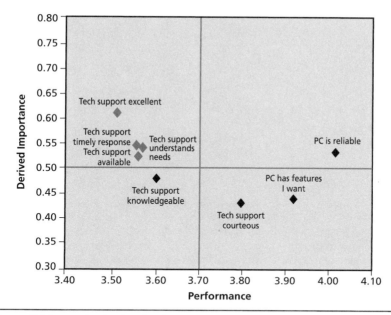

Figure 7.16   Purchasing loyalty driver analysis—PC manufacturer.

separate loyalty matrices, each for the specific customer loyalty index. The loyalty matrix for the PC manufacturer survey using the purchasing loyalty index appears in Figure 7.16.

With regard to purchasing loyalty, however, we see that many of the technical support attributes (excellence, timeliness, availability, understanding of needs) have a relatively big impact on purchasing loyalty. It's interesting to note that product attributes do not have a big impact on purchasing loyalty.

Using the two loyalty matrices, we can draw some conclusions regarding how this particular PC manufacturer can increase advocacy loyalty and purchasing loyalty. The driver analysis appears to be inconclusive regarding advocacy loyalty. While PC features are big determinants of advocacy, they are rated as relatively good. Consequently, there is not much room for improvement in these attributes. The technical support attributes, while rated relatively low, do not have a large impact on advocacy loyalty.

If this PC manufacturer wants to improve purchasing loyalty, however, the driver analysis indicates that it should focus on improving technical support attributes; these have a relatively large impact on purchasing loyalty and there is much room for improvement.

The different results from this analysis suggest that "improving customer loyalty" is more complex than simply using a single metric. If the

Table 7.5 Summary of micro and macro approaches to loyalty management.

Micro Approach	Macro Approach
Addresses special causes of disloyalty	Addresses common causes of disloyalty
Focus on changing individual issues	Focus on improving systemic issues
Customer-specific improvements	Organization-wide improvements
Short-term solutions	Long-term solutions

company were to use advocacy loyalty as its only measure of loyalty (as is commonly done), it would not identify ways in which to improve purchasing loyalty of the customer base. Inclusion of the two different dimensions of customer loyalty ensures the company fully understands how to improve both advocacy loyalty and purchasing loyalty.

SUMMARY OF MICRO VS. MACRO APPROACH

The two approaches to survey-based loyalty management should not be viewed as competing. Instead, by design, the survey-based loyalty management system should help a company deal with specific customer complaints while at the same time identifying systemic reasons for dissatisfaction and disloyalty. This approach ensures that both short-term concerns and long-term concerns are dealt with effectively.

Table 7.5 summarizes the features of two approaches to loyalty management. The micro (individual) approach focuses on special causes of customer disloyalty and addresses individual customer concerns with customer-specific improvements; these are short-term solutions to improving customer loyalty. The macro (organizational) approach addresses common causes of disloyalty and focuses on improving systemic issues with organization-wide improvements that are long-term solutions to improving customer loyalty.

MAKING IMPROVEMENTS AND ROOT CAUSE ANALYSIS

A customer loyalty survey, while providing great insight into systemic reasons for disloyalty, is not the final step in driving increases in customer loyalty. Conducting a customer survey does not cause improvement. We might think of the loyalty matrix results as a great first step; it provides insight into where organizational improvement should occur. Depending on the specificity of the survey questions, the loyalty matrix provides specific or general direction as to where the organization should make investment (in time and resources) in order to improve customer loyalty (or maintain existing loyalty). In either case, the next step an organization must take is to translate this investment into tangible operational changes that will transform its business strategy to improve customer satisfaction and loyalty.

An organization can employ root cause analysis (RCA) to identify root causes of quality problems that might eventually result in customer disloyalty. Rather than simply addressing the symptoms of the problem (for

Uses	Important Issues
1. Present current standing of customer satisfaction.	• Present means and standard deviations of specific items as well as overall scores of each dimension.
2. Identify important customer requirements.	• Use correlational analysis relating customer requirements to overall satisfaction scores.
3. Monitor satisfaction levels over time.	• Use control charting techniques.
	• Control chart method depends on the type of response format you select (checklist–attribute data versus Likert-type–variable data).
	• Types of control charts include p chart, c chart, u chart, x chart, and s chart.
4. Provide organizational comparisons.	• Comparisons should be made on companies using the same questionnaire.
	• An independent research firm could conduct comparisons.
5. Determine program effectiveness.	• Evaluate effect of training programs.
	• Conduct benchmarking studies.
6. Customer loyalty management.	• Micro approach deals with special causes of disloyalty
	• Macro approach deals with common causes of disloyalty

Figure 7.17   Uses of customer satisfaction questionnaires.

example, low satisfaction with technical staff knowledge, responsiveness of technical support), this popular continuous improvement technique identifies the underlying, or root, causes for problems. RCA tries to identify the root causes for the symptoms in hopes to eliminate them. Addressing these root causes will decrease the likelihood that the symptoms will reoccur. While there is no single method for identifying the root causes for a problem, RCA provides guidelines that can be applied in many situations. A full discussion on RCA is beyond the scope of this book, but the interested reader can find more information about this topic. (See Andersen & Fagerhaug 2006, for a variety of RCA tools.)

SUMMARY

The utility of customer satisfaction questionnaires is dependent, in part, on the use of the data. This chapter covered effective presentation of data. It also demonstrated other uses for customer satisfaction questionnaires: determining the quality dimensions of the product or service that strongly predict overall customer satisfaction, monitoring business processes over time, making organizational comparisons, and determining effectiveness of intervention programs. Figure 7.17 summarizes these uses.

8

Examples of Customer Satisfaction Questionnaires

This chapter presents specific examples of customer satisfaction questionnaire development and use in three service businesses: dental offices, newspaper publishers, and coffee shops. It is one thing to talk about survey guidelines in the abstract and quite another thing to put these guidelines to practice. You will see that the survey process varies quite a bit from one company to another. These differences are due to various factors that affect the ease with which a particular company is able to subscribe to the guidelines outlined in this book. For example, you will see that some companies were not able to conduct a sampling plan, while others were confined to using general items in their questionnaires. Although each of these examples differs from the rest, all of the examples demonstrate the usefulness of customer satisfaction data.

DENTAL PATIENT SATISFACTION

House of Teeth Insurance, Inc., a large company that provides dental insurance, developed a patient satisfaction survey to determine patients' perceptions regarding the quality of care they receive from the dentists on their provider list. Additionally, the survey was designed to provide feedback regarding patients' perceptions regarding the quality of the insurance the company provided its customers. The survey team consisted of the director of marketing and two external consultants who specialized in survey development.

Questionnaire Development

The survey team examined a previous patient satisfaction survey in order to determine what content should be included in the new survey. The team inspected the items and analyzed some existing data in order to determine whether there were any factors that could be identified in a factor analysis of the data. Figure 8.1 includes some of the old items.

In addition to examining the previous survey, the survey team also reviewed current literature on the measurement of dental patient satisfaction, knowing that these studies might lead to the inclusion of important quality factors missed in the previous survey. This literature review covered recent articles in scientific, peer-reviewed journals. Some journal articles used in this literature review, and their conclusions, are included in Figure 8.2. As can be see in this figure, researchers have identified various factors that define the quality of dental care. Some researchers found more dental patient satisfaction factors than other, and there is some overlap. In any case, these articles provided useful information regarding the content of the questionnaire the survey team wanted to develop.

Using information from the previous survey and from the literature review, the survey team developed a new dental patient satisfaction survey that reflected the team's four primary goals:

1. The survey was short.

2. The survey comprehensively covered the important quality factors identified in the literature review.

3. The survey provided specific feedback to the dentists.

4. The survey included items that assessed patient satisfaction with the insurance company itself, not just dental care.

The process of developing the survey was one of compromise. On the one hand, the team wanted a reliable instrument, which meant including multiple items in the scale. However, the team also wanted a survey instrument that was short enough to facilitate the patients' completion of it. With these goals in mind, the survey team developed the customer satisfaction questionnaire presented in Figure 8.3.

---

1. My dentist's office was clean and orderly.

2. I feel the wait time to schedule a dental appointment at my dentist's office was reasonable.

3. The insurance personnel did not seem to be concerned about my well-being.

4. The insurance personnel I spoke with on the toll-free telephone line were courteous.

Figure 8.1 Items from the previous dental patient satisfaction survey.

Sampling Plan

The survey team decided to allow all patients the opportunity to provide feedback regarding the quality of dental care and their satisfaction with the insurance company's coverage. Consequently, a sampling plan was not needed. However, because each doctor was to be given feedback regarding his or her service quality, a sample of returned surveys was examined in

Authors	Quality Factors
Andrus and Buchheister (1985)	• Technical competence • Interpersonal skills
Factor analysis was used to determine the quality dimensions	• Office organization • Financial considerations
Koslowsky, Bailit, and Valluzzo (1974)	• Technical competence • Dentist personality • Office organization • Financial considerations
Davies and Ware (1981) They used principal components, not recommended when looking at underlying constructs. However, they report it supported their five-facet hypothesis. Scale reliabilities ranged from .52–.81. There are single-item scales.	• Access • Availability convenience • Cost • Pain • Quality
Chapko, Bergner, Green Beach, Milgrom, and Skalabrin (1985) Scale reliabilities range from .46 to .79. Some are single-item scales. The interscale correlations are low but the low reliabilities may have attenuated these correlations; thus, the scale measures fewer facets of dental patient satisfaction.	• Dentist-patient relations • Technical quality of care • Access • Patient waiting time • Cost • Facilities • Availability • Continuity • Pain • Auxiliaries performing expanded duties • Staff-patient relations • Staff technical quality of care • Office atmosphere

Figure 8.2   Facets of dental patient satisfaction.

House of Teeth Insurance, Inc., is concerned about your satisfaction as our customer. We are striving to provide the best dental plan available. Please take a few moments to answer the following questions, as they relate to your dental office visit and the insurance plan benefits. Please return the completed survey within the next 10 days. Thank you.

	Strongly Agree	Agree	Neutral	Disagree	Strongly Disagree	Not Applicable
1. I was able to schedule an appointment at a good time.	☐	☐	☐	☐	☐	☐
2. The dental office is inconsiderate of my time.	☐	☐	☐	☐	☐	☐
3. The front office staff was courteous.	☐	☐	☐	☐	☐	☐
4. The front office staff was helpful in explaining my insurance dental benefits.	☐	☐	☐	☐	☐	☐
5. I was treated poorly because I had insurance benefits coverage.	☐	☐	☐	☐	☐	☐
6. The dentist treated me fairly.	☐	☐	☐	☐	☐	☐
7. The office was clean.	☐	☐	☐	☐	☐	☐
8. The office uses outdated equipment.	☐	☐	☐	☐	☐	☐
9. The dental office used sterilized instruments.	☐	☐	☐	☐	☐	☐
10. Gloves, masks, and glasses were used by the staff during dental procedures.	☐	☐	☐	☐	☐	☐
11. The dentist/staff told me how much the dental work would cost before beginning the treatment.	☐	☐	☐	☐	☐	☐
12. The dentist/staff explained the treatment procedures with me.	☐	☐	☐	☐	☐	☐
13. The treatment prescribed was inappropriate for my needs.	☐	☐	☐	☐	☐	☐
14. The dental work done for me was top quality.	☐	☐	☐	☐	☐	☐
15. The dentist reduced my discomfort during the dental treatment.	☐	☐	☐	☐	☐	☐
16. The hygienist was rough during my teeth cleaning appointment.	☐	☐	☐	☐	☐	☐
17. There were plenty of available dental offices on the insurance list from which to choose.	☐	☐	☐	☐	☐	☐
18. The offices on the insurance list require me to travel a long distance.	☐	☐	☐	☐	☐	☐

Figure 8.3   Dental patient satisfaction survey.   *(Continued)*

(Continued)

	Strongly Agree	Agree	Neutral	Disagree	Strongly Disagree	Not Applicable
19. I received superior benefit coverage under the insurance plan.	☐	☐	☐	☐	☐	☐
20. The information I received from the insurance company fully explained my dental benefits.	☐	☐	☐	☐	☐	☐

	1 week	2 weeks	3 weeks	4 weeks	4+ weeks	N/A
21. How long did you have to wait to schedule an appointment?	☐	☐	☐	☐	☐	☐

	5 min.	10 min.	15 min.	20 min.	20+ min.	N/A
22. How long did you have to wait in the dentist's waiting room before seeing your dentist?	☐	☐	☐	☐	☐	☐

	Yes	No	Not sure
23. I would recommend this office to a friend or relative.	☐	☐	☐
24. I would recommend the insurance dental plan to a friend or relative.	☐	☐	☐

	Very Satisfied	Satisfied	Neutral	Dissatisfied	Very Dissatisfied
25. Overall, how satisfied were you with the dental office visit?	☐	☐	☐	☐	☐
26. Overall, how satisfied were you with the insurance dental benefits plan?	☐	☐	☐	☐	☐

Figure 8.3 Dental patient satisfaction survey.

order to ensure a desired level of confidence for an acceptable level of tolerable error. That is, the survey team wanted to ensure that the results for each doctor were reliable. The team decided to use a 95 percent confidence level and a tolerable error of .20. These criteria were to be attained before each doctor received results for his or her quality of care. An appropriate sample size was determined that would satisfy these criteria.

Because some doctors were used more frequently than others, the frequency with which they received feedback results varied accordingly. Given a constant response rate across doctors, we would expect doctors with a higher patient load to receive more frequent feedback because the confidence interval (CI) of 95 percent and a level of tolerable error of .20 would be reached more quickly compared to doctors with a lower patient load.

The survey team used the standard formula for estimating sample size to guide them in their survey plan.

$$n = (t^2 \times s^2)/e^2$$

where n equals the sample size, t equals the level of confidence, s equals the standard deviation, and e equals tolerable error.

Recall that this formula allows us to determine what our sample size should be for our desired levels of confidence and tolerable error with a specific standard deviation. For the House of Teeth Insurance, Inc. Dental Health Satisfaction Survey, we have set these parameters: $t = 2.0$ (95 percent confidence interval) and $e = .20$. Using previous survey research conducted at House of Teeth Insurance, Inc. and other survey research, we found that s for survey items, on average, equals 1.0. To achieve a tolerable error of .20 (in the same unit of measurement as the scale being used), requires a sample size of 100. In other words, we need a sample size of 100 to obtain a 95 percent confidence interval with a .20 level of tolerable error.

We must also take response rates into consideration. We see that we need a sample size of 100 to ensure the specified level of confidence and tolerable error. Because many survey recipients will not respond, we must mail out more than 100 surveys in order to ensure that we have 100 returned surveys in the end. With a history of a 10 percent response rate, we know that we must mail out 1000 surveys in order to ensure that 100 surveys are returned. Several hypothetical examples presented to the survey team are illustrated in Table 8.1.

Given these factors, the survey team decided to take the following approach regarding feedback provision to a given dental clinic. First, the team decided that clinics with a large patient base would require larger samples for feedback. Although sampling error is not associated with the size of the population, dentists in larger clinics may perceive the data to be more valid when based on larger sample sizes. Thus, the distribution of the survey for larger clinics (those clinics with sample sizes greater than 300) will be set at a given number (mailout = 176, so $n = 44$ and tolerable error =.30). For smaller clinics, sample size will be set to obtain an acceptable level of tolerable error. However, due to the small client base and low response rates, the desired sample sizes may not be reached within a given quarter. Thus, feedback would be delayed until an acceptable level of tolerable error is obtained for a given office. This would result in feedback being conducted only twice per year rather than four times per year.

Survey Administration

The survey was administered through the U.S. mail. After each patient received treatment, he or she was mailed a customer satisfaction survey, the completion and return of which was voluntary. To improve the response rate, postage was provided for return of the survey. Additionally, the

Table 8.1 Number of surveys needed to be mailed (mailout) for a 95 percent confidence interval, standard deviation of 1.0, and varying degrees of tolerable error.

Tolerable error	Sample size	Mailout (25% response rate)	Mailout (40% response rate)
.20	100	400	250
.30	44	176	110
.40	25	100	63
.50	16	64	40

Note: If s is less than 1.0, then the sample size given *(n)* would result in a smaller level of tolerable error.

customers were told that House of Teeth Insurance, Inc. would donate $1 to a charity of the patient's choosing for every survey returned. Because this survey process required a large sample size, the surveys were created so as to allow electronic scanning of the responses. This procedure greatly reduced time and money normally required for manual input of data.

Survey Results

The survey results presented in Figure 8.4 represent a one-quarter period. In this particular quarter, the company received 14,062 completed patient satisfaction surveys.

Items in the survey were coded for numerical analysis. The coding scheme was conducted so that higher scores represented higher levels of customer satisfaction. For positively phrased items (such as "The front office staff was courteous" or "The office was clean"), the following coding was used: Strongly Agree = 5, Agree = 4, Neutral = 3, Disagree = 2, Strongly Disagree = 1. For negatively phrased items (such as "The office used outdated equipment" or "The treatment prescribed was inappropriate for my needs"), the following coding scheme was used: Strongly Agree = 1, Agree = 2, Neutral = 3, Disagree = 4, Strongly Disagree = 5. For scheduling availability and wait time items (questions 21 and 22), items were coded such that a shorter wait time reflected a higher score (5—higher scores indicate higher levels of satisfaction) and a longer wait time reflected a lower score (1—lower scores indicate lower levels of satisfaction). For the recommend/not recommend items (items 23 and 24), the following coding scheme was used: Yes = 3, Not sure = 1, No = 0.).

To get a general idea of the satisfaction levels of the patients, the survey team calculated the statistics (the mean and the standard deviation) for each item in the survey. The results of this analysis are presented in Figure 8.4.

	Percentage of respondents						
	SA	A	N	D	SD	Mean	StD
1. I was able to schedule an appointment at a good time.	44.7	38.7	16.8	15.3	14.6	4.14	1.06
2. The dental office was inconsiderate of my time.	10.2	11.6	19.4	29.4	39.4	3.76	1.35
3. The front office staff was courteous.	48.0	40.9	17.0	12.4	11.7	4.31	1.84
4. The front office staff was helpful in explaining my insurance dental benefits.	25.9	37.7	23.7	18.1	14.6	3.72	1.07
5. I was treated poorly because I had insurance benefits coverage.	14.5	15.1	10.6	32.3	47.5	4.13	1.08
6. I was treated fairly by the dentist.	44.7	41.1	17.4	13.6	13.2	4.21	1.95
7. The office was clean.	50.6	41.9	14.8	12.0	11.6	4.37	1.80
8. The office uses outdated equipment.	14.7	17.3	14.5	35.8	37.7	3.94	1.11
9. The dental office used sterilized instruments.	38.7	49.4	19.6	11.3	11.0	4.24	1.75
10. Gloves, masks, and glasses were used by the staff during dental procedures.	51.4	43.3	12.4	12.1	11.8	4.42	1.72
11. The dentist/staff told me how much the dental work would cost before beginning the treatment.	29.1	38.4	12.4	14.2	15.9	3.71	1.19
12. The dentist/staff explained the treatment procedures to me.	34.6	46.9	19.5	16.2	12.9	4.04	1.97
13. The treatment prescribed was inappropriate for my needs.	15.9	18.7	10.3	35.3	39.9	3.95	1.17
14. The dental work done for me was top quality.	34.0	40.7	15.3	15.9	14.1	3.95	1.05
15. The dentist tried to reduce my discomfort during the dental treatment.	36.0	44.4	13.1	14.0	12.6	4.07	1.94
16. The hygienist was rough during my teeth cleaning appointment.	14.3	16.8	11.1	38.9	38.9	4.01	1.08
17. There were plenty of available dental offices on the insurance list from which to choose.	10.4	27.3	20.4	21.6	20.3	2.86	1.30
18. The offices on the insurance list require me to travel a long distance.	17.6	12.5	17.3	39.7	22.9	3.58	1.19
19. I received superior benefit coverage under the insurance plan.	21.8	41.0	21.9	19.1	16.2	3.63	1.11
20. The information I received from the insurance company fully explained my dental benefits.	21.2	56.4	14.5	15.6	12.3	3.89	1.88

Figure 8.4 Descriptive statistics for each item in the patient satisfaction survey. *(Continued)*

(Continued)

	1 week	2 weeks	3 weeks	4 weeks	4+ weeks	Mean	StD
21. How long did you have to wait to schedule an appointment?	32.0	25.2	14.0	19.8	19.0	3.42	1.49

	5 min	10 min	15 min	20 min	20+ min	Mean	StD
22. How long did you have to wait in the dentist's waiting room before seeing your dentist?	29.1	31.9	19.3	17.8	10.9	3.62	1.28

	Yes	No	Not sure			Mean	StD
23. I would recommend this office to a friend or relative.	69.6	16.9	13.5			2.22	1.21
24. I would recommend the insurance dental plan to a friend or relative.	68.3	11.1	20.6			2.26	1.13

	VS	S	N	D	SD	Mean	StD
25. Overall, how satisfied were you with the dental office visit?	46.1	33.5	18.6	16.5	15.3	4.08	1.13
26. Overall, how satisfied were you with the insurance dental benefits plan?	31.7	45.7	13.4	16.5	12.7	3.97	1.98

Figure 8.4 Descriptive statistics for each item in the patient satisfaction survey.

As we can see from the survey results, the responses vary from unfavorable to favorable. On the average, however, most of the items have a favorable response; many items with a five-point scale have an average response above 4.0.

Factor Analysis of the Client Satisfaction Survey

Although we have 26 items in the survey, we might be able to combine some responses into fewer categories. Factor analysis is the statistical method used to determine whether this may be appropriate (see Appendix K). The factor analysis tells us whether we may be able to combine some of the items in our scale in order to obtain subscale scores. For example, rather than thinking that items 3 and 4 measure two distinct quality factors, we might combine them in order to obtain a score that we could call *dentist office professionalism*. Additionally, items 8, 9, and 10 might be combined to obtain a score we would call *equipment quality*. Factor analysis is a method that allows us to see whether combining these items may be appropriate.

The results of the factor analysis of items 1 through 20 are presented in the factor pattern matrix located in Table 8.2. The elements in this factor pattern matrix tell us how well each item is related to the underlying dimension. Although this particular factor pattern matrix is not as clear as we would like, it still provides some useful information. Some items clearly load onto a single factor (such as items 1, 2, 3, and 4), measuring only one

Table 8.2 Rotated factor pattern matrix of the 26 items in the dental patient satisfaction survey.

	Factor 1	Factor 2	Factor 3	Factor 4
Q1	**.40**	.33	.16	.23
Q2	.08	**.43**	.07	.06
Q3	**.51**	.35	.22	.15
Q4	**.66**	.25	.15	.15
Q5	.28	**.62**	.14	.17
Q6	**.44**	**.45**	.37	.17
Q7	.26	.31	**.56**	.12
Q8	.07	**.45**	.39	.12
Q9	.27	.23	**.61**	.17
Q10	.27	.14	**.59**	.14
Q11	**.57**	.05	.24	.08
Q12	**.58**	.24	.40	.13
Q13	.15	**.51**	.20	.13
Q14	**.45**	**.44**	**.44**	.23
Q15	**.44**	.32	**.40**	.16
Q16	.19	**.40**	.22	.14
Q17	.12	.04	.10	**.58**
Q18	−.03	.19	.08	**.43**
Q19	.35	.25	.17	**.47**
Q20	.30	.07	.09	**.43**

underlying thing. Some items, however, do not load clearly onto a single factor. For example, items 6, 14, and 15 load onto more than one factor, suggesting that these items measure more than one underlying thing.

From this rotated factor pattern matrix, we see that there are four underlying factors, each with corresponding items:

1. Interpersonal skills (items 1, 3, 4, 11, 12)

2. Technical competence (items 2, 5, 8, 13, 16)

3. Sterilization of office (items 7, 9, 10)

4. Insurance quality (items 17, 18, 19, 20)

The survey team labeled these factors based on the items that loaded onto them. It is possible that other people would choose different labels for these same factors. The actual labels are not important; what is important is that we understand that some items are measuring the same thing and that it is possible to obtain summary scores based on the responses to these items. Based on the factor analysis, subscale scores were calculated for each of the four factors using the items that represented the factors. These subscale scores were calculated by averaging the items within each factor. Due to the content of items 6, 14, and 15, these items were included in the interpersonal skills subscale score.

We can now present the results at a more general level. Additionally, we can calculate an estimate of reliability (internal consistency) for each of the subscales derived from the factor analysis. The descriptive statistics for the subscales are presented in Table 8.3.

Correlational analysis. Next, we can use the data to determine which of the four factors of dental satisfaction (technical competence, interpersonal skills, sterilization of office, or insurance quality) is correlated with some of the other items in the customer satisfaction survey. The insurance company would be interested to know which of these four factors best predicts overall satisfaction with the dental office visit (question 25) or the extent to which the patient makes recommendations about the dentist's office (question 23) or insurance plan (question 24). One method to determine the relative predictive power of each subscale is to examine the correlation coefficients of each subscale with the remaining items in the customer satisfaction questionnaire. This correlation matrix is presented in Table 8.4. Included in the correlation matrix are the reliability estimates (Cronbach's alpha) for each of the four subscales.

From Table 8.4, we find that the overall satisfaction rating of the insurance plan (question 26) was most highly related to the insurance quality subscale. That is, patients who said they were satisfied overall with the insurance plan also indicated that there were plenty of offices from

Table 8.3 Descriptive statistics for subscale scores for the patient satisfaction survey.

Variable	Mean	StD	Cases
Interpersonal skills	4.03	.73	14062
Technical competence	3.94	.81	13976
Sterilization of office	4.34	.62	14056
Insurance quality	3.50	.78	14053

Note: StD = standard deviation

Table 8.4   Correlations among the subscales and the remaining items in the patient satisfaction questionnaire.

	1	2	3	4	5	6	7	8	9	10
1. Interpersonal	(.87)									
2. Technical	.57	(.69)								
3. Sterilization	.66	.49	(.75)							
4. Insurance	.48	.35	.38	(.60)						
5. Q21	.38	.22	.20	.23	—					
6. Q22	.43	.37	.31	.25	.27	—				
7. Q23	.66	.51	.48	.39	.27	.40	—			
8. Q24	.38	.30	.28	.48	.18	.21	.48	—		
9. Q25	.78	.57	.57	.45	.31	.45	.77	.45	—	
10. Q26	.44	.33	.34	.58	.19	.24	.41	.66	.52	—

Note: All correlations significant at the .01 level. Reliability estimates (Cronbach's alpha) is located in diagonal. Reliability estimates cannot be calculated for single-item measures. *N* ranges from 11662 to 14062; Interpersonal = Interpersonal skills; Technical = Technical competence; Sterilization = Sterilization of office; Insurance = Insurance quality.

which to choose, they didn't have to travel long distances to get to the dentist's office, they thought they received superior benefits, and their benefits were fully explained to them. Also, we see that the interpersonal skills subscale was the best predictor of overall satisfaction with the dental office visit (question 25), wait time for scheduling an appointment (question 21), wait time in the dentist's waiting room (question 22), and whether the patient would recommend the dentist's office to a friend or relative (question 23). Finally, we see that the insurance quality subscale was the best predictor of whether or not the patient would recommend the insurance plan to a friend or relative (question 24).

Regression analysis. From the correlational analysis, we found that the interpersonal skills factor was good at predicting some important customer behaviors and attitudes (questions 23 and 25). The correlations of the three other subscales with these same customer behaviors and attitudes are also quite high and might still be important in the understanding of customer satisfaction and behavior. A more powerful approach for determining which of the four subscales best predicts the other variables is through a statistical method called *regression analysis* (see Appendix J).

The specific type of regression analysis conducted here is referred to as *stepwise regression analysis.* For these analyses, the predictor variables were the four subscales. A total of four stepwise regression analyses were conducted, one for each of the outcome variables. This form of regression analysis allows you to see the unique contribution of all four subscales in predicting a given outcome variable. The results of the stepwise regression analysis are presented in Table 8.5.

As we can see from the results of the stepwise regression analysis, all of the subscales uniquely contribute in the explanation of the customer satisfaction and customer recommendation variables. However, a degree of caution must be noted. Due to the large sample size, even small effect sizes are statistically significant. The ΔR^2 shows us the effect size of the given subscale. We see that, after the first subscale has been entered into the equation, not much more of the variance can be explained by the remaining

Table 8.5 Stepwise regression analysis of the dental patient satisfaction questionnaire.

	Subscale	ΔR^2	p
Question 23	Interpersonal skills	.4339	.01
(recommend office)	Technical competence	.0274	.01
	Insurance quality	.0049	.01
	Sterilization of office	.0007	.01
	Total for four variables in the equation	.4669	.01
Question 24	Insurance quality	.2299	.01
(recommend plan)	Interpersonal skills	.0308	.01
	Technical competence	.0038	.01
	Total for three variables in the equation	.2645	.01
Question 25	Interpersonal skills	.6065	.01
(office satisfaction)	Technical competence	.0257	.01
	Insurance quality	.0060	.01
	Sterilization of office	.0013	.01
	Total for four variables in the equation	.6395	.01
Question 26	Insurance quality	.3348	.01
(insurance satisfaction)	Interpersonal skills	.0357	.01
	Technical competence	.0027	.01
	Sterilization of office	.0002	.05
	Total for four variables in the equation	.3734	.01

Note: $N = 14062$, ΔR^2 = percent of variance accounted for at each step in the analysis.

subscales. It is best to examine not only the significance of the effect but the actual effect size (R^2) when interpreting the results. For example, many of the subscales, even though statistically significant, explain less than .5 percent of the variance in the outcome variables.

Some interesting findings can still be seen from the results. We found that interpersonal skills and technical competence are both important predictors of customer satisfaction of and customer recommendation for dentist's office. Additionally, insurance quality and interpersonal skills are both important predictors of customer satisfaction of and customer recommendation for the insurance plan. Interpersonal skills of the office staff are related to two areas: office quality and insurance quality. Consequently, the insurance company might be best served by focusing resources on increasing the interpersonal skills of the dental office staff. Increases in interpersonal skills scores might be reflected in increases in customer satisfaction scores for both the dental office and insurance quality.

Summary

The development and use of the dental patient satisfaction questionnaire was labor intensive. The importance of providing reliable and valid information to the dentist's office warranted an in-depth review of current literature on the topic of dental patient satisfaction research. It was important that the survey team members not miss important quality dimensions in their development of the survey. Additionally, the customer satisfaction survey allowed customers to rate the quality of the insurance program. We saw that the dental patient satisfaction survey provided useful information regarding the factors that were highly related to customer recommendation behavior. Additionally, the survey performed two very useful functions. On the one hand, survey results supplied the insurance provider with a measure of the quality of its insurance benefits. Survey results also supplied the insurance company with a measure of the quality of the dentists in its provider network and provided feedback to the individual dentists, allowing them to ensure a high degree of customer satisfaction.

READER SURVEY

Our next customer survey example takes place on a much smaller scale than our dental patient satisfaction example. A small company publishes a monthly newspaper, *The Parent,* filled with articles and information about children. The purpose of the reader survey was to provide the publisher with reader demographics and information about lifestyles and shopping habits. The survey asked questions about the extent of computer use, readership of other newspapers, and recreational activities. Additionally, the publisher of *The Parent* wanted to get a general sense of the customer satisfaction with the newspaper.

Questionnaire Development

The survey team consisted of the owner of the publishing company and a survey consultant. They used a survey from the previous year as a starting point for the new survey, modifying some questions and adding others. The survey instructions and a partial list of questions are included in Figure 8.5.

Administration of the Survey

The reader survey was administered through the newspaper itself, printed on one side of a single page in the newspaper. Readers were instructed to send completed surveys to an independent consulting firm that was responsible for data management and analysis. Readers were asked to provide their own stamps and envelopes. To increase response rates, the publisher offered chances in a drawing to readers who turned in a completed survey. Because all readers had the opportunity to complete the survey, no sampling plan was developed.

Results

A total of 201 readers completed the reader survey. The results of the survey are presented in Figure 8.6.

From the standard deviations in Figure 8.6, we could calculate the standard error of the mean for each item to be .05. Consequently, the 95 percent confidence interval for each mean is:

Question 1 $CI = 4.10 \pm 2 \times .05$; $CI = 4.00 < X < 4.20$

Question 2 $CI = 4.13 \pm 2 \times .05$; $CI = 4.03 < X < 4.23$

Question 3 $CI = 4.31 \pm 2 \times .05$; $CI = 4.21 < X < 4.41$

From these results, we see that we can be fairly certain that our observed means using our sample of 201 customers are good estimates of the population mean (all our customers). We have a fairly tight confidence interval around our estimate of each of the means. In addition, we are fairly confident that our population means for each item all fall above 4.00 (satisfied), indicating that our customers are generally satisfied with the newspaper.

Overall Newspaper Satisfaction Score

The correlation among the three customer satisfaction questionnaires ranges from .74 to .78, suggesting that the items may be measuring a single underlying construct. Therefore, an overall satisfaction score was calculated by averaging the three customer satisfaction items. The internal consistency estimate (Cronbach's alpha) for this overall satisfaction score is .91. This high reliability estimate for the three-item scale also suggests that these items measure one underlying construct. The descriptive statistics for this overall satisfaction score are presented in Table 8.6.

Please take a few moments to complete this survey. Your participation will help us to serve you better. Please return your completed survey by January 24 to enter a drawing to win a $100 gift certificate from one of our advertisers.

1. Are you: ☐ Male   ☐ Female

2. What is your age?   ☐ Under 18   ☐ 30–34   ☐ 45–49
   ☐ 18–24   ☐ 35–39   ☐ 50–54
   ☐ 25–29   ☐ 40–44   ☐ 55 or older

3. What is your marital status?   ☐ Married   ☐ Single (never married)
   ☐ Divorced/separated/widowed

4. Are you currently employed full or part time?
   ☐ Employed full time, that is, 30 hours or more a week.
   ☐ Not employed
   ☐ Employed part time, that is, less than 30 hours per week

5. What was your total household income, before taxes, in 2008? Please include all family members' incomes from all sources.
   ☐ Less than $20,000   ☐ $40,000–$49,999   ☐ $100,000–$149,999
   ☐ $20,000–$29,999   ☐ $50,000–$74,999   ☐ $150,000–$199,999
   ☐ $30,000–$39,999   ☐ $75,000–$99,999   ☐ $200,000–$299,999
   ☐ $300,000 or more

6. What is the highest level of education that you have attained? (Please check only one.)
   ☐ Some high school or less   ☐ Graduated four-year college
   ☐ Graduated high school   ☐ Postgraduate study without degree
   ☐ Attended college less than one year   ☐ Master's degree
   ☐ Attended college 1–3 years   ☐ Doctoral degree

7. Please select the category that best describes your type of employment. (Please check only one.)
   ☐ Full-time parent   ☐ Professional health care related
   ☐ Technical/administration/   ☐ Educator
      Sales/service   ☐ Executive/management
   ☐ Not employed   ☐ Other (please specify): _____

8. How frequently do you read a copy of *The Parent?*
   ☐ Monthly   ☐ Every other month   ☐ Less than every other month

9. Does your spouse read *The Parent?*   ☐ Yes   ☐ No

10. Including yourself, how many adults usually read or look through your copy of *The Parent?* (check one)
    ☐ 1   ☐ 2   ☐ 3   ☐ 4   ☐ 5   ☐ 6 or more

11. Please estimate how much time you spend reading *The Parent.*
    ☐ About 15 minutes   ☐ About 45 minutes   ☐ More than 1 hour
    ☐ About 30 minutes   ☐ About 1 hour

Customer Satisfaction Survey—Please indicate how much you agree with each of the following statements concerning *The Parent.*

	Strongly Disagree	Disagree	Neutral	Agree	Strongly Agree
1. Overall, I am satisfied with the quality of the articles in *The Parent.*	☐	☐	☐	☐	☐
2. The articles in *The Parent* are informative.	☐	☐	☐	☐	☐
3. I enjoy reading *The Parent.*	☐	☐	☐	☐	☐

Figure 8.5   *The Parent* reader survey.

1. Are you: Male Female	Percent
Male	3.0
Female	97.0

2. What is your age?	Percent
Under 18 years	1.5
18–24 years	3.5
25–29 years	15.7
30–34 years	20.2
35–39 years	30.3
40–44 years	20.7
45–49 years	6.1
50–54 years	1.5
55 or older	1.5

3. What is your marital status?	Percent
Married	85.4
Divorced/separated/widowed	9.0
Single (never married)	5.5

4. Are you currently employed full or part time?	Percent
Employed full time	34.5
Not employed	37.6
Employed part time	27.9

5. What is your total household income?	Percent
Less than $20,000	10.6
$20,000–$29,999	5.0
$30,000–$39,999	12.8
$40,000–$49,999	16.1
$50,000–$74,999	28.3
$75,000–$99,999	15.6
$100,000–$149,999	9.4
$150,000–$199,999	.6
$200,000–$299,999	1.7
$300,000 or more	0.0

6. What is the highest level of education that you have attained?	Percent
Some high school or less	.5
Graduated high school	2.1
Attended college less than one year	6.8
Attended college 1–3 years	19.5
Graduated four-year college	33.2
Postgraduate study w/o degree	12.1
Master's degree	21.6
Doctoral degree	4.2

7. Please select the category that best describes your type of employment.	Percent
Full-time parent	37.5
Technical/administration/ sales/service	18.8
Not employed	6.8
Professional health care related	10.8
Educator	14.8
Executive/management	7.4
Other (please specify):	4.0

8. How frequently do you read a copy of *The Parent?*	Percent
Monthly	74.1
Every other month	18.9
Less than every other month	7.0

9. Does your spouse read *The Parent?*	Percent
Yes	21.0
No	79.0

10. Including yourself, how many adults usually read or look through your copy of *The Parent?* (check one)	Percent
1	67.7
2	24.7
3	6.6
4	1.5
5	1.0
6 or more	1.5

11. Please estimate how much time you spend reading *The Parent.*	Percent
About 15 minutes	11.2
About 30 minutes	32.5
About 45 minutes	21.3
About 1 hour	21.8
More than 1 hour	13.2

	Percentage of respondents						
	SA	A	N	D	SD	Mean	StD
1. Overall, I am satisfied with the quality of the articles in *The Parent.*	1.5	0.5	9.0	64.3	24.6	4.10	0.69
2. The articles in *The Parent* are informative.	1.5	1.0	7.5	63.2	26.9	4.13	0.71
3. I enjoy reading *The Parent.*	1.5	1.0	2.6	53.6	41.3	4.32	0.72

Note: StD = standard deviation

Figure 8.6 Descriptive statistics of the reader survey.

Next, we can use this overall satisfaction score to make comparisons with other variables in our reader survey. For example, we might find that readers who spend more time reading *The Parent* are more satisfied with the newspaper. Other variables can be examined to determine their relationship with overall customer satisfaction. We will use analysis of variance (ANOVA) to test these possibilities (see Appendix I). The results of the analyses are presented in Table 8.7. Note that not all of the variables from the survey are used in the ANOVAs; many of the variables had a limited number of responses for certain categories (such as questions 1, 2, 3, and 10). Conducting analysis using these variables would not lead to reliable results.

Based on the ANOVAs presented in Table 8.7, we find that there are significant differences using the overall satisfaction score for some of the reader variables. Readers who report that their spouse reads *The Parent* also report higher levels of overall customer satisfaction compared to readers who indicate their spouse does not read *The Parent*. Readers who are more satisfied with *The Parent* also indicate that they spend more time reading that newspaper compared to readers who are less satisfied with *The Parent*. We can see that some of the results approach statistical significance. It is possible that, with additional survey data, the observed difference for these results would have become statistically significant.

Summary

The reader survey was designed to allow the publisher to obtain information regarding reader behavior, reader demographics, and customer satisfaction. The survey team was able to demonstrate that it is possible to obtain a high degree of confidence with a small level of tolerable error even with relatively small samples sizes. Also, the survey team showed that overall customer satisfaction was related to some of the reader's behavior (such as time spent reading the newspaper and whether spouse reads the newspaper—recommendation behavior). This information might be useful when establishing advertising rates for the newspaper. Comparing these scores with competitors' scores could establish a pricing structure in which

Table 8.6 Descriptive statistics for the overall newspaper satisfaction score.

	Mean	Standard deviation	Minimum value	Maximum value	Number of cases
Overall satisfaction	4.18	.65	1.00	5.00	201

Table 8.7 ANOVA using the overall newspaper satisfaction score.

Question 4. Are you currently employed full or part time?

Source	df	Sum of squares	Mean squares	F ratio	F prob.
Between groups	2	2.28	1.14	2.76	.07
Within groups	194	80.22	.41		
Total	196	82.50			

Question 6. What is the highest level of education that you have attained?

Source	df	Sum of squares	Mean squares	F ratio	F prob.
Between groups	7	5.10	.73	1.75	.10
Within groups	182	75.89	.42		
Total	189	80.99			

Question 7. Please select the category that best describes your type of employment.

Source	df	Sum of squares	Mean squares	F ratio	F prob.
Between groups	6	5.16	.86	1.98	.07
Within groups	169	73.58	.44		
Total		175.00	78.74		

Question 8. How frequently do you read a copy of *The Parent*?

Source	df	Sum of squares	Mean squares	F ratio	F prob.
Between groups	2	.54	.27	.64	.53
Within groups	198	83.37	.42		
Total	200	83.91			

Question 9. Does your spouse read *The Parent*?

Source	df	Sum of squares	Mean squares	F ratio	F prob.
Between groups	1	1.51	1.51	4.03	.05
Within groups	184	69.07	.38		
Total	185	70.58			

Means for overall satisfaction score:
    Yes = 4.36[a]   No = 4.14[a]

Question 11. Please estimate how much time you spend reading *The Parent*.

Source	df	Sum of squares	Mean squares	F ratio	F prob.
Between groups	4	6.12	1.53	3.85	.00
Within groups	192	76.27	.40		
Total	196	82.39			

Means for overall satisfaction score:

	About 15 minutes	About 30 minutes	About 45 minutes	About 1 hour	More than 1 hour
Means:	3.83[ab]	4.11	4.18	4.38[b]	4.41[a]

Note: Within each ANOVA, means with common superscripts are significantly different from each other.

scores on the satisfaction scale dictate cost of advertising in a given newspaper. If satisfaction scores are related to reader behavior (such as time spent reading the newspaper or spouse more likely to read the newspaper), then an advertiser would want to advertise in a newspaper where readers are highly satisfied and, consequently, are more likely to be exposed to the advertisements in the newspaper.

COFFEE SHOP

The next customer satisfaction survey example involves Wake Up, Inc., a company that owns coffee shops. The company wanted to determine the quality of the products and services it provides to its customers in order to increase levels of customer satisfaction. The primary customer group consists of customers who purchase coffee drinks and foods on the premises of the various locations.

The survey team consisted of the president of Wake Up, Inc. and other corporate representatives of the company: marketing, operations, quality, and research. The goal of the survey process was to obtain reliable, valid information by means of a simple, short survey instrument.

Questionnaire Development

The survey team used a preliminary survey to determine the factors important in defining the quality dimensions of its products and services. Specifically, the team wanted to know which factors customers use when deciding which coffee house to patronize. In this preliminary survey, customers were asked to rate the quality of the service they received and then to rank the top four quality factors they consider when selecting a coffee house. The factors used in the preliminary survey were developed based on the expertise of the survey team members. A total of 100 people were surveyed in this process. Table 8.8 contains the results of this initial survey.

From these results, the survey team concluded several things. First, they observed that clients were less satisfied with important quality dimensions and rated those poorly:

- Wait time
- Barista friendliness
- Food quality
- Price
- Coffee drink flavor

Table 8.8   Results from the preliminary survey.

Thank you for visiting Wake Up, Inc. To better serve you, we would like your input regarding our products and services. Please take some time to complete the following survey. For each question, indicate your response using the scale below. If the questions do not apply to you, circle NA (Not Applicable). Feel free to make any additional comments.

	1 Very Dissatisfied	2 Dissatisfied	3 Neither Satisfied nor Dissatisfied	4 Satisfied	5 Very Satisfied	NA Not Applicable	
1. Merchandise	0	0	14	45	41	0	4.27
2. Wait time	0	14	27	36	18	0	3.62
3. Food quality	0	0	14	55	32	0	4.18
4. Coffee drink flavor	0	0	5	68	27	0	4.23
5. Barista friendliness	0	5	18	55	18	0	3.90
6. Barista responsiveness	0	0	0	45	55	0	4.52
7. Barista knowledge	0	0	5	41	45	0	4.45
8. Barista attire	0	0	5	18	77	0	4.73
9. Cleanliness of store	0	0	0	41	59	0	4.59
10. Price	0	0	18	55	18	0	4.00
11. Overall service quality	0	0	9	50	41	0	4.32
12. Overall product quality	0	0	5	55	41	0	4.36

What factors are important to you when selecting a coffee house? Please check the top four (4) most important dimensions from the list below.

	Percent
1. Barista friendliness	86
2. Price	23
3. Barista knowledge	27
4. Wait time	73
5. Coffee drink flavor	95
6. Location	45
7. Food quality	68
8. Special products	0
9. Jazz shows	0
10. Coffee publication	0
11. Reputation	5
12. Other:	9

The team also observed, from the ranking portion of the survey, which five of the 12 possible factors were checked most often:

- Wait time

- Barista friendliness

- Food quality

- Coffee drink flavor

- Location

The goal of the survey process was to obtain reliable and valid information from the customers regarding important quality dimensions of the services and products. With this survey, the company hoped to be able to monitor the levels of customer satisfaction and see improvement over time in satisfaction scores. Although the preliminary survey could have been used, its length precluded its final use. Such long surveys generally result in a lower response rate than a shorter survey. Additionally, many factors the survey team originally thought would define the company's products and services were not ranked by the customers. Furthermore, customers gave high marks on many of the dimensions; including those items in a survey would add minimal utility when compared to a brief questionnaire that focused on more important factors. As a result, the survey team decided to select only "important" factors for the final version of the questionnaire. The determination of these "important" factors was based on the results of the preliminary survey and the input of the survey team. Two additional questions were included to obtain overall ratings of service quality and product quality. The final survey instrument included the questions illustrated in Figure 8.7.

Administration of the Survey

Administration of the client satisfaction survey did not include a sampling component. Instead, 3-inch by 5-inch Business Reply Mail postcards were placed at the area where the purchase transaction takes place, available to all customers. Customers who wished to participate picked up a card, answered the survey questions, and dropped the card in the mail. This is an easy way to collect customer information, but it may not result in a random sample of customers. At the corporate office of Wake Up, Inc., the company president read each card. If scores were considered low (1s and 2s), customers were sent a letter of apology. Next, data from the survey cards were compiled in a database for later management and analysis.

Results

The results of the customer satisfaction survey, covering the first three quarters of 1995, are presented here. The response rate was around 5 percent, resulting in a total of 985 completed surveys. The percentage of response for each response option, and the mean and standard deviation for each item, are presented in Table 8.9.

Here we see that scores, overall, are generally positive, almost all above 4.0 (Satisfied). Because of an adequate sample size, there is not much sampling error associated with these survey results. Given a 95 percent confidence level, we can calculate the confidence interval for each item:

Wait time	$CI = 4.15 \pm 2 \times .03$; $CI = 4.09 < X < 4.21$
Barista friendliness	$CI = 4.42 \pm 2 \times .02$; $CI = 4.38 < X < 4.46$
Coffee drink flavor	$CI = 4.42 \pm 2 \times .02$; $CI = 4.38 < X < 4.46$
Food quality	$CI = 4.40 \pm 2 \times .03$; $CI = 4.34 < X < 4.46$
Overall service quality	$CI = 4.39 \pm 2 \times .02$; $CI = 4.35 < X < 4.43$
Overall product quality	$CI = 4.42 \pm 2 \times .02$; $CI = 4.38 < X < 4.46$

Please send us feedback on this report. For each of the following six questions, indicate your response using the scale below. If the questions do not apply to you, circle NA (Not Applicable). Feel free to make additional comments.

Name:_____

Address:_____

_____

Date of service:_____

	Very Dissatisfied	Dissatisfied	Neither Satisfied nor Dissatisfied	Satisfied	Very Satisfied	Not Applicable
1. Wait time	1	2	3	4	5	NA
2. Barista friendliness	1	2	3	4	5	NA
3. Coffee drink flavor	1	2	3	4	5	NA
4. Food quality	1	2	3	4	5	NA
5. Overall service quality	1	2	3	4	5	NA
6. Overall product quality	1	2	3	4	5	NA

Comments:_____

Figure 8.7 Wake Up, Inc. client satisfaction survey.

Table 8.9   Descriptive statistics (percentages, means, standard deviation, standard error of the mean) for each item.

Percentage	VD	D	N	S	VS	Mean	SD[1]	SE[2]
1. Wait time	3.0	5.2	14.3	28.8	48.7	4.15	1.04	.03
2. Barista friendliness	0.2	1.0	7.9	38.3	52.5	4.42	0.70	.02
3. Coffee drink flavor	0.7	1.3	6.5	38.7	52.8	4.42	0.73	.02
4. Food quality	0.9	1.9	8.0	34.7	54.6	4.40	0.79	.03
5. Overall service quality	1.0	1.8	7.3	37.2	52.7	4.39	0.78	.02
6. Overall product quality	0.7	2.4	6.5	35.6	54.9	4.42	0.77	.02

Note: N = 985; SD[1] = standard deviation; SE[2] = standard error of the mean

A next step would be to determine which quality factors are highly related to the general measures of service quality and product quality. This is accomplished by examining the correlations among the items in the customer satisfaction measure. These correlations are reported in Table 8.10.

As we can see, all items are somewhat correlated with each other. We see that wait time correlates more highly with service quality than with product quality. Additionally, we see that barista friendliness is correlated the highest (but just slightly more) with service quality than with the rest. Of these same four, food quality and coffee drink flavor are correlated the highest with product quality. These findings suggest that a good way to increase service quality would be to focus on issues related to the friendliness of the staff. Higher levels of satisfaction with the staff might lead to higher levels of overall satisfaction with the service. To increase satisfaction levels related to product quality, however, our efforts might best be focused on factors that directly affect the quality of the tangible products (such as food quality and coffee drink flavor). To study the effect these four factors had on the outcome variables, I conducted a stepwise regression analysis. The results of these two analyses are presented in Table 8.11.

In Table 8.11, we see that all variables are predictive of the two outcome variables. The two most important variables in predicting service quality were barista friendliness and wait time. The other two variables, although significantly predictive of service quality, do not account for a substantial amount of the variance in service quality. As for product quality, coffee drink flavor and food quality are the best predictors. The remaining variables do not account for a substantial amount of the variance in product quality after the first two variables have been included in the equation.

Table 8.10   Correlations among the items in the client satisfaction questionnaire.

	Q1	Q2	Q3	Q4	Q5
Q1: Wait time					
Q2: Barista friendliness	.4780				
Q3: Coffee drink flavor	.4366	.7676			
Q4: Food quality	.4126	.7263	.8269		
Q5: Service quality	.6539	.6893	.6723	.6724	
Q6: Product quality	.4720	.7474	.8078	.8294	.7589

Note: N = 898 to 917. All correlations significant at the .001 level.

Table 8.11   Stepwide regression analysis of the Wake Up, Inc. satisfaction questionnaire.

	Subscale	$\Delta R2$	*p*
Overall service quality	Barista friendliness	.4751	.01
	Wait time	.1364	.01
	Food quality	.0446	.01
	Coffee drink flavor	.0042	.01
	Total for four variables in the equation	.6603	.01
Overall product quality	Coffee drink flavor	.6879	.01
	Food quality	.0470	.01
	Barista friendliness	.0169	.01
	Wait time	.0059	.01
	Total for four variables in the equation	.7577	.01

With this knowledge, we can now create control charts using the customer satisfaction data to help us monitor our processes. For illustrative purposes, I will use the current data to calculate the control charts. Figures 8.8–8.11 are control charts for the four quality factors in the Wake Up, Inc. customer satisfaction questionnaire. The sample unit is one month. Each figure includes both the $\bar{x}$ chart and the s chart. Recall that the $\bar{x}$ chart monitors

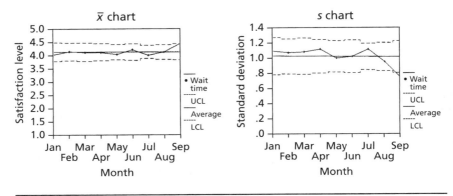

Figure 8.8 Control charts ($\bar{x}$ chart and s chart) for wait time.

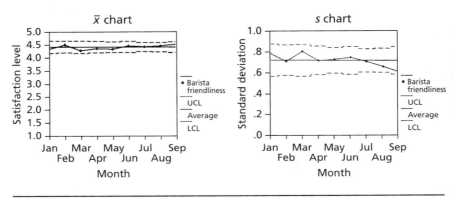

Figure 8.9 Control charts ($\bar{x}$ chart and s chart) for barista friendliness.

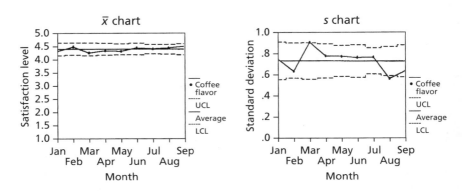

Figure 8.10 Control charts ($\bar{x}$ chart and s chart) for coffee drink flavor.

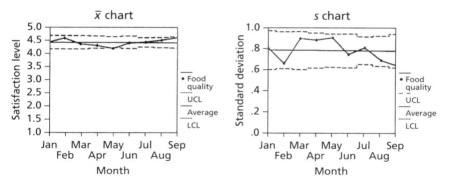

Figure 8.11   Control charts ($\bar{x}$ chart and s chart) for food quality.

the mean of the variable while the s chart monitors the standard deviation of the variable. These two types of control chart are typically presented together, allowing you to see how the mean and the range of data vary from sample to sample.

The upper and lower control limits vary from month to month due to the fluctuating sample size across the various months. Nonetheless, these control charts are interpreted the same way as those presented in Chapter 7.

We see that the respective processes related to wait time, barista friendliness, coffee drink flavor, and food quality are fairly stable across the first three quarters of the given year. For wait time in the last month reported (September), however, we see that the s chart indicates a process that is out of control. The variability in September is quite small relative to all the other months. This lack of variability might be associated with the high mean in the corresponding month in the $\bar{x}$ chart for wait time (notice that the average score in the corresponding month almost exceeds the UCL). Because possible scores can be only as high as the given scale (five-point scale), a high average score for that particular month indicates that most scores are clustered at the high end of the scale, thus minimizing the variability of possible responses. Subsequent monitoring of these control charts will help us determine whether this is a plausible finding.

The monitoring of these variables (barista friendliness and food quality) with control charts helps us determine the stability and change of the system that is driving the respective scores. Control charts would help the company determine if changes were due to common causes or special causes. Consequently, the company would know when, and if, changes were needed in the process.

Summary

We have seen that the development of the customer survey helped the survey team identify the important quality characteristics associated with their services and products. The use of a preliminary survey indicated what types of items should be used in the final, shorter version of the customer satisfaction questionnaire. The final six-item questionnaire was a useful vehicle with which customers could deliver feedback to the company on important quality dimensions. This survey was used for several purposes: (1) to determine current standing on customer satisfaction levels, (2) to identify what factors are most highly associated with overall satisfaction (both service and product), and (3) to monitor the work processes that are responsible for the scores through control charting techniques. Through these various uses of survey data, Wake Up, Inc. will ensure that its customers are an integral part of its quality-related measurements. Consequently, these data will allow Wake Up, Inc. to make informed decisions regarding quality improvement strategies that will increase customer satisfaction.

CONCLUSIONS

This book presents practical guidelines for the development and use of customer satisfaction questionnaires.

Chapter 2 discussed methods of determining customer requirements or quality dimensions. Customers judge services and products according to these dimensions. It is important to identify a comprehensive list of these quality dimensions because they determine the content of the questionnaire. If a customer requirement is not identified in this first step, the questionnaire will be unable to assess an important element.

Developing and evaluating questionnaires is another important step in understanding customer attitudes. In Chapter 3, measurement issues highlighted the importance of reliability and validity of scales. Reliability is important when determining the amount of error that is associated with our measures. The various methods of estimating the different forms of reliability were presented in this chapter. Validity deals with the meaning of the scores from our questionnaire.

Chapter 4 presented various rating formats used to quantify the quality of the service or product. Depending on the expected use of the data, either a checklist or a rating scale may be appropriate. A checklist format is useful for providing attribute data; a rating scale provides variable data. Chapter 4 also included characteristics of good items, as well as information that should be included in the introduction of the questionnaire.

Chapter 5 presented information on various methods of sampling and discussed two approaches to random selection sampling. The determination of sample size was presented to allow you to see how sample size affects the precision of our findings. Also discussed in this chapter were methods to increase response rates for mail surveys.

Chapter 6 included an in-depth look at the measurement and meaning of customer loyalty. Applied research illustrated the problems regarding the Net Promoter Score claims and helped clarify the multidimensionality of customer loyalty. The use of new customer loyalty indices highlighted how companies can grow their business through both new and existing customers.

In Chapter 7 we saw that customer satisfaction questionnaires can be used to monitor ongoing business processes, to highlight general strengths and weaknesses, to evaluate intervention programs, and to help determine the most important customer requirements. Finally, a discussion on customer loyalty management outlined how a company can improve customer loyalty at the individual- (micro approach) and group-level (macro approach).

Chapter 8 discussed companies that have used customer satisfaction questionnaires in various industries. The examples in this chapter illustrated how companies have applied some of the guidelines presented in this book and how they used the information obtained from the surveys.

The use of customer satisfaction questionnaires has increased greatly in the past few years. Companies want to distinguish themselves from their competitors in their ability to satisfy customers. The Baldrige Award places a strong emphasis on customer satisfaction. A company's ability to benefit from customer-related information is determined by the quality of the measurement system. The measurement system often takes the form of customer satisfaction questionnaires designed to assess various dimensions of service or product quality. If information obtained from questionnaires is to be useful, questionnaires should reflect reliable and valid information. I hope this book has provided users of customer satisfaction questionnaires with useful guidance for developing and using these instruments.

Introduction
to Appendices

There is an increasing use of data in aiding the decision-making process. To understand data and how it can help in decision making, we need to summarize and interpret the data. The appendices provide a basic foundation for the interpretation of data, including specific examples using data resulting from questionnaires and other business processes and general examples.

A basic understanding of statistics is desirable but not necessary to grasp the fundamental principles that will be presented. The appendices are not intended to make the reader proficient in these statistical techniques. Many textbooks cover these topics, and interested readers may consult the bibliography to learn more about these techniques. Although formulae for calculating various statistical indices are presented in this text, these statistical procedures usually require the assistance of a computer and appropriate statistical software because hand calculations are not practical with large data sets. The text presents formulae to allow you to see how these indices are, in fact, calculated. A final note: in some situations, you should consult an expert on these statistical techniques. Expert judgment is often necessary for interpreting statistical results.

The topics of the appendices fall into two major sections. The first (covered in Appendices C through F) deals with descriptive statistics and sampling distributions. Specifically, Appendix C introduces the measurement process and presents four levels of measurement often used in data collection. Appendix D discusses frequency as a way of summarizing data and also covers probability and distributions. Appendix E introduces measures of central tendency and variability as a means of summarizing data. Appendix F introduces one of the most important topics in the use of data in decision making: sampling error. Readers must thoroughly understand this topic to appreciate subsequent appendices.

The second section of topics deals with the use of data in hypothesis testing. Appendix G covers decision making and hypothesis testing. It outlines the elements involved in making a decision and formally presents the concept of hypothesis testing, including the types of errors that may occur in any decision-making situation. Appendix H introduces the *t*-test procedure, which allows us to examine the difference between two groups of numbers. Appendix I presents the analysis of variance procedure (ANOVA), which helps us examine the difference between two or more groups of numbers. Appendix J introduces the topic of correlational analysis, a procedure for summarizing the linear relationship between two variables. This appendix also includes a discussion on the regression equation for a straight line. Appendix K discusses the use of factor analysis. This appendix provides only a brief introduction to a powerful technique in questionnaire development. Appendix L contains a table of random numbers, which will help you in establishing your random samples.

Appendix A

Critical Incidents Interview Forms

Interview #_____ for critical incidents

Positive examples
1.
2.
3.
4.
5.
6.
7.
8.
9.
10.

Negative examples
1.
2.
3.
4.
5.
6.
7.
8.
9.
10.

Appendix B
Satisfaction Items and Customer Requirement Forms

Satisfaction item 1:
Critical incidents:

Satisfaction item 2:
Critical incidents:

Satisfaction item 3:
Critical incidents:

Customer requirement 1:

Satisfaction items:

1.

2.

3.

4.

5.

6.

7.

8.

Customer requirement 2:

Satisfaction items:

1.

2.

3.

4.

5.

6.

7.

8.

Customer requirement 3:

Satisfaction items:

1.

2.

3.

4.

5.

6.

7.

8.

Appendix C
Measurement Scales

Measurement scales are the means by which we assign a number to an object or entity. The number on the scale represents some characteristics of that object or entity. Stevens (1951) divided measurement scales into four types: nominal, ordinal, interval, and ratio. The degree to which these scales differ is reflected in the degree to which arithmetic operations make sense with the values of the entity represented by the numbers on the scale. The discussion of each scale will clarify this.

NOMINAL SCALE

A nominal scale categorizes objects. These objects are mutually exclusive, and the numbers on the nominal scale reflect only that the objects are different from one another. For example, we might use a nominal scale to categorize customers on the basis of their marital status.

Single people are assigned a 1.
Married people are assigned a 2.
Divorced people are assigned a 3.

We may also use a nominal scale to label a set of stores.

Bob's Barn is assigned a 1.
Tom's Tent is assigned a 2.
Stephen's Store is assigned a 3.
Marissa's Mall is assigned a 4.

Let's look at arithmetic operations using the scale values for customers' marital status. Some operations that would *not* make sense are addition and subtraction. For example, a Stephen's Store (3) minus a Tom's Tent (2) would not equal a Bob's Barn (1). The only arithmetic operations that can be used on a nominal scale are the equality and inequality operations. For example, within our present store categorization system, a Stephen's Store (3) is the same as another Stephen's Store (3). Also 1 ≠ 2 indicates that a Bob's Barn is not the same as a Tom's Tent.

Because the values on the nominal scale represent categories, they can also be identified by different symbols, such as letters of the alphabet. For example, a Bob's Barn might be labeled an "A," a Tom's Tent as "B," a Stephen's Store as "C," and a Marissa's Mall as "D."

ORDINAL SCALE

An ordinal scale uses numbers to order objects with respect to some characteristic. For example, we can place customers in order according to their satisfaction level. If person A is more satisfied than person B, and person B is more satisfied than person C, then person A is more satisfied than person C. Using an ordinal scale, we may assign a number to each of these people and rank them from least satisfied (person C) to most satisfied (person A). The numbers corresponding to this satisfaction ordinal scale could be:

> Person C is a 1.
> Person B is a 2.
> Person A is a 3.

Let's look at some arithmetic operations applied to ordinal scales. Equality/inequality operations can be applied to ordinal scales. For example, in an equality/inequality operation, we can say that person C (1) is not equal to person A (3). We can also use the operations of less than (<) and greater than (>) on ordinal scales. Statements such as 3 > 2 and 1 < 3 make sense, indicating that person A is more satisfied than person B and person C is less satisfied than person A, respectively.

Another example of ordinal scales is reflected in the ranking of companies on some variable. For example, in studying a wide variety of companies, a research firm may assess the satisfaction level of its customers. In a final report, the research firm ranks the companies from highest to lowest in terms of its customers' overall satisfaction level. Suppose the study included five companies. The company with the highest average score on the customer satisfaction questionnaire would be ranked 5; the company with the second highest score would be ranked 4; and so forth:

> Company A is a 5.
> Company B is a 4.
> Company C is a 3.
> Company D is a 2.
> Company E is a 1.

Although ordinal scales allow us to order objects, they do not allow us to determine the distance between the objects with respect to the characteristic being measured. For the example of ranking customers in terms of satisfaction, we know the order of the people but do not know how much more satisfied one person is relative to another. Also, ranking the companies does not tell us how much more satisfied company A's customers are compared to customers of other companies. This inability to determine differences between objects relates to the ordinal scale's lack of a unit of measurement.

INTERVAL SCALE

An interval scale orders things so that differences between scale values are equal, because the interval scale has a unit of measurement. One example is the Fahrenheit scale.

We can use more arithmetic operations with interval scale values. In addition to the equality/inequality and ordering operations, we can perform subtraction. For example, the difference between 50°F and 40°F equals the difference between 120°F and 110°F.

Attitude questionnaires are assumed to possess the features of an interval scale. If this assumption is true, we can perform useful arithmetic operations with the data from such questionnaires, which will aid in the interpretation of the data.

RATIO SCALE

A ratio scale is similar to the interval scale in that it possesses a unit of measurement. The ratio scale has one additional feature: a meaningful zero point. An example of a ratio scale is the measurement of length. All arithmetic operations are meaningful for the ratio scale. This includes equality/inequality, ordering, subtraction, addition, and division. Table C.1 summarizes the characteristics of measurement scales.

Table C.1 Types of measurement scales and the functional uses of each.

		Functional uses			
		Establish equality/ inequality	Establish rank ordering	Establish equal differences between scale points	Establish zero point
Scale types	Nominal	yes	no	no	no
	Ordinal	yes	yes	no	no
	Interval	yes	yes	yes	no
	Ratio	yes	yes	yes	yes

MEASUREMENT SCALES
IN CUSTOMER SATISFACTION

Some of the measurement scales can be used in customer satisfaction questionnaires to categorize customers (nominal scale) and differentiate customers along some continuum (interval scale). Development of questionnaires to assess customers' perceptions and attitudes is based on the notion that the scales possess features found in the interval scale. In addition, we imply the use of a scale when we rank companies on the basis of their quality (ordinal scale). The ranking of companies is best accompanied by evidence that the ranking reflects meaningful, statistically significant differences between companies (see Appendix F).

Example

A hospital wanted to determine the quality of its physicians and front office staff. The survey was to be used to track this information over time and to compare the various office locations across the western region, where the company has its offices. The survey is presented in Figure C.1.

We can divide the various questions into the types of measurement scales. Nominal scales are illustrated by the following questions: location of exam, name of patient, gender of patient, and name of physician. There is some debate as to the classification of rating scales for surveys. While some might classify rating scales as ordinal measures, we make the assumption that rating scales possess features of interval measures. Ratio scales are illustrated by the following questions: time with doctor and wait time (time you saw your doctor minus the time of your appointment).

The goal at Doc in a Box is to ensure you get the best service possible. Please take the time to answer the following questions. Your opinions are important to us. We will use this information to help us learn how to meet your needs in the best way we possibly can. To mail, please fold at the lines on the back of this sheet and seal with tape and drop in any mailbox. Thank you.

Date of exam:_____ Location of exam:_____

Name of patient: _____

Physician's name: _____

For each of the following questions, please indicate whether the phrase describes your experience at Doc in the Box. Please use the rating scale below. Circle your response for each question.

Y = Yes, describes my experience   N = No, does not describe my experience   ? = Not sure

Physician Quality

	Yes	No	Not Sure
1. Introduced himself/herself to me.	Y	N	?
2. Asked me how I was injured/became ill.	Y	N	?
3. Listened to me.	Y	N	?
4. Treated me with respect.	Y	N	?
5. Was professional in doing the examination.	Y	N	?
6. Spent enough time with me (not rushed).	Y	N	?

7. Please rate your overall experience of the exam, using the following scale (circle your response).

Terrible	Poor	Fair	Good	Excellent
1	2	3	4	5

Office Quality

	Yes	No	Not Sure
1. Appointment was at a convenient time.	Y	N	?
2. Waiting area was clean.	Y	N	?
3. Waiting room was comfortable.	Y	N	?
4. Examination room was clean.	Y	N	?
5. Office staff treated me with respect.	Y	N	?
6. I received a call from Doc in the Box reminding me of my appointment.	Y	N	?
7. Office staff answered my questions.	Y	N	?
8. Office staff was professional.	Y	N	?

9. Time of your appointment _____ A.M. P.M. Time you saw your doctor: _____ A.M. P.M.

Thank you for your time and for completing this survey. Please place in a mailbox. There is room for comments on the reverse side of this form.

Figure C.1   Patient satisfaction questionnaire.

Appendix D

Frequencies, Percentages, Probabilities, Histograms, and Distributions

D
ata can be overwhelming. Often we are confronted with large data sets consisting of hundreds of scores. We need a way of summarizing the data to make some sense of it. This appendix will discuss one way of summarizing large data sets with the use of frequencies and histograms.

FREQUENCIES

Table D.1 lists scores from a hypothetical study examining the level of customer satisfaction of a given company. The data set contains 48 scores, each representing one person's average score on the customer satisfaction questionnaire. Upon examination, we see that scores vary somewhat, ranging from a low of 1.4 to a high of 4.6. To gain a better understanding of the data, we need to summarize the scores in a simple format.

One way of summarizing data is to calculate the frequency of occurrence of a specific value, or how often that given value occurs in our data set. To calculate frequencies, we first rank the scores from lowest to highest (see Table D.2). After the ranking, we determine the frequency of occurrence of each value. We see that the value of 1.4 occurred only once. Therefore, 1.4 has a frequency of one. Likewise, the value of 2.5 has a frequency of four.

Although calculating frequencies for each specific value will help summarize the information, the amount of information can still be overwhelming. For example, with characteristics measured in small increments, we may obtain many values, each occurring with little frequency. Calculating the frequency of each value might not be enough to simplify the data. Therefore, when calculating frequencies, we usually group values with similar scores into a particular class. Then we calculate frequencies for these class values.

Table D.1   Hypothetical data set.

2.3	4.3	3.3	1.5
2.5	2.7	3.4	3.2
4.1	3.8	3.7	2.9
3.0	2.7	2.5	3.4
4.6	2.3	2.1	2.3
3.7	3.6	1.4	3.2
1.5	1.6	1.7	3.6
4.0	4.1	3.4	2.1
3.3	3.1	3.5	4.4
2.5	2.8	3.9	2.0
1.7	2.5	2.9	3.8
4.2	2.1	3.9	2.4

Table D.2   Data from Table D.1 ranked from smallest to largest.

1.4	2.3	3.1	3.7
1.5	2.4	3.2	3.8
1.5	2.5	3.2	3.8
1.6	2.5	3.3	3.9
1.7	2.5	3.3	3.9
1.7	2.5	3.4	4.0
2.0	2.7	3.4	4.1
2.1	2.7	3.4	4.1
2.1	2.8	3.5	4.2
2.1	2.9	3.6	4.3
2.3	2.9	3.6	4.4
2.3	3.0	3.7	4.6

CLASS INTERVALS

A class interval represents a range in which a set of values is included. Creating class intervals is a process of dividing the scores into specified equal intervals. Each class interval is defined by a lower bound and an upper bound. The lower bound represents the lowest possible score that can be included in the interval; the upper bound represents the highest possible score. Using the data set in Table D.2, we can create a class interval with the width of 0.4 to represent the scores. Starting with a lower bound of 1.0, the first class interval would include scores ranging from a low of 1.0 to a high of 1.4. The second class interval would include scores ranging from 1.5 to 1.9. The last class interval would include scores ranging from 4.5 to 4.9. Table D.3 presents these class intervals and the frequency of values that occur in the class.

We use arbitrary numbers to select class intervals and determine the width of each interval. It has been shown that, if continuous data are divided into intervals, you lose less information about the data by creating more intervals. A reasonable number of intervals is seven (Shaw, Huffman, and Haviland 1987), although more intervals would result in less information loss.

PERCENTAGES

Another way of looking at the frequency of values is through the use of percentages. A percentage reflects the proportion of scores of a particular value. The percentage for a particular value is calculated by dividing the frequency of a given value by the total number of scores in the data set. For

Table D.3 Frequencies for the class variable.

Class interval	Frequency	Percentage
1.0 to 1.4	1	2.1%
1.5 to 1.9	5	10.4%
2.0 to 2.4	8	16.7%
2.5 to 2.9	9	18.8%
3.0 to 3.4	9	18.8%
3.5 to 3.9	9	18.8%
4.0 to 4.4	6	12.5%
4.5 to 4.9	1	2.1%
Total	48	100.0%

our data, we see that the percentage of people with scores of 2.5 to 2.9 is 18.8 percent (9/48), and the percentage of people with scores ranging from 4.0 to 4.9 is 14.6 percent (7/48). The total of the percentages for a given question should be 100 percent (given rounding errors).

The percentage is sometimes preferred to the frequency since it incorporates the total number of scores into its calculation. A frequency of 50 may not tell us all we want to know about the data. A frequency of 50 in one sample of scores may indicate a large percentage (for example, when sample size is 60), while in another sample a frequency of 50 may indicate a minute percentage (for example, when sample size is 1,000,000). Thus, before interpreting the magnitude of the frequency, we should be aware of the total sample size.

CONSTRUCTING FREQUENCY DISTRIBUTIONS OF THE INTERVALS

We can graphically represent the frequencies of the class intervals. The graph is formally called a *histogram*. The histogram aids in summarizing the data beyond the lone use of frequencies since it captures many pieces of information in a single picture. The histogram not only indicates the frequency of each value, but also roughly indicates the range of the data (lowest to highest value) and the shape of the distribution.

The histogram has two axes. The horizontal axis (sometimes referred to as the *X axis* or *abscissa*) represents the variable or class interval. The vertical axis (sometimes referred to as the *Y axis* or *ordinate*) represents the frequency for a variable or class interval.

The horizontal axis is scaled by the midpoint of each class interval. Therefore, for the data in Table D.3, the horizontal axis would be scaled by eight values, each value representing the midpoint of it's class interval. The midpoints are 1.2, 1.7, 2.2, 2.7, 3.2, 3.7, 4.2, and 4.7. The histogram appears in Figure D.1.

Frequency tables and histograms are both useful tools for summarizing data. The frequency table reflects the frequency of occurrence of specific values or the frequency of values for a specific class interval. The histogram is a graphic illustration of the frequency table.

We can calculate frequencies for variables that are on any scale of measurement (nominal, ordinal, interval, and ratio). For example, a questionnaire could include various questions pertaining to satisfaction levels as well as questions asking for demographic information. The demographic portion could include questions pertaining to sex and age.

If the questionnaire was distributed to 150 people, we could subsequently calculate the frequency or proportion of males versus females and also determine the frequency or proportion of a given age group.

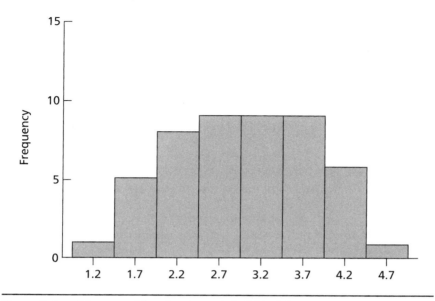

Figure D.1 Histogram of the class intervals in Table D.3.

The frequencies for the sex variable (nominal) and age variable (ratio) are listed in Table D.4. The frequencies indicate that the sample consists of more males than females. In terms of percentages, we see that males represent 58 percent (87/150) of respondents and females represent 42 percent of respondents. Also, this sample consists of a large group of people aged 36 to 45 years.

Table D.4 Frequencies and percentages for the variables of sex and age.

Sex	Frequency	%	Age	Frequency	%
M	87	58.0	0–15	0	0.0
F	63	42.0	16–25	3	2.0
			26–35	44	29.3
			36–45	64	42.7
			46–55	25	16.7
			56–older	44	9.3
Total	150	100.0%	Total	150	100.0%

DISTRIBUTIONS

The histogram in Figure D.1 can also be called a *distribution of scores*. Although there are many forms of distributions, such as a bimodal (two-humped) distribution and a unimodal (one-humped) distribution, I will present a special type called a *normal distribution*. The normal distribution is a symmetric, bell-shaped distribution. Many of the things we measure in our environment can be described by a symmetric, bell-shaped distribution. For example, if the heights of many people were plotted, the shape of the histogram would form a normal distribution.

DETERMINING PROBABILITIES FROM DISTRIBUTIONS

Given a distribution, we can calculate probabilities of various events. For example, we may have measured the height of 1000 people. The data of height forms a normal distribution described by some mean and variance (see distribution of $n = 1$ in Figure F.1). Now let's say we were to select one person at random from this sample. What is the probability that the height of that person is greater than 65″?

We determine the probability by dividing the number of people who are taller than 65″ by the total number of people in the sample. We can also determine the probability by calculating the area under the curve to the right of 65″. We can describe this area as a percentage of people who are taller than 65″. We can then transform this percentage into a probability by dividing the value by 100.

As we increase the height of our criterion to 70″, we see that the probability of selecting a person greater than that criterion decreases, since the area under the curve to the right of the criterion decreases.

Example

The percentage of respondents for each of the questions is presented in Table D.5.

As we can see in Table D.5, the distribution of scores is fairly evenly spread across the three quarters of the year. Additionally, the surveys are from all of the offices in the western region. Most of the surveys represent our San Jose, Yakima, Tacoma, and Spokane offices. San Diego and Sonoma have the least number of surveys in our sample. Furthermore, a little more than half of the surveys (53.4 percent) are from offices located in the state of Washington. Looking at the percentage of responses for our survey questions, many of the customers indicate a "Yes" to the questions. The percent of "Yes" responses range from a low of 53.4 percent to a high of 99.1 percent.

Table D.5 Frequencies and percentages for the patient satisfaction questionnaire.

Quarter of survey	Frequency	Percentage
1st quarter	462	34.4
2nd quarter	466	34.7
3rd quarter	414	30.8

Month of survey	Frequency	Percentage
January	153	11.4
February	149	11.1
March	160	11.9
April	155	11.5
May	169	12.6
June	142	10.6
July	133	9.9
August	138	10.3
September	143	10.7

Office location	Frequency	Percentage
Yakima	180	13.4
Seattle	176	13.1
San Francisco	150	11.2
Tacoma	180	13.4
San Jose	181	13.5
Sacramento	155	11.5
Spokane	180	13.4
San Diego	58	4.3
Sonoma	82	6.1

Office location	Frequency	Percentage
Washington	716	53.4
California	626	46.6

Physician Quality

	Yes	No	Not Sure
1. Introduced himself/herself to me.	1297 (97.4%)	23 (1.7%)	12 (0.9%)
2. Asked me how I was injured/became ill.	1268 (95.3%)	52 (3.9%)	11 (0.8%)
3. Listened to me.	1186 (90.5%)	60 (4.6%)	64 (4.9%)
4. Treated me with respect.	1256 (94.5%)	33 (2.5%)	40 (3.0%)
5. Was professional in doing the examination.	1261 (95.2%)	33 (2.5%)	31 (2.3%)
6. Spent enough time with me (not rushed).	1078 (83.2%)	118 (9.1%)	100 (7.7%)

7. Please rate your overall experience of the exam, using the following scale (circle your response.)

Terrible	Poor	Fair	Good	Excellent
21 (1.6%)	41 (3.2%)	178 (13.9%)	608 (47.4%)	435 (33.9)

(Continued)

(Continued)

Table D.5   Frequencies and percentages for the patient satisfaction questionnaire.

Office Quality

	Yes	No	Not Sure
1. Appointment was at a convenient time.	1156 (87.9%)	143 (10.9%)	16 (1.2%)
2. Waiting area was clean.	1319 (99.1%)	10 (0.8%)	2 (0.1%)
3. Waiting room was comfortable.	1288 (96.9%)	27 (2.0%)	14 (1.1%)
4. Examination room was clean.	1312 (98.7%)	10 (0.8%)	7 (0.8%)
5. Office staff treated me with respect.	1302 (98.1%)	18 (1.4%)	7 (0.5%)
6. I received a call from Doc in the Box reminding me of my appointment.	703 (53.4%)	554 (42.1%)	60 (4.6%)
7. Office staff answered my questions.	1205 (94.8%)	33 (2.6%)	33 (2.6%)
8. Office staff was professional.	1291 (97.9%)	16 (1.2%)	12 (0.9%)

Figure D.2 shows a histogram of the responses for the overall rating. As is indicated, most of the respondents indicate a "Good" or "Excellent" response.

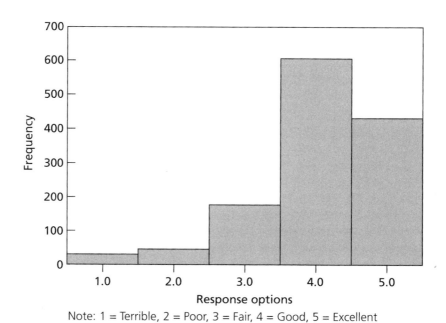

Note: 1 = Terrible, 2 = Poor, 3 = Fair, 4 = Good, 5 = Excellent

Figure D.2   Histogram of the overall rating of the exam.

SUMMARY

This appendix introduced various ways of describing and presenting data. Frequencies and percentages convey the occurrence of values in the data set. Histograms are a useful way of presenting data. They convey the frequency of values as well as the range of the data set. Histograms can also be thought of as distributions. The probability of a given event occurring can also be determined using the distribution.

Appendix E
Descriptive Statistics

The use of frequencies and histograms is one way of summarizing data (see Appendix D). Another way to summarize large data sets is with the use of summary indices, which describe the shape of the histogram. Two types of summary indices help us understand the data: central tendency and variability.

CENTRAL TENDENCY

One way of summarizing data is to determine the center or middle point of scores. Measures of central tendency allow us to determine roughly the center of the scores in the data set. For example, we may measure the satisfaction level of 10 customers. The data are presented in Table E.1. The scores vary considerably. We can capture a lot of information about these scores by determining the middle point. By doing so, we get an estimate of where the scores fall. Three statistics that describe the central tendency are the mean, median, and mode.

Table E.1 Hypothetical data set.

Customer	X
1	4
2	1
3	3
4	2
5	4
6	1
7	5
8	4
9	3
10	2

MEAN

The mean is the arithmetic average of all scores in the data set. It is calculated by adding all the scores in the data set and dividing by the total number of observations in the data set. The formula is

$$\bar{x} = \frac{\Sigma x_i}{n}$$

where n = the number of observations in the data set and Σx_i is the sum of all scores in the data set.

Using the formula, we can calculate the mean of the data in Table E.1.

$$\bar{x} = \frac{4 + 1 + 3 + 2 + 4 + 1 + 5 + 4 + 3 + 2}{10} = 2.9$$

MEDIAN

Another measure of central tendency is the median. The median is the middlemost score after the data have been rank ordered from either highest to lowest or lowest to highest. In other words, half of the scores have values larger than the median and half have values smaller than the median. If the data set has an odd number of scores, the median is the $(n + 1/2)$th largest score in the data set. If the data set has an even number of scores, the median is the average of two numbers, the $(n/2)$th largest score and the $(n/2 + 1)$th largest score. Table E.2 provides the rank order of data from Table E.1. Since the number of scores in the data set is even, the median is calculated as the average of the two middlemost scores. The median value in the data set is 3.

MODE

The third measure of central tendency is the mode. The mode is the score that occurs most often in the data set. In Table E.2, there are two 1s, two 2s, two 3s, three 4s, and one 5. Therefore, the mode of this data set is 4, since it is the most frequently occurring score. It is possible that a data set could have more than one mode. This occurs when two or more values in the data set have the highest frequency and the same frequency.

VARIABILITY

While measures of central tendency indicate the middle of the distribution, we also would like to know about the spread of data. The spread of data is indexed by measures of variability. Measures of variability indicate the extent to which scores are tightly packed together versus spread out. The measures of variability presented here are the variance and the standard deviation. Both measures indicate the spread of data around the mean.

Table E.2   Rank order of data from Table E.1.

Score	Customer	X
1	7	5
2	1	4
3	5	4
4	8	4
5	3	3 ◄─── (*n*/2)th score
6	9	3 ◄─── (*n*/2 + 1)th score
7	4	2
8	10	2 ◄─── The median is (3 + 3)/2 = 3
9	2	1
10	6	1

VARIANCE

Table E.3 contains four columns of numbers. The first column is x, the score; the second column contains a deviation score from the mean $(x - \bar{x})$; the third column contains the squared deviation score; and the last column is the squared value of each score.

One measure of variability is the variance. Variance, s^2, is the sum of the squared deviations about the mean *(SS)* divided by the number of scores in the data set less one. The formula for the variance is

$$s^2 = \frac{\Sigma(x_1 - \bar{x})^2}{n - 1} = \frac{SS}{n - 1}$$

The numerator is the sum of the squared deviations about the mean *(SS)* and the denominator is called the *degrees of freedom*. In general, the degrees of freedom for a particular statistic is the number of observations in the data set minus the number of estimated parameters used in the equation. The total number of observations used in the calculation is the sample size *(n)*, and the number of estimated parameters used in the equation is one (the sample mean). It should be noted that some people, in calculating the variance, divide the *SS* by n instead of $n - 1$. Usually, n is used when the variance is used to describe the present data set, while $n - 1$ is used to make inferences about the population variance from which the sample is drawn. A more complete discussion about the difference is available in various introductory statistics books. Using the previous equation, the variance of the data is calculated.

Table E.3 Deviation scores and squared deviation scores for hypothetical data.

	x	$x - \bar{x}$	$(x - \bar{x})^2$	x^2
	1	−2	4	1
	2	−1	1	4
	3	0	0	9
	4	1	1	16
	5	2	4	25
Totals	15	0	10	55

$$s^2 = \frac{4 + 1 + 0 + 1 + 4}{10} = 2.5$$

The formula for the sum of squared deviations *(SS)* can be simplified to facilitate hand computation of the variance. The formula for the sum of squares is

$$SS = \Sigma x_i^2 - \frac{(\Sigma x_i)^2}{n}$$

Using the data, the *SS* is calculated to be

$$SS = 55 - \frac{225}{5} = 10$$

The numerator for the formula of the variance is the squared deviation of each score from the mean. As the scores are widely spread out from the mean, the numerator increases. Therefore a large variance indicates that the scores are widely spread out, and a small variance indicates that the scores are tightly packed around the mean.

STANDARD DEVIATION

Another measure of variability is the standard deviation. The standard deviation is simply the square root of the variance; it is denoted by *s*. The standard deviation for the data in Table E.3 is calculated to be $s = 1.58$. The larger the standard deviation, the larger the spread in the data.

If the data are normally distributed, the standard deviation can be used to estimate the percentage of scores that fall within a specified range. By definition, 68 percent of the scores fall within a range of which the limits are (mean − 1*s*) and (mean + 1*s*), and 95 percent of the scores fall within a range whose limits are (mean − 2s) and (mean + 2s). If the standard deviation is small, a high percentage of the data falls closely around the mean. For our data, approximately 68 percent of the data falls within a range from 1.4 to 4.4.

Example

Before descriptive statistics were calculated, summary scores for physician quality and office quality were calculated by averaging the items within the respective scales. The descriptive statistics for the patient satisfaction questionnaire are presented in Table E.4.

As we can see from Table E.4, the descriptive statistics indicate that customers seem to be satisfied with the overall experience of the exam. Additionally, they seem to indicate that they are satisfied with the physician quality and overall quality of the exam. This information is not surprising to us given the information regarding the frequency of responses. Although this method of presenting the data (mean, median, and mode), compared to frequencies and percentages, summarizes the data even more, we conclude the same thing. This method of reporting the descriptive statistics is easier compared to reporting the frequencies if we just want to get a general idea of what the satisfaction data tell us. The wait time indicates that the patients typically had to wait about 15 minutes before seeing the physician. Once in to see the physician, the typical patient spent about 44 minutes with the physician.

Table E.4 Descriptive statistics of items in the patient satisfaction questionnaire.

Variable	Mean	Median	Mode	SD
Physician quality	2.81	3.00	3.00	.44
Overall experience of exam	4.09	4.00	4.00	.86
Office quality	2.74	2.75	3.00	.32
Time spent with physician (minutes)	43.53	40.00	30.00	28.93
Wait time (minutes)	16.24	15.00	0.00	23.90

SUMMARY

This section included measures of central tendency and measures of variability. Both types of measures summarize information contained in a sample of scores. The central tendency measures determine the score in the data set around which all other scores cluster. Measures of variability determine the extent of spread of the data.

Appendix F

Statistics, Parameters, and Sampling Distributions

A subset of observations can be randomly selected from a larger set of observations. The larger set of observations is called the *population*; the smaller set is called the *sample*. We are usually concerned with making conclusions about the population. Since the population can be extremely large, we often examine a sample to make conclusions about the larger population. For example, we may want to know the level of satisfaction of all our customers. Due to limited resources, we may only be able to measure the satisfaction level of a small set of customers. The population consists of all the customers; the sample consists of the small set of customers we measure.

We may examine the mean and the variance of a sample to make inferences about the mean and variance of the population. Numbers calculated from a sample of data are referred to as *statistics*. Therefore, the mean, variance, and standard deviation of the sample are statistics. Numbers calculated using the entire population are called *parameters*. Statistics are denoted with the following symbols: the mean is $\bar{x}$, the variance is s^2, and the standard deviation is s. Parameters are usually denoted with Greek symbols. The population mean is μ, the variance is σ^2, and the standard deviation is σ. Because the population parameters may not be easily obtained (due to limited resources), we have to estimate the parameters. We use the statistics as estimators of the parameters.

SAMPLING ERROR

Suppose we have a population of 1000 people and want to make conclusions about their mean height. We may have only the resources to measure 50 of these people. We use the mean from the sample to estimate the mean of the population.

For the sake of argument, suppose we knew the mean height of the population to be $\mu = 60''$ with a $\sigma^2 = 50''$. Based on our sample of 50 randomly selected people, we calculate the mean of their height. Suppose we found the mean height of the sample to be $\bar{x}_1 = 62''$. Now, let's place this sample back into the population of 1000 people and take another sample of 50 randomly selected people. Suppose we found the mean of this sample to equal $\bar{x}_2 = 55''$. We notice that there is some difference between the means of the first and second sample of people, both differing from the true population mean.

The difference of the sample means from population mean is referred to as sampling error. This error is expected to occur and is considered to be random. For the first sample, we happened to select, by chance, people who are slightly taller than the population mean. In the second sample, we selected, again by chance, people who are slightly shorter than the population mean.

STANDARD ERROR OF THE MEAN

In the preceding example, we witnessed the effect of sampling error; in one sample the mean $(\bar{x}_1) = 62''$ and in the second sample the mean $(\bar{x}_2) = 55''$. If we did not know the population mean (which is usually the situation), we could not determine the exact amount of error associated with any one given sample. We can, however, determine the degree of error we might expect using a given sample size. We could do so by repeatedly taking a sample of 50 randomly selected people from the population, with replacement, and calculating the mean for each sample. Each mean would be an estimate of the population mean.

If we collected 100 means, we could then plot them to form a histogram or distribution. This distribution is described by a mean and a standard deviation. This distribution of sample means is called a *sampling distribution*. The mean of this sampling distribution would be our best estimate of the population mean. The standard deviation of the sampling distribution is called the *standard error of the mean* (sem). The sem describes the degree of error we would expect in our sample mean. If the population standard deviation is known, we can calculate the sem. The standard error of the mean can be calculated easily using the following formula.

$$\text{Standard error of the mean} = \frac{\sigma}{\sqrt{n}}$$

where n is sample size and σ is the population standard deviation. If we do not know the population standard deviation, we can calculate the sem using the sample standard deviation as an estimate of the population standard deviation.

The sampling distributions for two different sample sizes are presented in Figure F.1. The population mean (μ) is $60''$ and the population variance

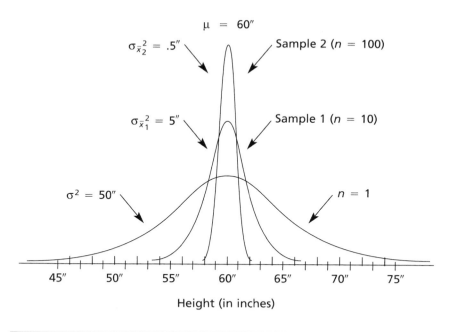

Figure F.1   Sampling distributions for sample sizes of *n* = 100 and *n* = 10 with a population mean of 60 and population variance of 50.

(σ^2) is 50″. The size of sample 1 is 10 and the size of sample 2 is 100. Using the equation above, the standard error of the mean is 2.24″ for sample 1 and .71″ for sample 2. As seen in Figure F.1, the degree of sampling error is small when the sample size is large. This figure illustrates the effect of sample size on our confidence in the sample estimate.

When the sample size is 100, we see that any one of our sample means will likely fall close to the population mean (95 percent of the sample means will fall within the range of 58.58″ to 61.42″). When the sample size is 10, our sample means will deviate more from the population mean than do our sample means when using a sample size of 100 (95 percent of the sample means will fall within the range of 53.68″ to 66.32″). In fact, when the sample size equals the population size, the standard error of the mean is 0. That is, when sample size equals population size, the sample mean will always equal the population mean.

Figure F.2 illustrates the relationship between sampling error and sample size. As sample size increases, sampling error decreases. When sample size equals one, the standard error of the mean is, by definition, the standard deviation of the observation. When sample size equals the size of

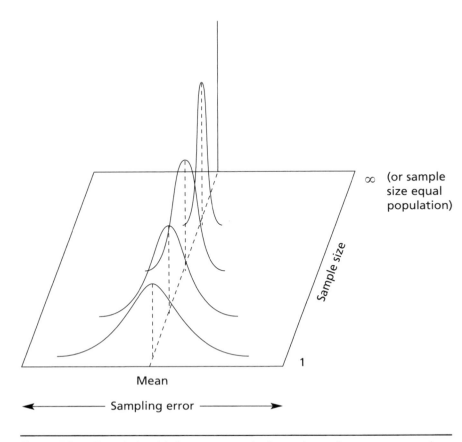

Figure F.2   The relationship between sample size and sampling error: as sample size increases, sampling error decreases.

the population, there is no error in the estimate of the population mean. Thus, the standard error of the mean is 0 when sample size equals the size of the population.

Example

The sampling error for some of the variables in the Patient Satisfaction Questionnaire are presented in Table F.1.

As we can see from the table, the sampling error is quite small, suggesting that there is not much error associated with our estimates of the population parameters. Given that we have a fairly large sample size, we can be fairly confident that our results will not vary if we were to conduct the same study using another sample of the same size. That is, if we were

Table F.1   Sampling error of the variables in the patient satisfaction survey.

Variable	Mean	SD	n (sample size)	Sampling error
Physician quality	2.81	.44	1335	.01
Overall experience of exam	4.09	.86	1283	.02
Office quality	2.74	.32	1337	.01
Time spent with physician (minutes)	43.53	28.93	1093	.88
Wait time (minutes)	16.24	23.90	827	.83

to take another 1500 or so surveys from our population of customers, our results would be very similar to the results we have here. For example, we would expect our mean for the physician quality score to vary only .01 (on the scale we are using) from sample to sample.

SUMMARY

Statistics are numbers derived from a sample of numbers. Parameters are numbers derived from a population. A sampling distribution is a distribution of a given statistic. Sampling error describes the degree of error associated with a given statistic for a specified sample size. As sample size increases, sampling error decreases. The concept of sampling error can be applied to many statistics (mean, t-value), and the concept of sampling error will be applied throughout the remaining appendices.

Appendix G
Decision Making and Hypothesis Testing

Decisions are made every day in the business world. On a small scale, we decide whether or not to leave early for a meeting being held on the other side of town. On a larger scale, companies select one supplier instead of another. We implicitly make decisions about some aspect of the world. In the former scenario, we might decide to leave early if the roads are icy and we need extra time to get to the meeting. In the second scenario, a company might select one supplier instead of another because one supplier makes parts of higher quality.

When we make decisions, we hope they are correct. A decision is correct if it is congruent with the state of the world. For example, a decision to leave early for the meeting is correct if the roads are icy and incorrect if the roads are not icy. In addition, a decision not to leave early for the meeting is correct if the roads are not icy and incorrect if the roads are icy.

REALITY AND DECISIONS

One morning, you are deciding whether or not to take your umbrella to work. To help you make this decision, you rely on some evidence (data). This evidence consists of several weather forecasts from various sources, each providing you with some data on the weather for the day. You must decide, based on this data, whether or not to take your umbrella with you.

You can make one of two choices based on your evaluation of the data. If you decide the data indicate it will rain today, you will take your umbrella. If you decide the data indicate it will not rain today, you will leave your umbrella at home.

There are four possible outcomes for this scenario. We can diagram these, crossing the two states of the world with the two possible decisions. The two states of the world constitute reality—the way the world truly is. The two decisions are based on the evaluation of the evidence (data), leading us to decide whether or not an umbrella is warranted. The diagram depicting the four possible outcomes is presented in Figure G.1 and illustrates the two correct decisions and the two types of error. For the sake of discussion, the errors are labeled *Type I* and *Type II*.

THE PROCESS OF DECISION MAKING

We can look at decision making as a process consisting of two important elements: the evidence and the criterion. The evidence is the data we evaluate in making our decision. In our previous umbrella-toting example, we may have gathered data from many local weather reports, the *Farmer's Almanac,* and other sources. The criterion reflects the amount of evidence or data we need to decide whether to carry an umbrella. Therefore, differences in our criterion will influence the likelihood of making a Type I versus a Type II error. We could have a stringent criterion, which means we need a lot of evidence to convince ourselves to carry an umbrella (for example, we will carry an umbrella only when all of the forecasts predict rain). With this stringent criterion, we will rarely end up carrying an umbrella on a day without rain (not likely to make a Type I error), but will likely end up not carrying an umbrella on a rainy day (likely to make a Type II error). On the other hand, we could have a lenient criterion, which means we need little evidence to convince us to carry an umbrella (for example, we will carry an umbrella if at least one forecast predicts rain). With this criterion, we would likely carry an umbrella on a day with no rain (likely to make a Type I error), but we will rarely end up without an umbrella on a rainy day (not likely to make a Type II error).

DECISION MAKING IN HYPOTHESIS TESTING

In business, we would like to know the real state of the world. To understand the true state of the world, we collect data. The data constitute

		State of the world	
		No rain	Rain
Your decision	Carry umbrella	Error (Type I)	Correct decision
	Do not carry umbrella	Correct decision	Error (Type II)

Figure G.1   Four possible outcomes, crossing the two states of the world with the two decisions.

the evidence we need to make conclusions about the world. Based on this evidence, we decide which state of the world is true.

Let's look at an example to illustrate the role of decision making in hypothesis testing. We may own two stores and have limited financial resources. We would like to give resources to the store that needs the most help (has the lowest level of customer satisfaction). We develop a customer satisfaction questionnaire and administer it to the stores' customers. Questionnaire scores constitute the data we need to make conclusions about the state of the world.

We can formally state our question: Do the two groups of customers have different levels of satisfaction? In hypothesis testing, we set up the world as consisting of two mutually exclusive hypotheses: the null hypothesis and the alternative hypothesis. The null hypothesis (HO) states:

There is no difference in satisfaction levels between the customers of the two stores.

The alternative hypothesis (HA) states:

There is a difference in the satisfaction levels between the customers of the two stores.

In the world, only one of these hypotheses is true. In our study, we will collect evidence to help us decide which is correct. In our hypothesis testing situation, we have a possibility of four outcomes. We have two possible states of the world crossed with two possible decisions. Each state of the world is represented by one of our hypotheses (there is no difference versus there is a difference). We also have two decisions we can make (deciding there is a difference between the two stores or that there is not a difference between the two stores). These decisions are unique to hypothesis testing. Formally, we state our decisions as either rejecting the null hypothesis (or accepting the alternative hypothesis that there is a difference between the two stores) or not rejecting the null hypothesis (not accepting the alternative).

We can construct a decision outcome matrix for this situation. This is presented in Figure G.2. The four cells, similar to the four cells in our umbrella-toting situation, can be characterized by probabilities, or likelihoods of occurrence. The probability of rejecting the null when the null is, in fact, true (upper left corner) is labeled α. The probability of not rejecting the null when the null is true is $1 - \alpha$. In addition, the probability of failing to reject the null when the alternative is true is labeled β. The probability of rejecting the null when the alternative is true is $1 - \beta$.

		State of the world	
		Null hypothesis true	Alternative hypothesis true
	Reject null hypothesis	Type I error (α)	Correct decision $(1 - \beta)$
Your decision			
	Do not reject null hypothesis	Correct decision $(1 - \alpha)$	Type II Error (β)

Figure G.2   The four possible outcomes in a hypothesis testing situation, crossing the two states of the world with the two decisions.

SOME EVIDENCE

We need to collect data to provide us with evidence of the true state of the world. Let's use our example concerning the level of satisfaction of customers from our two stores. We collect data from two samples, each representing one store. Higher scores on the questionnaire reflect higher levels of satisfaction. The data are presented in Table G.1.

Before examining the data, let's discuss the kind of evidence that would indicate whether or not we should reject the null. If the null is correct, then the two groups of scores should be roughly the same. If the alternative is true, then the two groups of scores should be different; one set should contain higher scores than the other.

We need a way of summarizing the data to allow us to decide which hypothesis is true. In this situation, we could look at the overall average of each group. The average score for Store 1 is $\bar{x}_1 = 3.5$, and the average for Store 2 is $\bar{x}_2 = 3.1$. The difference between these two scores is 0.4. We could use this difference score as the summary score. This summary score reflects the degree of difference between the two groups and is, essentially, the evidence.

DETERMINATION OF THE CRITERION

Summary scores are used to represent the state of the world, supporting either the null hypothesis or the alternative hypothesis. We need a criterion to judge whether the summary score reflects that the null hypothesis is true or that the alternative hypothesis is true. In hypothesis testing, we usually set the criterion to reflect that the alpha level (probability of rejecting the

Table G.1   Hypothetical data of satisfaction scores for two stores.

Store 1	Store 2
4	3
5	4
2	3
4	4
5	2
4	2
3	3
4	5
2	2
2	3

null when it is true) equal .05. That is, given that the null is true, we want to set a criterion with which we will incorrectly reject the null hypothesis, at the most, five times out of 100.

For our study, we found that the summary score (the difference between the two groups), is 0.4. Recall that, in Appendix F, the effect of sampling error would result in differences between two samples of scores even if the samples were selected from the same underlying population. Therefore, the difference of 0.4 revealed in our study might not indicate any real difference at all. The difference between the two samples could be due to sampling error.

For our example, the criterion we choose should reflect a difference between two samples that would occur by chance only five times out of 100 if the null were true. This criterion is established through formal methods discussed in the next three appendices.

Example

We could state some hypotheses for our study using our patient satisfaction data. Some explicit hypotheses are presented in Figure G.3.

There are many more hypotheses that can be generated using our current patient satisfaction questionnaire. We could examine the difference across the various offices using the other variables in the survey such as the office quality score, wait time, and time spent with the physician. Additionally, we could generate hypotheses examining the difference across the different months or quarters using these same variables.

Null hypothesis (H_{O1}): There is no difference in patient satisfaction levels for physician quality among the different offices.

Alternative hypothesis (H_{A1}): There is a difference in the patient satisfaction levels for physician quality among the different offices.

Null hypothesis (H_{O2}): There is no difference in the patient satisfaction levels for physician quality among the different months.

Alternative hypothesis (H_{A2}): There is a difference in the patient satisfaction levels for physician quality among the different months.

Null hypothesis (H_{O3}): There is no difference in the patient satisfaction levels for overall rating of the exam among the different offices.

Alternative Hypothesis (H_{A3}): There is a difference in the patient satisfaction levels for overall rating of the exam among the different offices.

Null hypothesis (H_{O4}): There is no difference in the patient satisfaction levels for overall rating of the exam among the different months.

Alternative hypothesis (H_{A4}): There is a difference in the patient satisfaction levels for overall rating of the exam among the different months.

Null hypothesis (H_{O5}): There is no difference in the patient satisfaction levels for overall rating of the exam between the two states.

Alternative hypothesis (H_{A5}): There is a difference in the patient satisfaction levels for overall rating of the exam between the two states.

Figure G.3 Hypotheses for the patient satisfaction questionnaire.

SUMMARY

Hypothesis testing involves determining the extent to which the differences between our samples is not likely due to sampling error. When the difference is likely due to sampling error, we do not reject the null hypothesis; the two samples are likely from the same population. When the difference is not likely due to sampling error (difference is large), then we reject the null hypothesis in favor of the alternative hypothesis.

The steps to hypothesis testing are presented in Figure G.4. The first step is to generate a null and an alternative hypothesis. The second step is to collect data to provide evidence of the state of the world (supporting the null or alternative hypothesis). The third step is determining a summary

1. Generate null and alternative hypothesis.
   - Null: there is no difference
   - Alternative: there is a difference
2. Collect data to provide evidence of the state of the world.
3. Using the data, determine the summary score that summarizes the difference between the groups.
4. Determine criterion to which to compare your summary score.
5. Decide to reject the null or not reject the null.

Figure G.4 Steps in hypothesis testing.

score using data that reflect the difference between the groups. The fourth step is determining the criterion, reflecting the point at which the summary score is likely to occur five times out of 100 if the null hypothesis is true. Fifth, if the summary score exceeds the criterion, we reject the null hypothesis and accept the alternate hypothesis.

Appendix H

T-Tests

We may want to compare two groups of people on some variable. Two companies in the retail business have a friendly competition. Bob of Bob's Barn claims that his customers are highly satisfied, while Tom, owner of Tom's Tent, claims he has more satisfied customers. Both owners would like to obtain empirical information to determine which company has the highest level of customer satisfaction.

An independent research firm was contacted to see whether it could settle the score. The research firm developed a customer satisfaction questionnaire to assess overall customer satisfaction. Higher scores on the questionnaire reflect higher satisfaction. This questionnaire was administered to two sets of customers. One set had received service from Bob's Barn and the other had received service from Tom's Tent. The research firm obtained 20 customers from each company to complete the questionnaire. The data appear in Table H.1.

The mean for the group from Bob's Barn is 2.85, and the mean for the group from Tom's Tent is 3.45. If we inspect only these mean values, we might conclude that customers from Tom's Tent are more satisfied with service than customers from Bob's Barn.

Recall that, when two small sets of data are compared, their means will almost always be different from each other, even when the two data sets come from the same population. This difference is due to sampling error (see Appendix F). This error arises because the observed mean is only an estimate of the population mean, which has inherent error because it is based on only a sample of data. Therefore, merely seeing if there is a difference between the two groups is not enough to say that the two data sets arise from two different populations.

The *t*-test provides a method by which we can more rigorously compare two data sets. Conducting a *t*-test informs us whether the degree of difference between the two data sets could be due to factors other than sampling error. If the results indicate that the difference between the groups is not

Table H.1   Hypothetical data for two companies.

	Bob's Barn		Tom's Tent	
1	3	2	3	
2	4	4	3	
3	3	5	4	
2	2	3	5	
4	1	3	3	
3	3	4	2	
3	4	2	1	
3	2	5	3	
4	4	4	4	
4	2	5	4	
Total =	57.00		69.00	
n =	20		20	
$\bar{x}$ =	2.85		3.45	
SS =	18.55		24.95	

likely due to sampling error, we believe that the two data sets probably do not come from the same population.

CALCULATION

The formulae for the calculation of the *t*-test vary, depending on whether the sample sizes for each group are equal. The following general equation can be applied to situations in which the sample sizes are either equal or not equal. The calculation of the *t*-test is

$$t(N-2) = \frac{\bar{x}_1 - \bar{x}_2}{\sqrt{\left(\dfrac{SS_1 + SS_2}{n_1 + n_2 - 2}\right)\left(\dfrac{1}{n_1} + \dfrac{1}{n_2}\right)}}$$

where $\bar{x}_1$ and $\bar{x}_2$ are the means for each group, SS_1 and SS_2 are the sum of squares for each group, n_1 and n_2 are the sample sizes for each group, and N is the sum of n_1 and n_2.

Also, $(N-2)$, associated with the t statistic, is the degrees of freedom. Recall that the degrees of freedom is the total number of observations (N) minus the number of estimated parameters. Using the data in Table H.1, the observed *t* value is calculated to be

$$t(38) = \frac{3.45 - 2.85}{.338} = 1.77$$

If we assume that the null hypothesis is true (there is no difference between the two groups), we would expect the *t* statistic to equal 0.0 (since $\bar{x}_1 - \bar{x}_2 = 0$). The *t* statistic, like the sample mean, can also be described by a sampling distribution with associated sampling error. That is, even though the null might be true, we would not expect to obtain a *t* statistic of zero every time we randomly sample two samples from the same population. Given that the null hypothesis is true, the mean of the *t* distribution is symmetric around zero. If we were to randomly sample *t* values from this distribution, we would likely see a majority of *t* values clustering around 0. We would not likely see extreme *t* values. Recall that 95 percent of the data falls within two standard deviations above or below zero. If the *t* value we obtain from our study is more than 2s away from the mean, we know this finding is highly unlikely; therefore, we think the two sample means do not come from the same population.

When the *t* values are extreme, we think the two samples come from different populations (reject the null hypothesis and accept the alternative hypothesis). We say the two sample means are *statistically significantly* different from each other. In significance testing, we set a critical value that our observed *t* value should exceed if we are to say the means are significantly different from each other. This critical *t* value is determined to be the *t* value above which the probability of obtaining a *t* value, by chance, is .05.

The spread of the *t* distribution is determined by the sample size used in the calculation of the *t* statistic. The spread of the *t* distribution is wider when sample size is small and becomes narrower as the sample size increases. A given *t* distribution (with associated degrees of freedom) describes the frequency with which we would see varying *t* values if we repeatedly performed independent *t*-tests with a given sample of subjects (20 in each group). For our example we would be interested in the probability of obtaining *t* values using a *t* distribution with 38 degrees of freedom.

The observed *t* value we obtain in our study is 1.77. We compare this *t* value to a critical *t* value. A *t* table containing critical *t* values is located in Appendix H. We select our critical *t* value to be 2.04 (.05 level with 30 degrees of freedom and a two-tailed test). Although our actual degrees of freedom is 38, we select 30 to provide a conservative test of significance. This critical *t* value represents the point above which our chance of obtaining an obtained *t* value is less than 5 percent if the null hypothesis were true. Our observed *t* value is below this critical *t* value. Thus, we conclude that the difference between our observed means (2.85 and 3.45) is likely due to sampling error, or that both sets of customers come from one underlying population; the customers from Bob's Barn and Tom's Tent are equally satisfied.

FACTORS AFFECTING SIGNIFICANCE TESTING

Power is the probability of finding a significant difference with our samples when there truly is a difference between the two populations. We always strive to have a high degree of power when we conduct significance testing. One way of increasing power is by increasing the sample size on which the *t*-test is conducted. Another is to use scales with high reliability. In our example, perhaps customers from Tom's Tent were more satisfied but our test lacked sufficient power to detect this difference.

Example

A *t*-test can be conducted to test hypothesis 5 (see Appendix G). Specifically this hypothesis tests to see if there is a difference between the two states (Washington and California) in the customers' overall rating of the exam. The summary information for this *t*-test is presented in Table H.2.

From the *t*-test, we compare the obtained *t* value with our critical value. Because we did not have a directional hypothesis, we will compare this obtained *t* value with the critical value for a two-tailed test. To be conservative, we use a critical *t* value associated with a smaller degree of freedom. The critical value for *t* given 180 degrees of freedom is 1.96. We see that the absolute value of the obtained *t* statistic does not exceed the critical value. Therefore, we conclude that there was no statistically significant difference between the two states with respect to the overall rating of the exam. That is, the observed differences we see between the states is due to chance factors (sampling error).

Table H.3 contains the critical values for the *t* statistic. The table is used to compare the absolute value of the obtained *t* statistic (from the study) with the critical value of the *t* statistics for a given critical value. If the absolute value of the observed *t* statistic exceeds the critical value, we reject the null (there are no differences between the groups) and conclude that the difference between the two groups is probably not due to chance.

Table H.2 Summary information for the *t*-test examining state differences for overall ratings of the exam.

	Washington	California
Mean	4.07	4.11
SD	0.89	0.84
SE of the mean	0.03	0.03
n	678	605

$$t(1281) = -.72, p > .05$$

Note: SD = standard deviation; SE = standard error; *n* = sample size.

Table H.3   Critical values of the *t* statistics.

Degrees of freedom	One-tailed significance level *p*		Two-tailed significance level *p*	
	.05	.01	.05	.01
3	2.35	4.54	3.18	5.84
4	2.13	3.75	2.78	4.60
5	2.02	3.36	2.57	4.03
6	1.94	3.14	2.45	3.71
7	1.89	3.00	2.36	3.50
8	1.86	2.90	2.31	3.36
9	1.83	2.82	2.26	3.25
10	1.81	2.76	2.23	3.17
11	1.80	2.72	2.20	3.11
12	1.78	2.68	2.18	3.05
13	1.77	2.65	2.16	3.01
14	1.76	2.62	2.14	2.98
15	1.75	2.60	2.13	2.95
16	1.75	2.58	2.12	2.92
17	1.74	2.57	2.11	2.90
18	1.73	2.55	2.10	2.88
19	1.73	2.54	2.09	2.86
20	1.72	2.53	2.09	2.85
21	1.72	2.52	2.08	2.83
22	1.72	2.51	2.07	2.82
23	1.71	2.50	2.07	2.81
24	1.71	2.49	2.06	2.80
25	1.71	2.49	2.06	2.79
26	1.71	2.48	2.06	2.78
27	1.70	2.47	2.05	2.77
28	1.70	2.47	2.05	2.76
29	1.70	2.46	2.05	2.76
30	1.70	2.46	2.04	2.75
40	1.68	2.42	2.02	2.70
50	1.68	2.40	2.01	2.68
60	1.67	2.39	2.00	2.66
70	1.67	2.38	1.99	2.65
80	1.66	2.37	1.99	2.64
90	1.66	2.37	1.99	2.63
100	1.66	2.36	1.98	2.63
120	1.66	2.36	1.98	2.62
140	1.66	2.35	1.98	2.61
160	1.65	2.35	1.97	2.61
180	1.65	2.35	1.97	2.60
>10000	1.65	2.33	1.96	2.58

SUMMARY

The *t*-test can determine if the difference between two samples is meaningful. We calculate the observed *t* value using our data and compare it to a critical *t* value. This critical *t* value is the cutoff point above which the probability of obtaining a *t* value is .05. If our observed *t* is greater than this critical *t* value, then we say the difference between the two means is not likely due to sampling error. That is, the data likely come from two different populations. On the other hand, if the observed *t* value falls below the critical *t* value, we say the observed difference between the two means is likely due to sampling error. That is, the data from the two groups likely come from the same population and the observed difference is the result of chance. The power of detecting true differences can be increased by increasing the sample size on which the *t*-test is conducted and also by using measures with high reliability.

Appendix I
Analysis of Variance

nalysis of variance (ANOVA) is used to compare groups. When conducting an ANOVA, we can compare more than two groups simultaneously. As the name of the analysis implies, ANOVA is a method of analyzing components of variance.

Let's look at an example. Suppose we have four independent sets of data. The data are presented in Table I.1. We will calculate the variance of the observations with two methods. The first method is to calculate the variability within each group. Four separate variances, one for each group, can be calculated. These four separate variances are each an estimate of the same variance. Therefore, we can get an overall variance measure by averaging these four variances. This average variance is the pooled variance estimate (s^2_p). This approach results in a variance estimate of .625.

The second method is to calculate the variance of the means (s^2_x). The variance of the means, however, is dependent on the sample size (see Appendix F). As sample size increases, the variance of the means decreases. Thus, to correct for sample size, we multiply the variance of the means by the sample size for each group ($n = 10$). This estimate now reflects the variability of the group means corrected for sample size (ns^2_x). This approach results in a variance estimate of 7.49.

If there is no true difference between the group means, then the two variance measures should be roughly the same. We see, however, that the variability using the group means approach is 7.49, and the variance using the within-group approach is .625. The magnitude of the former variance indicates that there is considerable variability between groups, more so than variability within groups. In ANOVA, we are comparing these variance components. If the variance calculated using the means is larger than the variance calculated using individual scores within groups, this might indicate that there is a significant difference between the groups.

Table I.1 Hypothetical data of four groups.

	Set 1	Set 2	Set 3	Set 4
	2	4	2	3
	1	5	3	2
	2	5	1	3
	1	4	4	2
	2	4	3	4
	2	4	3	3
	2	5	4	4
	3	3	3	2
	3	4	3	3
	2	3	2	4
Mean =	2.0	4.1	2.8	3.0
n =	10	10	10	10

$$SS_1 = 3.996 \quad SS_2 = 4.896 \quad SS_3 = 7.596 \quad SS_4 = 6.003$$

$$s^2_1 = .444 \quad s^2_2 = .544 \quad s^2_3 = .844 \quad s^2_4 = .667$$

$$s^2_p = (s^2_1 + s^2_2 + s^2_3 + s^2_4)/4 = .625$$

$$SS_B = 20.03 + 41.02 + 28.02 + 30.02 - (20 + 41 + 28 + 30)2/4 = 6.741$$

$$s^2_{\bar{x}} = SS_B/3 = .749$$

CALCULATIONS

The standard method for presenting the results of the ANOVA is the tabular format. The ANOVA table appears in Table I.2. The first row of the ANOVA table contains information about the variance of the groups. The second row contains information concerning the variance of the subjects within each group. The third row of the table represents total variance. Each of the rows contains specific information about the variability of its respective components.

The first column identifies the sources of variation. The differences between groups is denoted by Between *(B)*. The variation due to subjects within each group is denoted by Within *(W)*. The total variation is denoted by Total. The second column in the ANOVA table represents the sum of squared deviations *(SS)*. The SS_B and the SS_W should sum to SS_{TOT}. The third column represents the degrees of freedom for each SS. The degrees of freedom *(df)* for SS_B are the number of groups minus one. The *df* for SS_W are the total sample size minus the number of groups. The *df* for SS_{TOT} are the

Table I.2 Analysis of variance (ANOVA) table.

Source	Sum of squares	Degrees of freedom (df)	Mean square	$F(df_B, df_W)$
Between	SS_B	$k - 1$	$SS_B/(k - 1)$	MSB
Within	SS_W	$N - K$	$SS_W/(N - k)$	MSW
Total	SS_{TOT}	$N - 1$		

Note: N = total sample size, *k* = number of groups, *df* = degrees of freedom.

total sample size minus one. The df_B and the df_W should sum to df_{TOT}. The fourth column, mean square, represents the measure of variation of a particular source. The mean squares are calculated by dividing the sum of squares by the *df*. The last column represents the ratio of the MS_B to the MS_W and is referred to as the *F ratio*.

TESTING

The F value is a ratio of the variance of the means corrected for by sample size to variance within the groups. A large F value indicates that the between-group variance is larger than the within-group variance. Like the *t* statistic, the F value can also be described by a distribution, the F distribution. The F distribution has two different degrees of freedom, one associated with the estimate of the variance of the means $(k - 1)$ and the other associated with the variance within groups $(N - k)$. The exact shape of the distribution is determined by the df_B and df_W.

The concept of testing in ANOVA is the same as the testing using the *t*-test. We compare the observed F value from our study to a critical F value. This critical F value is a cutoff point, above which the probability of obtaining an F value is only .05 if the null hypothesis is true. Therefore, an observed F value above the critical value, because it is such an unlikely event, would lead us to believe that the different groups in our study do not come from the same population.

The ANOVA table for the data in Table I.1 is presented in Table I.3. We see that the resulting F value is large. The critical F value with 3 and 36 degrees of freedom is approximately equal to 2.9. Our observed F value equals 11.99, which is larger than the critical F. Thus, we conclude that all four groups do not come from the same underlying population; at least one group comes from a different population than the rest.

Table I.3   ANOVA table for the data in Table I.1.

Source	Sum of squares	Degrees of freedom	Mean square	$F(3, 36)$
Group	22.475	3	7.492	11.987
Within	22.5	36	.625	$p = .0001$
Total	44.975	39		

Note: p = the probability of our observed F value occurring by chance.

POST-HOC COMPARISONS

When we compare three or more groups and find a significant effect using the ANOVA method, we can conclude only that the group means are significantly different from each other. Unlike the *t*-test, in which only two groups are compared, the ANOVA method can be inconclusive. For example, if we find the *t*-test to be statistically significant, we examine the means of the two groups to see which group is higher. In the ANOVA with three or more groups, a significant *F*-test tells us only that the groups do not come from the same population. In other words, significant effect indicates that there is at least one statistically significant difference between two of the groups in our study. Some of the groups may not be significantly different from each other, while others might be significantly different.

To determine where the underlying differences lie, we must do further testing, referred to as *post-hoc testing*. There are various methods of post-hoc testing. All are somewhat related to the *t*-test method in which individual groups are compared to determine whether they are significantly different from each other. Readers are referred to the bibliography to learn more about these techniques.

Example

An ANOVA can be conducted to test the other hypotheses stated in Appendix G. The ANOVA table is presented in Table I.4. In the table, the summary *F*-test is presented. If the result is significant, more information regarding analysis is presented. Specifically, the descriptive statistics of the customer satisfaction measure are presented for each level of the independent variable, including the mean, standard deviation, standard error of the mean, and the 95 percent confidence interval. Additionally, the result of the post-hoc comparisons (Tukey-HSD test) is presented to show you where the differences are located.

Table I.4   ANOVA table for the hypotheses in Appendix G.   *(Continued)*

Null Hypothesis 1: No difference in physician quality across offices

Source	df	Sum of squares	Mean squares	F ratio	F prob.
Between groups	8	6.1902	.7738	4.1106	.0001
Within groups	1326	249.6067	.1882		
Total	1334	255.7969			

Group	Count	Mean	Standard deviation	Standard error	95% confidence interval for mean
Yakima	178	2.8577	.3060	.0229	2.8124 to 2.9029
Seattle	173	2.7371	.5685	.0432	2.6518 to 2.8224
San Francisco	150	2.8224	.5023	.0410	2.7414 to 2.9035
Tacoma	179	2.8467	.3420	.0256	2.7963 to 2.8972
San Jose	181	2.8726	.3172	.0236	2.8260 to 2.9191
Sacramento	155	2.7989	.4004	.0322	2.7354 to 2.8625
Spokane	180	2.7988	.4421	.0330	2.7338 to 2.8638
San Diego	58	2.9233	.2619	.0344	2.8544 to 2.9922
Sonoma	81	2.6140	.6830	.0759	2.4630 to 2.7650
Total	1335	2.8119	.4379	.0120	2.7884 to 2.8355

(*) Indicates significant differences, which are shown in the lower triangle

```
                                        S
                                        a
                                        n
                            S
                            a   F           S
                            c   r       S   a
                    S   S   r   a       a   n
                    S   e   p   a   n   T   Y   n
                    o   a   o   m   c   a   a       D
                    n   t   k   e   i   c   k   J   i
                    o   t   a   n   s   o   i   o   e
                    m   l   n   t   c   m   m   s   g
                    a   e   e   o   o   a   a   e   o
```

Mean	Office	
2.6140	Sonoma	
2.7371	Seattle	
2.7988	Spokane	*
2.7989	Sacramento	*
2.8224	San Francisco	*
2.8467	Tacoma	*
2.8577	Yakima	*
2.8726	San Jose	*
2.9233	San Diego	*

Table I.4   ANOVA table for the hypotheses in Appendix G.   *(Continued)*

Null Hypothesis 2: No difference in physician quality across months

Source	df	Sum of squares	Mean squares	F ratio	F prob.
Between groups	8	2.8366	.3546	1.8586	.0627
Within groups	1326	252.9604	.1908		
Total	1334	255.7969			

No significant differences

Null Hypothesis 3: No difference in overall rating of exam scores across offices

Source	df	Sum of squares	Mean squares	F ratio	F prob.
Between groups	8	27.7563	3.4695	4.7607	.0000
Within groups	1274	928.4666	.7288		
Total	1282	956.2229			

Group	Count	Mean	Standard deviation	Standard error	95% confidence interval for mean
Yakima	170	4.0824	.8244	.0632	3.9575 to 4.2072
Seattle	166	3.8976	1.0481	.0813	3.7370 to 4.0582
San Fran	147	4.2041	.8019	.0661	4.0734 to 4.3348
Tacoma	168	4.0893	.7802	.0602	3.9704 to 4.2081
San Jose	172	4.2035	.7409	.0565	4.0920 to 4.3150
Sacramento	150	4.0400	.7408	.0605	3.9205 to 4.1595
Spokane	174	4.2069	.8553	.0648	4.0789 to 4.3349
San Diego	58	4.2931	.6756	.0887	4.1155 to 4.4707
Sonoma	78	3.6923	1.1877	.1345	3.4245 to 3.9601
Total	1283	4.0873	.8636	.0241	4.0400 to 4.1346

(*) Indicates significant differences, which are shown in the lower triangle

```
                                    S
                                    a
                                    n
                          S
                          a   F         S
                          c   r     S   a
                    S  S  r   a     a   n
              S  e  p  a   n  T  Y   n
              o  a  o  m   c  a  a       D
              n  t  k  e   i  c  k   J   i
              o  t  a  n   s  o  i   o   e
              m  l  n  t   c  m  m   s   g
              a  e  e  o   o  o  a   a   e  o
```

Table I.4   ANOVA table for the hypotheses in Appendix G.   *(Continued)*

Mean	Office			
3.6923	Sonoma			
3.8976	Seattle			
4.0400	Sacramento			
4.0824	Yakima	*		
4.0893	Tacoma	*		
4.2035	San Jose	*	*	
4.2041	San Fran	*	*	
4.2069	Spokane	*	*	
4.2931	San Diego	*		

Null Hypothesis 4: No difference in overall rating of exam scores across months

Source	df	Sum of squares	Mean squares	F ratio	F prob.
Between groups	8	16.9757	2.1220	2.8782	.0035
Within groups	1274	939.2472	.7372		
Total	1282	956.2229			

Group	Count	Mean	Standard deviation	Standard error	95% confidence interval for mean
January	144	4.2708	.7684	.0640	4.1443 to 4.3974
February	144	4.1736	.8050	.0671	4.0410 to 4.3062
March	157	4.1783	.7638	.0610	4.0579 to 4.2988
April	149	4.0940	.8648	.0708	3.9540 to 4.2340
May	158	4.0506	.9155	.0728	3.9068 to 4.1945
June	135	3.9407	.9601	.0826	3.7773 to 4.1042
July	128	4.0781	.8749	.0773	3.9251 to 4.2312
August	134	4.1045	.8341	.0721	3.9620 to 4.2470
September	134	3.8657	.9322	.0805	3.7064 to 4.0250
Total	1283	4.0873	.8636	.0241	4.0400 to 4.1346

(*) Indicates significant differences, which are shown in the lower triangle

```
S
e                 F
p                 e    J
t           A     b    a
e        A  u  r  M  n
m  J  J  p  g  u  a  u
b  u  M  u  r  u  a  r  a
e  n  a  l  i  s  r  c  r
r  e  y  y  l  t  y  h  y
```

Table I.4 ANOVA table for the hypotheses in Appendix G. *(Continued)*

Mean	Month		
3.8657	September		
3.9407	June		
4.0506	May		
4.0781	July		
4.0940	April		
4.1045	August		
4.1736	February		
4.1783	March		
4.2708	January	*	*

As can be seen in Table I.4, there are significant differences seen across the different offices on the measure of physician quality and overall rating of the exam. Patients in the Sonoma office rated their physician lower compared to all other offices (except Seattle patients). Additionally, Sonoma and Seattle patients tended to be less satisfied with the overall exam compared to the rest of the patients from the other offices. There was a significant difference across the months with respect to the overall rating of the exam. The months of June and September had significantly lower scores compared to the month of January of that same year, suggesting a downward trend.

Appendix J
Regression Analysis

To understand the application of regression analysis, let's first look at an example of the relationship between two variables: (1) a person's level of satisfaction with perceived quality of service received from a company in terms of availability; and (2) the person's level of overall satisfaction with service. Perceived quality of availability is defined as the extent to which the customer perceives the company as being available to provide service whenever he or she needs it. Overall satisfaction with the service is defined as the extent to which the customer is generally satisfied with the way he or she was treated by the company. Measures were developed to assess both variables on a five-point scale. A higher number on either scale represents better service.

We use these measures on a sample of 10 people and subsequently obtain two scores: X_i, which represents perceived quality of availability, and Y_i, which represents overall satisfaction. The data are presented in Table J.1. The first column in the table provides the names of 10 people who were given the questionnaire. The second and third columns present the scores on perceived availability and overall satisfaction, respectively, for each of the 10 people.

A graphic representation called a *scatterplot* indicates the relationship between these two variables. This is seen in Figure J.1. As one would expect, there is a positive relationship between these two variables. That is, customers who perceive the company as more available to provide services when needed have higher levels of satisfaction. The relationship can be summarized by a line, a regression line, which indicates the degree of relationship between X and Y. This relationship can also be described by an equation

$$Y = a + bX + e$$

where b and a are constants representing the slope and intercept of the regression line, respectively. The error associated with the prediction is labeled as e.

Table J.1 Hypothetical data for variables *X* and *Y*.

Customer	*Xi*	*Yi*	*(Xi)²*	*(Yi)²*	*XiYi*
Lance A.	3	5	9	25	15
Jackson B.	1	2	1	4	2
Brian F.	3	3	9	9	9
Joe F.	5	4	25	16	20
Kim P.	2	2	4	1	2
Lamona F.	2	2	4	4	4
Bob H.	4	4	16	16	16
Tom H.	3	4	9	16	12
Jenifer K.	1	1	1	1	1
Wade G.	4	3	16	9	12

$$\Sigma Xi = 28 \quad \Sigma Yi = 29 \quad \Sigma Xi^2 = 94 \quad \Sigma Yi^2 = 101 \quad \Sigma XiYi = 93$$

$$r = \frac{10(93) - (28 \times 29)}{\sqrt{([10(94) - (28)^2][10(101) - (29)^2])}} = .726$$

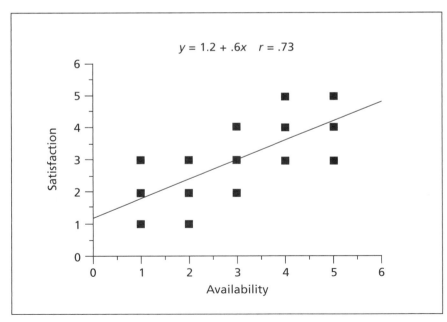

$$y = 1.2 + .6x \quad r = .73$$

Figure J.1 A scatterplot representing the relationship between perceived availability and overall satisfaction with service.

The intercept is the predicted score for Y when X is equal to zero, the point at which the line intersects the Y axis. The slope represents the change in Y given a unit change in X. The values of a and b describe the regression line. Different values of each will necessarily lead to different regression lines. For a given relationship between two variables, there is a regression line that best fits the scatterplot. The parameters, a and b, for the best fitting regression line are calculated by the following equations.

The formula for b is

$$b = \frac{n\Sigma X_i Y_i - (\Sigma X_i)(\Sigma Y_i)}{n\Sigma X_i^2 - (\Sigma X_i)^2}$$

We use b to calculate a.

$$a = \frac{\Sigma Y_i - b\Sigma X_i}{n}$$

These two equations are used to calculate the best fitting regression line. For the data in Table J.1, the regression slope is calculated to be

$$b = .756$$

and the intercept is calculated to be

$$a = .782$$

Therefore, the regression equation for predicting Y (overall satisfaction) from X (perceived availability) is

$$Y = .782 + .76X$$

This equation can be used to make predictions of Y for any given level of X. If a person had an X score of 4.5, their predicted score for Y would be 4.2. If a person had an X score of 1.25, their predicted score for Y would be 1.73.

DETERMINING THE DEGREE OF FIT

An important step in regression analysis is to determine how well the regression line represents the data or how well the regression line fits the data. We determine this fit with an index called *Pearson r^2*. This index varies from 0 to 1.0. This index approaches 1.0 as the data lie closely near the regression line. The index approaches 0 as the data are widely dispersed around the regression line. The formula for the *Pearson r^2* is

$$r^2 = \frac{[n\Sigma X_i Y_i - \Sigma X_i \Sigma Y_i)]^2}{[n\Sigma X_i^2 - (\Sigma X_i)^2][n\Sigma Y_i^2 - (\Sigma Y_i)^2]}$$

This index can be interpreted as the percentage of variance in Y (the criterion) that is accounted for by X (the predictor). So, if r^2 is equal to .70, we say that 70 percent of the variance in Y is accounted for by differences in X. Conversely, we could also say that 30 percent of the variance in Y is not accounted for by differences in X (this is essentially the variance that is unexplained by the X variable). The r^2 for data presented in Table J.1 is calculated to be

$$r^2 = \frac{[10(93) - (28)(29)]^2}{[10(94) - (28)^2][10(101) - (29)^2]} = .528$$

The r^2 indicates that about 53 percent of the variance in Y is accounted for by differences in X.

PEARSON *r*

The r^2 is an index that describes how well the data fit a straight line. However, the r^2 does not tell us the direction of the relationship between the two variables. The linear relationship between two variables can be indexed by a single number, the *Pearson correlation coefficient*, denoted by the letter r. The Pearson r indicates the strength and direction of relationship between two variables. It can vary from -1 (a perfectly negative relationship between two variables) to 1 (a perfectly positive relationship between two variables). A negative relationship indicates that, as one variable increases, the other variable decreases. A positive relationship indicates that, as one variable increases, the other variable also increases.

The equation for the Pearson r is

$$r = \frac{n\Sigma X_i Y_i - \Sigma X_i \Sigma Y_i}{\sqrt{[n\Sigma X_i^2 - (\Sigma X_i)^2][n\Sigma Y_i^2 - (\Sigma Y_i)^2]}}$$

Table J.1 includes data on two variables, X and Y. Using the previous equation, we determine the extent to which variables X and Y are related to each other. The direction of their relationship is positive, and the strength of their relationship is $r = .73$. The amount of variance in Y accounted for by X (r^2) is calculated by squaring the correlation coefficient ($r^2 = .73^2 = .53$).

Figure J.2 illustrates various strengths and directions of relationships. A high correlation (either positive, Figure J.2(a), or negative, Figure J.2(b)) indicates that there is a substantial relationship between the two variables. Figures J.2(c) and (d) indicate that there is a moderate relationship between the two variables. In fact, we know, by the size of the correlation coefficient, that the relationship between X and Y is stronger in the two former figures. For example, the two variables in Figure J.2(a) have a positive correlation of .84, while the two variables in Figure J.2(c) have a moderate positive correlation of .45.

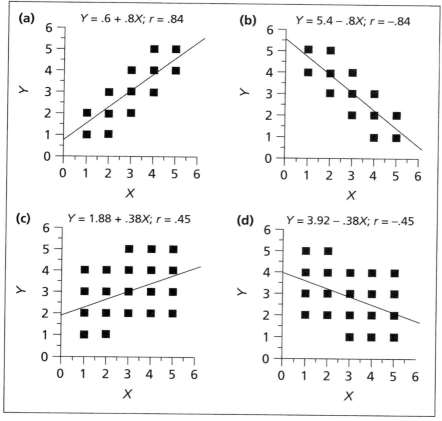

Figure J.2 Scatterplots indicating various strengths and directions of relationships between two variables.

TESTING SIGNIFICANCE OF FIT

We test the significance of the r by first transforming the r statistic to a t statistic. The formula for the transformation is

$$t(n - 2) = \frac{r\sqrt{n - 2}}{r\sqrt{1 - r^2}}$$

We can calculate the t from the r in our present example. In our example $n = 10$ and

$$t(8) = \frac{.73\sqrt{8}}{\sqrt{1 - .53}} = 3.01$$

We can determine if the t represents a significant effect (see Appendix H).

SUMMARY

The relationship between two variables can be described by a straight line, a regression line. The regression line allows us to predict values of Y (with a degree of error) from given values of X. The degree of fit of data around the regression line is indexed by the correlation coefficient, denoted by r. It is an index of the linear association between the two variables. The correlation coefficient can range from -1 (perfect negative relationship) to 1 (perfect positive relationship). A correlation of zero indicates no linear relationship between two variables.

MULTIPLE REGRESSION

In simple linear regression, we examine the relationship between two variables. We might want to examine the relationship of overall satisfaction with many other factors within the customer survey, such as reliability, availability, and professionalism. Instead of examining each factor separately (for example, calculating simple correlation coefficients), another approach would be to examine all factors simultaneously in their prediction of overall customer satisfaction. This method is referred to as *multiple regression analysis*. Multiple regression analysis allows us to determine which variable or variables best predict overall customer satisfaction. For example, it might be conceivable to think of overall satisfaction as a result of several factors, some factors more important than others. Although all the variables may be significantly correlated with overall customer satisfaction, multiple regression analysis determines which factors are *the best* predictors of overall customer satisfaction. *Best* is defined as factors that uniquely predict customer satisfaction.

Essentially, multiple regression analysis examines all the factors and selects the factors that account for most of the variance in customer satisfaction with the criterion that the factors account for a unique and significant amount of the variance in customer satisfaction. So, it is possible that, although five factors may be significantly correlated with overall customer satisfaction, a multiple regression analysis could result in a finding that only one factor accounts for a unique portion of the variance in customer satisfaction. The other factors, due to overlap with the first factor, may not add any explanation to the prediction of customer satisfaction. Graphically, we could look at this in a Venn diagram (see Figure J.3).

In this diagram, the circles represent the variance in each of the variables. The overlapping portions of the circles represent shared variance among the variables. We see that one factor, availability, explains most of the variance in customer satisfaction (larger overlap) compared to professionalism. Additionally, we see that professionalism does share a large amount of variance with customer satisfaction. However, we see that the unique

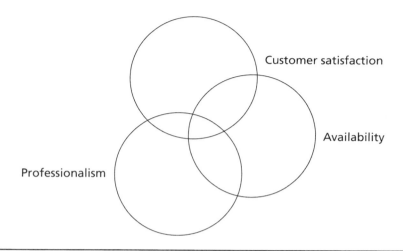

Customer satisfaction

Availability

Professionalism

Figure J.3 A Venn diagram.

variance professionalism shares with customer satisfaction is almost cut in half after we take into account the variance professionalism and availability both share with customer satisfaction. Multiple regression analysis could be used to see whether the unique variance of professionalism significantly predicts customer satisfaction.

There are various methods of multiple regression analysis. The different multiple methods vary with respect to how the factors are included (or retained) in the final regression equation. These methods are forward selection, backward elimination, and stepwise selection. Using the *forward selection* method, the variable that has the highest correlation with customer satisfaction is entered into the equation first. Next, the factor that explains the greatest and unique amount of variance (after the first factor has been entered) is entered into the equation and tested for its significance. If the factor is significant, it remains in the equation and the next factor that explains the greatest and unique amount of variance (after the first two factors have been entered) is entered in the equation and tested for significance. This process is conducted until the remaining factors do not contribute any significant variance to the prediction of customer satisfaction.

Using *backward elimination,* all factors are included into the equation from the start. Each factor's unique contribution to the explanation of customer satisfaction (after controlling for the other factors) is tested. The factor whose unique variance does not account for a significant amount of variance and explains the least amount of variance in customer satisfaction is dropped from the equation. Each factor is again tested to see if its unique variance accounts for a significant amount of variance. The process of elimination is iterated until all factors in the equation account for a significant amount of variance in customer satisfaction.

In *stepwise selection*, both forward selection and backward elimination procedures are used. In the first step, the variable that has the highest correlation with customer satisfaction is entered into the equation. Next, the factor that explains the greatest and unique amount of variance (after the first factor has been entered) is entered into the equation and tested for its significance. In the next step, however, the first variable that was entered into the equation is tested to see if it explains a unique amount of variance in customer satisfaction after the second variable has been added to the equation. If the first variable does add unique explanation to customer satisfaction, it remains in the equation. If it does not, it is dropped. This process is conducted with the remaining variables. With this method, it is possible to determine which factors were initially good at predicting customer satisfaction at the early stages of the analysis but may have lost their usefulness at later stages after more variables have entered the equation.

These methods of multiple regression are presented here to show you the various methods you can use to determine the factors that best predict overall customer satisfaction. Readers are referred to the bibliography to learn more about multiple regression analysis.

Example

Using the patient satisfaction questionnaire, we are able to use simple linear regression to determine the relationship of office quality and physician quality. Specifically, we will regress office quality *(Y)* on physician quality *(X)*. First, the two variables are plotted to give us a general idea of the relationship between them. This scatterplot is presented in Figure J.4. As can be seen in this figure, the relationship between the two variables is positive.

In the next step, we conduct a simple regression analysis. The results of this regression analysis are presented in Table J.2. As we can see, the relationship between physician quality and office quality is slightly positive $(r = .27)$. Also, the percent of variance of physician quality that is accounted for by office quality is only 7 percent. Table J.2 also includes the final regression equation for the prediction of physician quality *(Y)* from office quality *(X)*.

Next, we could determine which variables are related to the overall rating of the exam. First, let's examine the simple correlations among the variables. These are located in Table J.3. As we can see from the correlation matrix, overall rating of the exam is positively correlated with physician quality and office quality. Overall rating of the exam is negatively correlated with wait time; patients who spend more time waiting for the doctor also report lower levels of satisfaction with the exam compared to patients who spend less time waiting for their doctor.

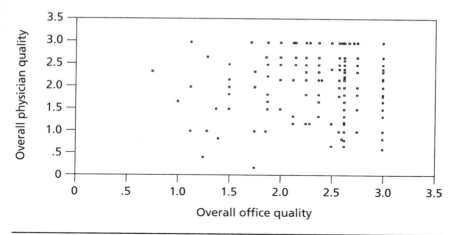

Figure J.4   Scatterplot of the relationship between physician quality and office quality.

Table J.2   Regression analysis predicting physician quality from office quality.

r	.27
r^2	.07
Regression equation:	$Y = a + bX$; $Y = 1.78 + .376X$
Significance test:	$t(1329) = 10.21$; $p < .0001$

Table J.3   Correlations among the patient satisfaction variables.

	Physician	Office	Wait time
Physician quality	—		
Office quality	.34	—	
Wait time (minutes)	−.07	−.14	—
Overall rating of the exam	.60	.30	−.11

Note: N for correlations ranges from 797 to 1336. All correlations significant at the .05 level.

Next, we conduct a multiple regression analysis (using a stepwise approach) using physician quality, office quality, and wait time as the predictor variables and overall rating of the exam as the outcome variable. The results of the analyses are presented in Table J.4. As we can see from the multiple regression approach, the best predictor of the overall rating of the exam is physician quality, followed by office quality, and wait time. The effects of the latter two variables are significant but not that substantial. Thus most of the variance in overall rating of the exam can be explained by the satisfaction level with the physician.

The next appendix covers another procedure that extends the concept of correlational analysis. This procedure, factor analysis, determines the relationship between observed variables and hypothetical variables.

Table J.4 Stepwise regression analysis of the patient satisfaction questionnaire.

	Scale	ΔR^2	p
Overall rating of the exam	Physician quality	.3554	.01
	Office quality	.0189	.01
	Insurance quality	.0031	.05
	Total for four variables in the equation	.3774	.01

Appendix K
Factor Analysis

actor analysis is a general term that refers to a number of statistical techniques used in questionnaire development. There are several types of factor analysis, each with its own particular method for generating results. Because these methods often result in the same conclusions regarding interpretation of the data, this discussion will be very general and will not focus on one particular method of factor analysis; it will instead describe the general factor analytic technique.

Generally, factor analysis is used when you have a large number of variables in your data set and would like to reduce the number to a manageable size. For example, the 12 items presented in Figure K.1 might be used to assess service quality of a particular organization. You might think that they represent 12 dimensions of customers' attitudes, but upon inspection, we see that they might not really represent 12 different dimensions.

For example, items 1, 2, and 3 are similar to each other and might be represented by a broader dimension called *availability of the provider*. In addition, items 4, 5, and 6 might represent *responsiveness of the provider,* and items 7, 8, and 9 represent *professionalism*. Items 10, 11, and 12 represent *overall satisfaction with the service.*

Let's say that we had a large number of people complete the questionnaire. A factor analysis of the resulting data would tell us whether there is a smaller set of more general dimensions (like availability and responsiveness). We reduce the original number of variables to a smaller number of dimensions so we can more easily interpret the information contained in the data. If we want to see the interrelationship (correlation coefficients) between these 12 variables, we would have to calculate and interpret 60 correlations. This may be difficult, since we are not able to understand what all of the interrelationships would indicate. By reducing the number of dimensions—say, reducing the 12 variables to the four dimensions suggested earlier—we now have to calculate and interpret only six relationships.

1. I could get an appointment with the merchant at a time I desired.

2. The merchant was available to schedule me at a good time.

3. My appointment was at a convenient time for me.

4. The merchant was quick to respond when I arrived for my appointment.

5. The merchant immediately helped me when I entered the premises.

6. My appointment started promptly at the scheduled time.

7. The merchant listened to my opinion about what I wanted.

8. The merchant conducted herself/himself in a professional manner.

9. The merchant was courteous.

10. The quality of the way the merchant treated me was high.

11. The way the merchant treated me met my expectations.

12. I am satisfied with the way the merchant treated me.

Figure K.1 Customer opinion statements concerning service quality and overall satisfaction.

In general, factor analysis examines the relationships between a large set of variables and tries to explain these correlations using a smaller number of variables. Initially, factor analysis uses the overall correlation matrix of the variables and determines which items share an underlying dimension. Factor analysis mathematically identifies the number of factors or underlying dimensions that best represent the observed correlations between the initial set of items. Generally, in the set of existing items, those that are highly correlated with each other will be represented by a single factor or dimension.

After the number of factors or dimensions has been identified, the next step in factor analysis is to determine which items fall within their respective dimensions. This is done by a mathematical procedure called *rotation*. This rotation will clarify the dimensions' relationships with the items. As with the general method of factor analysis, various methods of rotation exist. Generally, these different rotation methods result in the same conclusions regarding which dimensions represent a given set of items.

EXPLORATORY AND CONFIRMATORY USES OF FACTOR ANALYSIS

Factor analysis explores the possibility that our variables can be reduced to a smaller, undetermined number of factors. That is, we do not know the number of factors that represent our variables nor which variables load on which factors. Factor analysis, in this situation, will identify which variables load on their respective factors. Factor analysis can also be used in a confirmatory manner in which we go into the analysis with some guess as to the outcome. In other words, we think we know the number of factors and which variables load on which factors. (The term *confirmatory factor analysis* is used here to illustrate how factor analysis can be used and is different from the more sophisticated approach of confirmatory factor analysis using significance testing.) This use of factor analysis is guided more by hypothesis testing. We expect the results from the factor analysis to confirm our hypothesis of the variables in our data set. For example, if we develop a questionnaire designed to assess certain dimensions of service quality, we expect that the items on our scale represent their respective factor or dimension.

HYPOTHETICAL FACTOR ANALYSIS

The results of the factor analysis (the number of factors and factor rotation) are presented in a tabular format called a *factor pattern matrix*. The elements in the factor pattern matrix represent the regression coefficient (like a correlation coefficient) between each of the items and the factors. These elements indicate the degree of relationship between the variables and the factors.

Table K.1 presents a hypothetical factor pattern matrix representing the results of a factor analysis that identified the existence of three factors that represented nine items. Items 1 through 3 have a high loading on factor I and small loadings on the other factors. Items 4 through 6 load highly on factor II, and items 7 through 9 load highly on factor III. A factor's definition is determined by the content of the items that load on it.

This hypothetical factor analysis indicates it would be reasonable to think of the data set as containing three variables rather than nine. Therefore, instead of looking at each variable as its own separate dimension, we would believe that there are three dimensions, each composed of three items. To obtain a score for each of the dimensions, we might combine the variables associated with a given factor to represent that dimension. That is, we would combine all the items that loaded highly on factor I to get a measure of that dimension. We would do the same for the items associated with factor II and factor III.

Table K.1   A factor pattern matrix with the factor loadings from the results of a hypothetical factor analysis of the responses to nine items.

	Factor		
Items	I	II	III
1	.80	.05	.07
2	.77	.04	.21
3	.45	.11	.13
4	.02	.55	.04
5	.10	.77	.21
6	.11	.88	.16
7	.09	.08	.72
8	.30	.21	.77
9	.21	.22	.67

Now we would have three dimensions with which to work. These dimensions are useful summary variables for drawing conclusions about the data. Furthermore, we could now more easily interpret the interrelations (correlation coefficients) among these dimensions.

ACTUAL FACTOR ANALYSIS

This next example is taken from actual data obtained from a beauty salon using a customer satisfaction questionnaire. Although the questionnaire contained the items listed in Figure K.1, only items 1 through 6 are included in this example. The first three items were written to reflect an availability dimension, while the last three items were written to reflect a responsiveness dimension. A method of factor analysis, called *principle factor analysis,* was performed. This initial factor analysis resulted in the factor pattern matrix presented in Table K.2.

As this factor pattern indicates, the factor analysis identified the existence of two factors or dimensions representing these six items. We expected this. However, it might be unclear as to which items represent factor 1 and which represent factor 2. All of the six items seem to load fairly high on factor 1. Factor 2 seems to reflect a bipolar scale; some items load positively on the factor, while others load negatively on the factor. The interpretation of the factor pattern matrix becomes even more difficult as the number of items and factors increases. To make the results of the factor analysis more meaningful, we use *rotation.*

On the initial factor pattern matrix, a method of rotation, called *varimax rotation,* was conducted. Other methods of rotation were used and, as

Table K.2   The factor pattern matrix resulting from the factor analysis of six items designed to measure perceived availability and perceived responsiveness.

Unrotated factor matrix

	Factor 1	Factor 2
Item 1	.727	.683
Item 2	.842	.425
Item 3	.321	.861
Item 4	.807	−.537
Item 5	.604	−.652
Item 6	.84	−.361

expected, resulted in the same pattern of results as varimax rotation. Therefore, this presentation will only include the results of varimax rotation. The rotated factor pattern matrix appears in Table K.3. In this factor pattern matrix, the interpretation of the factors is more clear. Factor 1 is clearly represented by the last three items, while factor 2 is clearly represented by the first three items.

As expected, we found the existence of two factors that underlie these six items. In a sense, we used factor analysis to confirm our expectations. By design, the first three items reflected an availability dimension of service while the last three items reflected a responsiveness dimension. The factor analysis confirmed our hypothesis as to the number of factors that these six items represent, thus making us more confident that the items measure what they were designed to measure.

Example

From the patient satisfaction questionnaire, we derived an overall measure of physician quality by averaging the responses to the six questions related to physician quality. We can use factor analysis to determine whether this method of averaging the items is reasonable. The factor analysis would tell us the number of underlying factors that describe the correlations among the six items of physician quality. The six items measuring physician quality are presented in Figure K.2.

The next step would be to determine the correlations among these six items. The correlation matrix for the six physician quality items is presented in Table K.4.

Table K.3   The result of the factor analysis after rotating the factors.

Orthogonal transformation solution—varimax

	Factor 1	Factor 2
Item 1	.14	.987
Item 2	.391	.858
Item 3	−.288	.873
Item 4	.966	.086
Item 5	.879	−.131
Item 6	.881	.244

Physician quality			
	Yes	**No**	**Not sure**
1. Introduced himself/herself to me.	Y	N	?
2. Asked me how I was injured/became ill.	Y	N	?
3. Listened to me.	Y	N	?
4. Treated me with respect.	Y	N	?
5. Was professional in doing the examination.	Y	N	?
6. Spent enough time with me (not rushed).	Y	N	?

Figure K.2   Physician quality items.

As we can see from the correlation matrix, all items are positively correlated with each other. The pattern of correlations, however, is not clear. Some items show high correlations with other items ($r = .58$) while other items show low correlations with other items (.14). A factor analysis examines the entire correlation matrix and helps us make sense of these correlations. Perhaps one underlying factor can explain the pattern of correlations we see in Table K.4.

The results of the factor analysis (factor pattern matrix) is presented in Table K.5.

Table K.4 Correlation matrix for the six physician quality items.

	1	2	3	4	5	6
Question 1	1.00					
Question 2	.22	1.00				
Question 3	.15	.22	1.00			
Question 4	.31	.20	.56	1.00		
Question 5	.26	.14	.48	.58	1.00	
Question 6	.17	.22	.47	.42	.41	1.00

Table K.5 Factor pattern matrix for the six physician quality items.

	Factor 1
Question 1	.35531
Question 2	.26187
Question 3	.69985
Question 4	.78311
Question 5	.69716
Question 6	.59329

The results of the factor analysis suggest that the six items could be described by one underlying factor. As is indicated in the factor pattern matrix, one factor can explain the correlations among the variables, suggesting that all six items are measuring one underlying factor that is responsible for the variance in the items. Therefore, the creation of a new variable called overall *physician quality* by averaging the six items does make sense, both logically and statistically.

Summary

Factor analysis identifies the number of underlying dimensions that account for the relationship between many items. Since factor analysis allows you to determine which items measure similar things, it is often used as a means of data reduction.

Appendix L
Table of Random Numbers

These random numbers were generated with a computer program and range from 1 to 99,999. Each number had an equal chance of being generated.

92513	21156	20618	78167	87337	80703	00468	84107	58120	15456
17743	07198	90623	93143	58624	99172	90774	32892	43015	03868
64861	63732	82018	99240	11925	87715	08917	64625	51627	20766
79728	09753	43999	23550	20290	45512	06476	50545	49641	68162
20515	97350	04927	87226	11553	40866	70782	20944	65761	08406
55469	10628	09666	09906	94742	11203	99330	38092	26386	38890
95834	67434	10367	25356	03517	11773	12159	61605	79374	73538
38344	94791	86959	90375	39792	31626	16217	75227	59118	48758
58805	62440	80292	69705	80900	53725	19260	63853	52996	41111
13310	73409	14683	72271	83141	31214	06020	36270	89706	59971
63713	76433	82594	13916	49596	51822	19609	27454	85470	89592
74104	73061	81653	70740	30044	11351	97125	92733	73051	84786
78861	42464	71587	29797	69687	98987	73885	91051	56021	55387
36915	77574	29370	77071	38475	39808	26999	61025	74503	48624
04771	12920	35438	84635	57077	71178	05781	95589	19444	50655
38792	98613	08548	65459	46643	31589	26608	93722	71904	98448
22358	87444	47701	58366	28319	66264	90515	16041	62258	35767
85925	79736	54218	88132	33224	19743	29210	26962	79052	44391
52972	54548	85857	60644	12414	63024	30719	47093	57483	98950
01504	34410	87397	45152	13270	70784	40097	74700	36362	27201
47310	81172	43366	95102	12440	66368	71484	84735	78198	65864
52773	71303	43874	52350	50081	87145	08226	45971	87660	77714
10822	41517	94528	27204	34618	21898	92037	77282	00834	91593
45122	47428	78536	16203	47494	40969	75182	44961	04057	75998
57860	98766	70665	22204	50186	92901	43092	01484	94901	38907
97394	86975	63503	83789	66147	18745	98056	56883	09887	68377
04824	69980	08281	08365	81162	14938	15126	14297	97930	87086
72933	93269	88155	37800	46676	45646	93489	83874	82111	62150
16305	67104	66060	28206	53165	79230	01372	53440	27867	09628
02674	21739	07376	51503	39818	77886	66043	53012	66435	65773
72311	39822	42810	19800	96401	27412	36409	69962	93899	11187
20706	35672	86437	61921	65572	92677	95636	57183	58219	63017
42718	18888	63674	90418	40960	08617	24701	31349	72595	34379
24010	42118	44494	68694	33997	26586	86540	52297	74910	56444
32067	87027	19144	18467	40376	35642	05817	27684	19042	03323
44569	68369	59771	39055	17045	64723	65400	66571	75542	65935
08487	63190	89557	44757	52447	62902	87699	50010	63877	96156
85834	44712	33304	54909	75046	49907	64365	42403	61689	72287
05150	00751	15552	87821	72474	73283	88592	61628	12753	78396
17670	88611	90535	04493	23554	07028	19741	00796	12694	65857
05221	65192	51547	52682	81566	94180	78802	47901	76064	54259
20977	74751	03998	78282	64292	48037	09946	02345	61880	45268
57906	12627	93767	06761	55512	53175	26354	73948	55615	53165
28352	33164	93269	93833	58574	62083	13382	00109	46278	49877
94165	27864	64602	68693	53619	64668	07040	33622	33066	40964
56693	42385	00601	65723	54104	63014	05768	07673	88769	42281
09131	74506	63078	30882	59738	70331	63669	16305	60160	72148
17652	95540	87088	89126	16730	79871	48653	37999	25753	89591
63576	61256	93052	49509	39740	39844	73818	30614	29605	62099
40912	46784	97819	67113	23390	79137	50734	33970	71863	79725

Bibliography

Allen, M.J. and Yen, W. M. *Introduction to Measurement Theory*. Long Grove, IL: Waveland Press, 2002.

American Educational Research Association, American Psychological Association, and National Council on Measurement in Education. *Standards for Educational and Psychological Testing*. Washington, DC: American Psychological Association, 1985.

Anastasi, A. *Psychological Testing*. New York: Macmillan, 1988.

Andersen, B. and Fagerhaug, T. *Root Cause Analysis: Simplified Tools and Techniques*, 2d ed. Milwaukee: ASQ Quality Press, 2006.

Balakrishnan, P. V., Chawla, S. K., Smith, M. F., and Michalski, B. P. "Mail survey response rates using a lottery prize giveaway incentive." *Journal of Direct Marketing* 6, no. 3 (1992): 54–59.

Bejou, D., Keiningham, T., and Aksoy, L. *Customer Lifetime Value: Reshaping the way we manage to maximize profitability*. Binghamton, NY: Haworth Press, 2007.

Brennan, M. "The effect of a monetary incentive on mail survey response rates: New data." *Journal of the Market Research Society* 34, no. 2 (1992): 173–177.

Brennan, M., Hoek, J., and Astridge, C. "The effects of monetary incentives on the response rate and cost-effectiveness of a mail survey." *Journal of Market Research Society* 33, no. 3 (1991): 229–241.

Brown, F. G. *Principles of Educational and Psychological Testing*. New York: Holt, Rinehart and Winston, 1983.

Camp, R. C. *Benchmarking: The Search for Industry Best Practices That Lead to Superior Performance*. Milwaukee: ASQC Quality Press, 1989.

Campbell, D. T. and Fiske, D. W. "Convergent and discriminant validation by the multitrait-multimethod matrix." *Psychological Bulletin* 56 (1959): 81–105.

Campbell, D. T. and Stanley, J. C. *Experimental and QuasiExperimental Designs for Research.* Boston: Houghton Mifflin, 1966.

Chandler, C. H. "Beyond customer satisfaction." *Quality Progress* 22, no. 2 (1989): 30–32.

Chapko, M. K., Bergner, M., Green, K., Beach, B., Milgrom, P., and Skalabrin, N. "Development and validation of a measure of dental patient satisfaction." *Medical Care* 23, no. 1 (1985): 39–49.

Chawla, S. K., Balakrishnan, P. V., and Smith, M. F. "Mail response rates from distributors." *Industrial Marketing Management* 21, no. 4 (1992): 307–310.

Corah, N. L., O'Shea, R. M., Bissell, G. D., Thines, T. J., and Mendola, P. "The dentist-patient relationship: Perceived dentist behaviors that reduce patient anxiety and increase satisfaction." *Journal of the American Dental Association* 116 (1988): 73–76.

Corah, N. L., O'Shea, R. M., Pace, L. F., and Seyrek, S. K. "Development of a patient measure of satisfaction with the dentist: The Dental Visit Satisfaction Scale." *Journal of Behavioral Medicine* 7, no. 3 (1984): 367–373.

Cottle, D. W. *Client-Centered Service: How to Keep Them Coming Back for More.* New York: John Wiley and Sons, 1990.

Cronbach, L. J. *Essentials of Psychological Testing,* 4th ed. New York: Harper and Row, 1984.

Cronbach, L. J. "Coefficient alpha and the internal structure of tests." *Psychometrika* 16, no. 3 (1951): 297-334.

Cronbach, L. J. and Meehl, P. E. "Construct validity in psychological tests." *Psychological Bulletin* 52 (1955): 281–302.

Davies, A. R. and Ware, J. E. Jr. "Measuring patient satisfaction with dental care." *Social Science and Medicine* 15A (1981): 751–760.

Dawes, R. M. *Fundamentals of Attitude Measurement.* New York: John Wiley and Sons, 1972.

Dillman, D.A., Tortora, R.D., and Bowker, D. (1998). Principles for constructing Web surveys. Retrieved February 12, 2008 from http://survey.sesrc.wsu.edu/dillman/papers/websurveyppr.pdf

Dillman, D.A., Tortora, R.D., and Bowker, D. (1998). Principles for constructing Web surveys. Retrieved February 14, 2008 from http://survey.sesrc.wsu.edu/dillman/papers/websurveyppr.pdf

Edwards, A. L. and Kenney, K. C. "A comparison of the Thurstone and Likert techniques of attitude scale construction." *Journal of Applied Psychology* 30 (1946): 72–83.

Fishbein, M. *Readings in Attitude Theory and Measurement.* New York: John Wiley and Sons, 1967.

Flanagan, J. C. "The critical incident technique." *Psychological Bulletin* 51 (1954): 327–358.

Fornell, C., Mithas, S., Morgensen, F. V., and Krishan, M. S. "Customer satisfaction and stock prices: High returns, low risk." *Journal of Marketing* 70 (January 2006): 1-14.

Fox, R. J., Crask, M. R., and Kim, J. "Mail survey response rate: A meta-analysis of selected techniques for inducing response." *Public Opinion Quarterly* 52, no. 4 (1989): 467–491.

Gale, E. N., Carlsson, S. G., Eriksson, A., and Jontell M. "Effects of dentists' behavior on patients attitudes." *Journal of the American Dental Association* 109 (1984): 444–446.

Goodman, J. "The nature of customer satisfaction." *Quality Progress* 22, no. 2 (1989): 37–40.

Guion, R. M. *Personnel Testing.* New York: McGraw-Hill, 1965.

Gulliksen, H. *Theory of Mental Tests.* Hillsdale, New Jersey: Lawrence Erlbaum Associates, Publishers, 1987.

Gupta, S. *Managing Customers as Investments: The Strategic Value of Customers in the Long Run.* Upper Saddle River, New Jersey: Wharton School Publishing, 2005.

Guttman, L. L. "The basis for scalogram analysis." Vol. 4 of Stouffer, S. A., Guttman, L., Shuchman, E. A., Lazarfeld, P. W., Star, S. A., and Clausen, J. A. (eds.) *Studies in Social Psychology—World War II.* Princeton: Princeton University Press, 1950.

Handleman, S. L., Fan-Hsu, J., and Proskin, H. M. 1990. "Patient satisfaction in four types of dental practices." *Journal of the American Dental Association* 121: 624–630.

Hannan, M. and Karp, P. *Customer Satisfaction: How to Maximize, Measure, and Market Your Company's "Ultimate Product."* New York: American Management Association, 1989.

Hawkins, D. I., Coney, K. A., and Jackson, D. W. Jr. "The impact of monetary inducement on uninformed response error." *Journal of the Academy of Marketing Science* 16, no. 2 (1988): 30–35.

Hayes, B. E. *Measuring Customer Satisfaction*, 2d ed. Milwaukee: ASQ Quality Press, 1997.

James, J. M. and Bolstein, R. "The effect of monetary incentives and follow-up mailings on the response rate and response quality in mail surveys." *Public Opinion Quarterly* 54, no. 3 (1990): 346–361.

Johnson, J. D., Scheetz, J. P., Shugars, D. A., Damiano, P. C., and Schweitzer, S. O. "Development and validation of a consumer quality assessment instrument for dentistry." *Journal of Dental Education* 54, no. 1 (1990): 644–652.

Keiningham, T. L., Cooil, B., Andreassen, T.W., and Aksoy, L. "A longitudinal examination of net promoter and firm revenue growth." *Journal of Marketing* 71 (July 2007): 39-51.

Kennedy, D. A. and Young, B. J. "Managing quality in staff areas." *Quality Progress* 22, no. 10 (1989): 87–91.

Kenny, D. A. *Statistics for the Social and Behavioral Sciences*, 2d ed. Boston: Little, Brown and Co., 1987.

Kepes, S. Y. and True, J. E. "Anonymity and attitudes toward work." *Psychological Reports* 21, no. 2 (1967): 353–356.

Kerlinger, F. N. *Foundations of Behavioral Research*, 2d ed. New York: Holt, Rinehart, and Winston, 1973.

Koslowsky, M., Bailit, H., and Vallugo, P. "Satisfaction of the patient and the provider: Evaluation by questionnaire." *Journal of Public Health Dentistry* 34 (1974): 188–194.

Latham, G. P., Fay, C., and Saari, L. "The development of behavioral observation scales for appraising the performance of foremen." *Personnel Psychology* 32 (1979): 299–311.

Latham, G. P., Saari, L., and Fay, C. "BOS, BES, and baloney: Raising Kane with Bernardin." *Personnel Psychology* 33 (1980): 815–821.

Latham, G. P. and Wexley, K. N. "Behavioral observation scales for performance appraisal purposes." *Personnel Psychology* 30 (1977): 255–268.

Likert, R. A. "Technique for the measurement of attitudes." *Archives of Psychology* 60 (1932): 140.

Lissitz, R. W. and Green, S. B. "Effect of the number of scale points on reliability: A Monte Carlo approach." *Journal of Applied Psychology* 60 (1975): 10–13.

Locke, E. A., Shaw, K. N., Saari, L. M., and Latham, G. P. "Goal setting and task performance: 1969–1980." *Psychological Bulletin* 90 (1981): 125–152.

Loftus, G. R. and Loftus, E. F. *The Essence of Statistics,* 2d ed. New York: Alfred A. Knopf, 1988.

Lorenzi, P., Friedmann, R., and Paolillo, J. "Consumer mail survey responses: More (unbiased) bang for the buck." *Journal of Consumer Marketing* 5, no. 4 (1988): 31–40.

Montgomery, D. C. *Introduction to Statistical Quality Control,* 3d ed. New York: John Wiley & Sons, 1996.

Morgan, N.A. and Rego, L.L. "The value of different customer satisfaction and loyalty metrics in predicting business performance." *Marketing Science* 25, no. 5 (2006): 426-439.

Morrison, D. F. *Applied Linear Statistical Methods.* Englewood, New Jersey: Prentice Hall, 1983.

Morrison, D. F. *Multivariate Statistical Methods,* 2d ed. New York: McGraw-Hill, 1976.

Murine, G. E. "Integrating software quality metrics with software QA." *Quality Progress* 21, no. 11 (1988): 38–43.

Neter, J., Wasserman, W., and Kutner, M. H. *Applied Linear Statistical Models,* 2d ed. Homewood, Illinois: Richard D. Irwin, Inc., 1985.

Nunnally, J. M. *Psychometric Theory,* 2d ed. New York: McGraw-Hill, 1978.

Parasuraman, A., Zeithaml, V. A., and Berry, L. L. "A conceptual model of service quality and its implications for future research." *Journal of Marketing,* Fall (1985): 41–50.

Parasuraman, A., Zeithaml, V. A., and Berry, L. L. "SERVQUAL: A multiple-item scale for measuring consumer perceptions of service quality." *Journal of Retailing* 64 (1988): 12–40.

Pedhazur, E. J. *Multiple Regression in Behavioral Research: Explanation and Prediction,* 2d ed. New York: Holt Rinehart Winston, 1982.

Pritchard, R. D., Jones, S. D., Roth, P. L., Stuebing, K. K., and Ekeberg, S. E. "Effects of group feedback, goal setting, and incentives on organizational productivity." *Journal of Applied Psychology* 73 (1988): 337–358.

Reckase, M. D. *Scaling Techniques: Handbook of Psychological Assessment.* New York: Pergamon Press, 1990.

Reichheld, F. F. "The One Number You Need to Grow." *Harvard Business Review* 81 (December 2003): 46-54.

Reichheld, F. F. *The Ultimate Question: Driving Good Profits and True Growth.* Boston: Harvard Business School Press, 2006.

Reichheld, F. F. and Sasser, W. E. "Zero defections: Quality comes to service." *Harvard Business Review* (Sept-Oct. 1990): 301–307.

Rouse, R. A. and Hamilton, M. A. "Dentists' technical competence, communication, and personality as predictors of dental patient anxiety." *Journal of Behavioral Medicine* 13, no. 3 (1990): 307–319.

Shank, M. D., Darr, B. D., and Werner, T. C. "Increasing mail survey response rates: Investigating the perceived value of cash versus noncash incentives." *Applied Marketing Research* 30, no. 3 (1990): 28–32.

Shaw, D. G., Huffman, M. D., and Haviland, M. G. "Grouping continuous data in discrete intervals: information loss and recovery." *Journal of Educational Measurement* 24, no. 2 (1987): 167–173.

Society for Industrial and Organizational Psychology, Inc. *Principles for the Validation and Use of Personnel Selection Procedures*, 3d ed. College Park, Md.: SIOP, 1987.

Soelling, M. E. and Newell, T. G. "Effects of anonymity and experimenter demand on client satisfaction with mental health services." *Evaluation and Program Planning* 6, no. 3–4 (1983): 329–333.

Stevens, S. S. *Handbook of Experimental Psychology*. New York: John Wiley and Sons, 1951.

Thurstone, L. L. "Theory of attitude measurement." *Psychological Bulletin* 36 (1929): 224–241.

Watkins, D. "Relationship between desire for anonymity and responses to a questionnaire on satisfaction with university." *Psychological Reports*, 42, no. 1 (1978): 259–261.

Yammarino, F. J., Skinner, S. J., and Childers, T. L. "Understanding mail survey response behaviors: A meta-analysis." *Public Opinion Quarterly* 55, no. 4 (1991): 613–639.

Zeithaml, V. A., Parasuraman, A., and Berry, L. L. *Delivering Quality Service: Balancing Customer Perceptions and Expectations*. New York: The Free Press, 1990.

Index